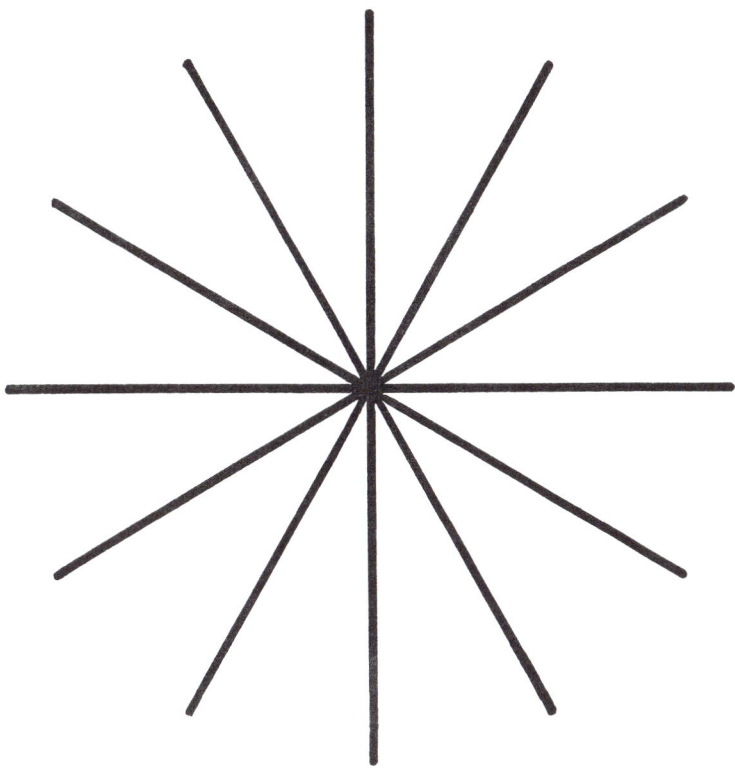

ECONOMICS—*A HALF CENTURY OF RESEARCH 1920-1970*

50th ANNUAL REPORT
SEPTEMBER 1970
NATIONAL BUREAU
OF ECONOMIC
RESEARCH, INC.

COPYRIGHT © 1970 BY
NATIONAL BUREAU OF ECONOMIC RESEARCH, INC.
261 MADISON AVENUE, NEW YORK, N. Y. 10016

ALL RIGHTS RESERVED

PRINTED IN THE UNITED STATES OF AMERICA

The National Bureau of Economic Research was organized in 1920 in response to a growing demand for objective determination of the facts bearing upon economic problems, and for their interpretation in an impartial manner. The National Bureau concentrates on topics of national importance that are susceptible of scientific treatment.

The National Bureau seeks not merely to determine and interpret important economic facts, but to do so under such auspices and with such safeguards as shall make its findings carry conviction to all sections of the nation.

No report of the research staff may be published without the approval of the Board of Directors. Rigid provisions guard the National Bureau from becoming a source of profit to its members, directors, or officers, and from becoming an agency for propaganda.

By issuing its findings in the form of scientific reports, entirely divorced from recommendations on policy, the National Bureau hopes to aid all thoughtful men, however divergent their views of public policy, to base their discussions upon objective knowledge as distinguished from subjective opinion.

The National Bureau assumes no obligation toward present or future contributors except to determine, interpret, and publish economic facts for the benefit of the nation at large, and to provide contributors with copies of its publications.

RELATION OF THE DIRECTORS
TO THE WORK AND PUBLICATIONS
OF THE NATIONAL BUREAU OF ECONOMIC RESEARCH

1. The object of the National Bureau of Economic Research is to ascertain and to present to the public important economic facts and their interpretation in a scientific and impartial manner. The Board of Directors is charged with the responsibility of ensuring that the work of the National Bureau is carried on in strict conformity with this object.

2. The President of the National Bureau shall submit to the Board of Directors, or to its Executive Committee, for their formal adoption all specific proposals for research to be instituted.

3. No research report shall be published until the President shall have submitted to each member of the Board the manuscript proposed for publication, and such information as will, in his opinion and in the opinion of the author, serve to determine the suitability of the report for publication in accordance with the principles of the National Bureau. Each manuscript shall contain a summary drawing attention to the nature and treatment of the problem studied, the character of the data and their utilization in the report, and the main conclusions reached.

4. For each manuscript so submitted, a special committee of the Board shall be appointed by majority agreement of the President and Vice Presidents (or by the Executive Committee in case of inability to decide on the part of the President and Vice Presidents), consisting of three directors selected as nearly as may be one from each general division of the Board. The names of the special manuscript committee shall be stated to each Director when the manuscript is submitted to him. It shall be the duty of each member of the special manuscript committee to read the manuscript. If each member of the manuscript committee signifies his approval within thirty days of the transmittal of the manuscript, the report may be published. If at the end of that period any member of the manuscript committee withholds his approval, the President shall then notify each member of the Board, requesting approval or disapproval of publication, and thirty days additional shall be granted for this purpose. The manuscript shall then not be published unless at least a majority of the entire Board who shall have voted on the proposal within the time fixed for the receipt of votes shall have approved.

5. No manuscript may be published, though approved by each member of the special manuscript committee, until forty-five days have elapsed from the transmittal of the report in manuscript form. The interval is allowed for the receipt of any memorandum of dissent or reservation, together with a brief statement of his reasons, that any member may wish to express; and such memorandum of dissent or reservation shall be published with the manuscript if he so desires. Publication does not, however, imply that each member of the Board has read the manuscript, or that either members of the Board in general or the special committee have passed on its validity in every detail.

6. Publications of the National Bureau issued for informational purposes concerning the work of the Bureau and its staff, or issued to inform the public of activities of Bureau staff, and volumes issued as a result of various conferences involving the National Bureau shall contain a specific disclaimer noting that such publication has not passed through the normal review procedures required in this resolution. The Executive Committee of the Board is charged with review of all such publications from time to time to ensure that they do not take on the character of formal research reports of the National Bureau, requiring formal Board approval.

7. Unless otherwise determined by the Board or exempted by the terms of paragraph 6, a copy of this resolution shall be printed in each National Bureau publication.

(Resolution adopted October 25, 1926, and revised February 6, 1933,
February 24, 1941, and April 20, 1968)

NATIONAL BUREAU OF ECONOMIC RESEARCH

OFFICERS

Arthur F. Burns, *Honorary Chairman*
Theodore O. Yntema, *Chairman*
Walter W. Heller, *Vice Chairman*
John R. Meyer, *President*
Thomas D. Flynn, *Treasurer*
Douglas H. Eldridge, *Vice President-Executive Secretary*
Victor R. Fuchs, *Vice President-Research*
F. Thomas Juster, *Vice President-Research*
Hal B. Lary, *Vice President-Research*
Robert E. Lipsey, *Vice President-Research*
Edward K. Smith, *Vice President*
Joan R. Tron, *Director of Publications*

DIRECTORS AT LARGE

Joseph A. Beirne, *Communications Workers of America*
Arthur F. Burns, *Board of Governors of the Federal Reserve System*
Wallace J. Campbell, *Foundation for Cooperative Housing*
Erwin D. Canham, *Christian Science Monitor*
Robert A. Charpie, *The Cabot Corporation*
Solomon Fabricant, *New York University*
Frank W. Fetter, *Hanover, New Hampshire*
Eugene P. Foley, *Dreyfus Corporation*
Marion B. Folsom, *Rochester, New York*
Eli Goldston, *Eastern Gas and Fuel Associates*
Crawford H. Greenewalt, *E. I. du Pont de Nemours & Company*
David L. Grove, *IBM Corporation*
Walter W. Heller, *University of Minnesota*
Vivian W. Henderson, *Clark College*
John R. Meyer, *Yale University*
J. Irwin Miller, *Cummins Engine Company, Inc.*
Geoffrey H. Moore, *Bureau of Labor Statistics*
J. Wilson Newman, *Dun & Bradstreet, Inc.*
James J. O'Leary, *United States Trust Company of New York*
Robert V. Roosa, *Brown Brothers Harriman & Co.*
Boris Shishkin, *AFL-CIO*
Lazare Teper, *ILGWU*
Donald B. Woodward, *Riverside, Connecticut*
Theodore O. Yntema, *Oakland University*

DIRECTORS BY UNIVERSITY APPOINTMENT

Moses Abramovitz, *Stanford*
Gary S. Becker, *Columbia*
Charles H. Berry, *Princeton*
Francis M. Boddy, *Minnesota*
Tom E. Davis, *Cornell*
Otto Eckstein, *Harvard*
Walter D. Fisher, *Northwestern*
R. A. Gordon, *California*
Robert J. Lampman, *Wisconsin*
Maurice W. Lee, *North Carolina*
Lloyd G. Reynolds, *Yale*
Robert M. Solow, *Massachusetts Institute of Technology*
Henri Theil, *Chicago*
Thomas A. Wilson, *Toronto*
Willis J. Winn, *Pennsylvania*

DIRECTORS BY APPOINTMENT OF OTHER ORGANIZATIONS

Emilio G. Collado, *Committee for Economic Development*
Thomas D. Flynn, *American Institute of Certified Public Accountants*
Nathaniel Goldfinger, *AFL-CIO*
Harold G. Halcrow, *American Agricultural Economics Association*
Douglas G. Hartle, *Canadian Economics Association*
Walter E. Hoadley, *American Finance Association*
Douglass C. North, *Economic History Association*
Murray Shields, *American Management Association*
George Cline Smith, *National Association of Business Economists*
Willard L. Thorp, *American Economic Association*
W. Allen Wallis, *American Statistical Association*

DIRECTORS EMERITI

Percival F. Brundage
Gottfried Haberler
Albert J. Hettinger, Jr.
George B. Roberts
Jacob Viner
Joseph H. Willits

SENIOR RESEARCH STAFF

Gary S. Becker
Charlotte Boschan
Philip Cagan
Alfred H. Conrad
James S. Earley
Solomon Fabricant
Milton Friedman
Victor R. Fuchs
Raymond W. Goldsmith
Jack M. Guttentag
Daniel M. Holland
F. Thomas Juster
C. Harry Kahn
John F. Kain
John W. Kendrick
Irving B. Kravis
Hal B. Lary
Robert E. Lipsey
John R. Meyer
Jacob Mincer
Ilse Mintz
Geoffrey H. Moore *
M. Ishaq Nadiri
Nancy Ruggles
Richard Ruggles
Anna J. Schwartz
Robert P. Shay
George J. Stigler
Victor Zarnowitz

* On leave.

Contents

	PAGE
I. PAPERS PRESENTED TO THE BOARD OF DIRECTORS AT THE SPRING MEETING, 1970	1
Introduction—*John R. Meyer*	3
On the Measurement of Economic and Social Performance—*F. Thomas Juster*	8
II. STAFF REPORTS ON RESEARCH UNDER WAY	25
1. ECONOMIC GROWTH	26
Productivity, Employment, and Price Levels—*Solomon Fabricant*	26
Price Trends and Economic Growth—*Solomon Fabricant*	26
Interrelated Factor Demand Functions—*M. I. Nadiri* and *Sherwin Rosen*	28
Problems in the Measurement of Nonresidential Fixed Capital—*Robert J. Gordon*	29
Problems in Predicting the Rate of Inflation—*Robert J. Gordon*	30
Postwar Productivity Trends in the United States—*John W. Kendrick*	31
Other Studies	33
Public Finance	33
Introduction—*John Bossons*	33
Measuring the Effects of Tax Substitutions—*John Bossons* and *Carl S. Shoup*	34
Industry Price/Output Effects of Substituting a Value-Added Tax for a Corporate Profits Tax—*Bruce L. Petersen*	35
The Initial Differential Incidence of Alternative Income Tax Systems—*John Bossons*	35
The Cost and Incidence of Transfer Payment Programs in Canada—*John Bossons, Colin J. Hindle,* and *T. Russell Robinson*	36
Negative Income Taxation and Poverty in Ontario—*Colin J. Hindle*	36
Effect of Taxation on Personal Effort—*Daniel M. Holland*	38
The Effects of Alternative Unemployment Insurance Programs—*John Bossons* and *James Hosek*	38
Inter- and Intrastate Analyses of Grants-in-Aid and Local Fiscal Activity—*Stephen P. Dresch* and *Raymond J. Struyk*	39
2. NATIONAL INCOME, CONSUMPTION, AND CAPITAL FORMATION	40
Introduction—*F. Thomas Juster*	40
Household Capital Formation and Savings—*F. Thomas Juster*	41
The Design and Use of Economic Accounts—*Nancy D. Ruggles* and *Richard Ruggles*	43
Studies in the National Income Accounts—*John W. Kendrick*	44
Measurement and Analysis of National Income (Nonincome Income)—*Robert Eisner*	44
Capital Gains and the Theory and Measurement of Income—*Michael B. McElroy*	45
3. URBAN AND REGIONAL STUDIES	46
Introduction—*John F. Kain*	46
Modeling the Urban Housing Market—*Gregory K. Ingram*	48
The Detroit Housing Consumption–Residential Location Study—*Stephen P. Dresch*	49
Residential Location Decisions—*Stephen Mayo*	50
Metropolitan Moving Behavior—*John F. Kain* and *H. James Brown*	51
Housing Consumption, Housing Demand Functions, and Market-Clearing Models—*Mahlon R. Straszheim*	52
The Demand for Housing—*Irving R. Silver*	53
A Housing Market Model—*Irving R. Silver*	54
An Analysis of Ghetto Housing Markets—*John F. Kain* and *John M. Quigley*	55
Industrial Location within Metropolitan Areas—*Franklin James* and *Raymond J. Struyk*	56
Ghetto Employment Problems—*David Gordon*	56
Migration and Employment in Southern Metropolitan Areas—*Joseph J. Persky*	57
Research on Regional Unemployment—*Masanori Hashimoto*	58

	PAGE
4. HUMAN RESOURCES AND SOCIAL INSTITUTIONS	61
Introduction—*F. Thomas Juster* and *Gary S. Becker*	61
Education Studies	63
Human Capital Analysis of Personal Income Distribution—Jacob Mincer	63
A Theory of Life-Cycle Consumption—Gilbert R. Ghez	63
Education and Consumption Patterns—Robert T. Michael	64
Time Spent In and Out of the Labor Force by Males—Gary S. Becker	65
Economic Growth and the Distribution of Labor Income—Michael Tannen	65
Net Returns to Education—Paul Taubman and *Terence Wales*	65
Learning and Knowledge in the Labor Market—Sherwin Rosen	67
Education and Savings Behavior—Lewis C. Solmon	68
Education and Family Size—Robert T. Michael	70
NBER-Thorndike Sample—F. Thomas Juster	70
The Use Value of Education—Finis Welch	71
Aptitude, Education, and Earnings Differentials—John C. Hause	72
Comparison of Measures of the Growth in Educational Output—Roger E. Alcaly and V. K. Chetty	73
Economics of the Legal System	74
An Economic Analysis of the Courts—William M. Landes	74
Participation in Illegitimate Activities and the Effectiveness of Law Enforcement— Isaac Ehrlich	76
5. BUSINESS CYCLES	78
Introduction—*F. Thomas Juster*	78
Business Cycle Turning Points—*Ilse Mintz*	79
Money—*Milton Friedman* and *Anna J. Schwartz*	79
Study of Short-Term Economic Forecasting—*Victor Zarnowitz*	81
An Analysis of the Forecasting Properties of U.S. Econometric Models— *Michael K. Evans, Yoel Haitovsky,* and *George I. Treyz*	82
Business Cycle Analysis of Econometric Model Simulations—*Victor Zarnowitz, Charlotte Boschan,* and *Geoffrey H. Moore*	84
Econometric Model of Business Cycles—*Gregory C. Chow*	85
Determinants of Investment—*Robert Eisner*	86
6. FINANCIAL INSTITUTIONS AND PROCESSES	86
Interest Rates—*Jack M. Guttentag*	86
Interest Rates and Other Characteristics of Income Property Mortgage Loans— Royal Shipp, Robert Moore Fisher, and *Barbara Opper*	87
A Study of the Gibson Paradox—Thomas J. Sargent	88
Institutional Investors and the Stock Market—Raymond W. Goldsmith	89
Unions as Financial Institutions—Leo Troy	89
Performance of Banking Markets	90
Performance of Banking Markets in the Provision of Services to Business— Donald P. Jacobs	90
Banking Structure and Performance in Consumer Credit Markets—Paul F. Smith	91
Behavior of the Commercial Banking Industry, 1965-67: A Microeconometric Study—David T. Kresge	91
Other Studies	92
7. STUDIES IN INDUSTRIAL ORGANIZATION	92
Economics of Health	92
An Econometric Analysis of Spatial Variations in Mortality Rates by Race and Sex—Morris Silver	92
The Demand for Health: A Theoretical and Empirical Investigation—Michael Grossman	93
An Economic Analysis of Accidents—William M. Landes	95
Expenditures for Physicians' Services—Victor R. Fuchs and *Marcia J. Kramer*	96
Socioeconomic Determinants of Hospital Use—K. K. Ro	96
The Ownership Income of Management—Wilbur G. Lewellen	96
Diversification in American Industry—Michael Gort	97

	PAGE
8. INTERNATIONAL STUDIES	98
Introduction—*Hal B. Lary*	98
The Relation of U.S. Manufacturing Abroad to U.S. Exports—	
Robert E. Lipsey and *Merle Yahr Weiss*	99
The Role of Prices in International Trade—*Irving B. Kravis* and *Robert E. Lipsey*	99
The Diffusion of New Technologies—*Alfred H. Conrad*	100
Exchange Control, Liberalization, and Economic Development—	
Jagdish N. Bhagwati and *Anne O. Krueger*	103
The Pattern of Exports and Import-Substitution in an Outward-Looking Economy:	
Korea—*Seiji Naya*	104
Foreign Holdings of Liquid Dollar Assets—*J. Herbert Furth* and *Raymond F. Mikesell*	105
Credit, Banking, and Financial Flows in Eastern Europe—*George Garvy*	106
9. ECONOMETRICS AND MEASUREMENT METHODS	107
Analysis of Long-Run Dependence in Time Series: The R/S Technique—	
Benoit B. Mandelbrot	107
Analysis of Time Series—*John C. Hause*	108
Papers on Statistical and Economic Methodology—*Yoel Haitovsky*	109
Experimentation with Nonlinear Regression Programs—*Sidney Jacobs*	110
A Study of the Properties of the Minimum-Sum-of-Absolute-Errors Estimator—	
Thomas J. Sargent	111
10. ELECTRONIC COMPUTER SERVICES IN SUPPORT	
OF ECONOMIC RESEARCH	111
Introduction—*Charlotte Boschan*	111
Operations of the Data Processing Unit—*Charlotte Boschan*	112
NBER Computer Operations at New Haven—*Sanford Berg*	113
Progress Report on Project RIPP—*Richard Ruggles* and *Nancy D. Ruggles*	113
The National Bureau Data Bank—*Charlotte Boschan*	113
Programmed Determination of Cyclical Turning Point and Timing Measures—	
Charlotte Boschan	114
III. *CONFERENCES ON RESEARCH*	117
Conference on Research in Income and Wealth	118
Universities-National Bureau Committee for Economic Research	118
Universities-National Bureau Conference on the Application of the Computer	
to Economic Research	120
IV. *REPORT ON NEW PUBLICATIONS*	121
Introduction—*Joan R. Tron*	122
Reports Published Since June 1969	122
Publications Forthcoming	126
V. *ORGANIZATION*	127
Directors and Officers—*Douglas H. Eldridge*	128
Research Fellowships—*Victor R. Fuchs*	129
Staff Seminars—*W. M. Landes*	130
The National Bureau's Fiftieth Anniversary Program—*Nancy Steinthal*	132
VI. *ROSTER OF NATIONAL BUREAU STAFF*	135
VII. *PUBLICATIONS 1920–1970*	139
VIII. *FINANCES AND SOURCES OF SUPPORT*	153

I

Papers Presented to
the Board of Directors
at the
Spring Meeting, 1970

INTRODUCTION
John R. Meyer

Strong historical antecedents support the view that economic research has been best when it has been relevant. Certainly, that historical lesson seems authenticated when one looks back over the NBER's first fifty years. Indeed, the Bureau was started because men of affairs, of many political and philosophical viewpoints, perceived a strong need to establish as objectively as possible the facts about certain economic policy issues of their times.

At the Bureau's inaugural, two central policy questions dominated all others. The first of these was how income and wealth were distributed among different groups in society. The second was a concern with how to avoid major economic depressions and all the social and human losses attendant thereon. Both of these issues, that of distribution of the national wealth and the avoidance of business cycles, still remain with us. But I think it is safe to assert that the urgency and perceived severity of these issues, particularly the cyclical one, is a good deal less today than it was fifty years ago—and in no small part because of the NBER's contributions. The distribution question, for example, though it remains quite cogent, has assumed new dimensions. No longer is the focus exclusively on the allocation to different wealth classes. Increasingly, the issues of concern are how different minority groups, regions, and organizations participate in the national wealth and its growth over time.

In its fifty years of existence the NBER has not concentrated, of course, on only two problems. As the years have gone by, the Bureau has undertaken research in many other areas of policy concern. To a considerable extent these other interests have focused on what makes the national economy grow. Among the questions addressed have been: How do we measure productivity? How do we mobilize financial resources for investment in the human and physical capital needed to increase productivity? How do we organize our industry and market structure so as to provide the proper incentives for growth?

Certain practical lessons about quantitative economic research seem also to have been learned over the course of the last half century at the Bureau. We have learned, for example, that good quantitative research in economics can be expensive, both in terms of time and money. We have also learned that, to be done properly, it usually requires some minimum scale, again of time and money. As a rough rule of thumb, I would guess that effective quantitative research in economics involves projects of at least two or three years duration and no fewer than three to four professionals simultaneously. But I should immediately confess that these numbers are based more on intuition than on any hard empirical research or information!

Nevertheless, if correct, certain important conclusions about the organization of good empirical research flow from these observations. The first of these, quite simply, is that the basic problem in designing quantitative research programs in economics is to identify problems as early as possible, and ones that are likely to be with us for some time into the future.

The negative inferences to be drawn from this rule are quite as important, perhaps more so, than the positive ones. The rule obviously suggests, for example, that the more transitory policy problems are probably well avoided as topics for serious quantitative research. It would imply, in short, a focus on structural problems—on avoiding investigation of the symptomatic as contrasted with basic causal or behavioral relationships.

An emphasis on longer-term structural problems has several implications. First, in today's context it suggests a concentration on the study of growth processes. Second, it implies the need for a fairly broad historical perspective underlying the research design. Third, it suggests an emphasis on dynamic as contrasted with static models. Fourth, it would argue for less concern about equilibrium conditions and more involvement with the processes by which we move from one equilibrium to another. Finally, it would point toward a very considerable focus on technological change and the processes by which that change is achieved.

All this was very well summarized years ago when it was said, I believe by Schumpeter, that "the really important economic problems are typically identified with what the economist puts in *ceteris paribus.*" Changes in technology, tastes, and income distribution are typical items economists hold constant, and they are surely among the least constant of forces in our real world.

In designing a good research program in quantitative economics the major problem thus becomes that of identifying the substantive issues that will concern economic policy makers five years or a decade hence. That must be the constant preoccupation. With that in mind, we at the Bureau have sought the help of others in making such identifications, and have organized the effort into a series of colloquia to commemorate our fiftieth anniversary. The details of these colloquia are discussed elsewhere in this report (p. 132). Suffice it to say here that we have organized these meetings under six major headings, representing research interests of long-standing concern and involvement: (1) business cycles and forecasting; (2) public finance and expenditures; (3) human capital and its development; (4) financial institutions and markets; (5) the processes of economic growth; and (6) industrial organization and the functioning of markets.

As we begin this systematic survey of our research priorities for the next decade, I suspect that we shall find that the future policy problems quite naturally fall under three major headings. The first of these will be what we might call problems that "constitute more of the same." The second will be mutations or adaptations of present interests and problems. The third, and by far the most difficult to identify, will be entirely new departures and policy interests.

Thus, I shall hardly be surprised if we conclude that some problems of the 70's are nothing other than a continuation of problems already with us. To include these in our research interests it is really only necessary to decide that they are not likely to be solved quickly. A few examples quickly come to mind: understanding urban structure, that is, the ways in which urban complexes evolve and change over time in response to economic, political, legal, and social conditions; better comprehension of the impact of inflation and changes in industrial, demographic, and market composition on the ways in which we save and allocate investable funds; the relationships between local, state, and federal public finance as outlined in our last *Annual Report* by Bossons and Shoup; or the problems and questions raised by changes in international comparative advantage as suggested by Lary's survey in last year's *Annual Report*. One hardly needs much insight to suspect that all of these problems will be of concern for at least one more decade or so!

Similarly, certain problems of the 70's can be forecast simply because they will represent mutations of present problems. For example, economists almost surely will try to measure some of the negative aspects or externalities of economic activity. Certain environmental effects, such as air and water pollution, are perhaps the most obvious subjects for such attention; at least the most widely discussed. But there are many others. For example, deterioration in performance caused by increased congestion on major public transport facilities, such as highways or airports, clearly constitutes another area of important negative externalities worthy of investigation.

In general, the study of negative externalities is a quite natural extension of efforts, already under way at the Bureau, to better understand the contributions of nonmarket activities in our economy. Thomas Juster discusses these problems, the measurement of externalities and nonmarket activities, more thoroughly in a special report which immediately follows this one.

Concern with negative externalities, moreover, may lead us into some entirely new departures and research interests. We may be led to substantially rework our entire theory of consumer behavior, for example, to reflect new information and concepts on the allocation of time, or on the role of expectations in conditioning savings behavior under different regimes of price stability or instability. Perhaps, too, this new theory of consumer behavior might be more psychological and behavioral and less normative than the conventional theory. Furthermore, it might lead us into some radically different policy conclusions, perhaps by providing us with an improved capability to forecast the effects of tax or other policy changes under inflationary expectations.

I suspect that an interest in negative externalities will also lead us to investigate how we might use the price system in rather new and different ways, particularly to achieve stipulated social objectives in sectors where we have not relied extensively on the price system to date. The only alternative to better use of the price system to mitigate some problems may well be detailed planning beyond the present state of the art or conventional planning capabilities. Several possible areas for application of the price system to achieve efficiency or other objectives suggest themselves: major airports, urban streets and highways, parking facilities, postal services, legal and court services, communication services, common carrier freight services, commuter and transit services, military manpower recruitment, airline fares, and medical and hospital services. One can see by scanning the staff progress reports later in this *Annual Report* that many of these problems are already of concern to economists. Incidentally, only by better understanding the price system, its applicability and its limits, will we be able to estimate many of the benefits of various public and private programs aimed at correcting environmental and similar problems. And, only by the application of the price system will we be able in many cases to keep the costs of corrective action for such problems within reasonable bounds. After all, only in that way will we be able to identify the relevant margins of costs and benefits to be equated in an efficient solution.

This very brief list of new research possibilities is of course not exhaustive. I am sure that our fiftieth anniversary colloquia will uncover many suggestions and possibilities totally unrelated to those mentioned. Furthermore, I am sure that as a result of our deliberations we shall be able to define our research interests and objectives far more precisely than now. In essence, this list represents nothing more than a very simple and exceedingly brief summary of where we stand in our staff evaluations at this point in time.

Defining research priorities also involves, of course, more than simply recognizing or forecasting future areas of policy concern. There are also important problems of "research logistics," that is, of providing supporting data and methods to do the research. Indeed, one might suspect that an organization like the Bureau has at least as much of a role to play in meeting these needs as in the research itself.

I advanced some speculations in last year's *Annual Report* as to what some of these new methodological developments might be. One particular aspect of these developments that warrants special emphasis is the role of the computer and the technological revolution it is creating in economic research. As suggested earlier, there are reasons for believing that the emphasis in economics will increasingly be on complex dynamic models, often of a continuous disequilibrium character. The only feasible way now known for handling such efforts is through computer simulation. With the computer one can embody in the model nonlinearities, interdependencies, and other complications that defy simple mathematical representation. Mathematical modeling may also undergo a revolution in language as a result of the computer, with macrocomputer languages replacing the calculus and algebra as the major mode of expression.

With complex computer models, complex data bases will also be needed. During the next ten years the multivariate cross section will probably be the basic data source for most empirical research in economics. These cross sections, moreover, will increasingly be augmented by special surveys and censuses. The emphasis on cross-sectional microdata follows almost automatically once it is observed that these samples must contain as much information as the aggregates created from them. The major reason for relying exclusively on the aggregates in the past has simply been that we did not have the capability to handle the bookkeeping or data reduction problems posed by these large cross-section samples. And, of course, there are important privacy or secrecy problems that should keep us from using totally disaggregated and identifiable data on individual businesses, households, or establishments. The computer, properly used, provides a sensible way of meeting some of these problems; that is, of doing the data reduction and the bookkeeping while still maintaining the privacy and guarding the identity of individual sources.

As suggested in last year's *Annual Report,* and as many of the individual staff progress reports within this report indicate, new statistical techniques may also be required when employing these new data bases. In general, I suspect that these new data will increasingly move us beyond the traditional econometric preoccupation with regression analysis, and will involve economists increasingly in other multivariate analytic techniques.

This new emphasis on microdata does not mean, however, that economists will lose all interest in the economic aggregates. These will continue to be of prime importance in setting and evaluating much of fiscal and monetary policy. Even here, though, particularly in the analysis of aggregate time series, there is considerable room for improvement. Specifically, we in the profession need better ways of disseminating our macromodels, so as to facilitate their replication and further development. We also need faster, more accurate, and less expensive ways of maintaining widely used time series data on aggregate economic performance.

Toward meeting these various needs, the Bureau has now established its third "Conference Series," a collaborative effort with other institutions and individuals. The initial objective of this new undertaking is to improve the dissemination of computer software and "machine-readable data" to those doing quantitative research in economics. We have also continued to explore the possibility of establishing an experimental "computer utility" for economic and related research, an innovation which could do much to meet the identifiable needs for better aggregate data and time series analyses.

We have also given considerable thought during the past year to realizing Wesley Clair Mitchell's ambition, expressed in the *Fifteenth Annual Report*, that the Bureau become truly national in reality as well as in name. As a step toward that goal, we hope to establish within the next several months or so a West Coast branch of the Bureau, on land leased gratis to us by Stanford University. The proposed site would be just off the Stanford Campus and directly adjacent to the Center for Behavioral Studies. The major remaining obstacle to the creation of this establishment is to assemble the financial resources needed to construct and furnish the building that will house the forty or so researchers and aides planned for the facility. Toward that goal, the Bureau has already received a commitment of approximately $250,000 from an anonymous donor; however approximately $200,000 to $250,000 more is needed before the undertaking can be formally launched. If this experiment with a detached branch facility proves successful, it could be a prototype for similar experiments elsewhere, if and as resources permitted.

In sum, the problems and techniques of economic research, even its physical locale, have been and are undergoing change. We at the Bureau should respond to these changes as they emerge. I am sure that we can and will. In that way, but only in that way, can we have as productive a second fifty years as we have had in our first fifty.

ON THE MEASUREMENT OF ECONOMIC AND SOCIAL PERFORMANCE

F. Thomas Juster

Introduction

Although most economic concepts remain a mystery to the majority of even well-informed laymen, the "Gross National Product" has become part of our everyday vocabulary. The widespread use of this concept, both at professional and popular levels, attests to the fact that GNP is generally thought to be a simple, unambiguous, and comprehensive measure of economic performance. But what has always been recognized by professionals is now beginning to be recognized by others: that the GNP is neither simple, nor unambiguous, nor comprehensive; and that it is not necessarily a good measure of economic performance.

The National Bureau, and, in particular, Simon Kuznets, played a major role in developing a conceptual and empirical framework for the measurement of national income and output. The structure of the U.S. National Income Accounts was largely the creation of Milton Gilbert and his colleagues at the U.S. Department of Commerce, while the present system of accounts in the U.S. has been greatly influenced by George Jaszi. Kuznets' work tended to focus more on the normative aspects (what should be included in real national output and has total output grown or declined?), while Gilbert, Jaszi, and their colleagues have tended to focus more on the behavioral aspects (what economic activities have firms, households, and governments actually engaged in).[1]

Many of the conceptual problems raised in the course of developing the

---

[1] The concept and measurement of aggregate income and output are discussed in several National Bureau publications. In particular, see Simon Kuznets, *National Income and Its Composition, 1919-1938*, 1941, Vols. I and II. Also, Kuznets, *National Product in Wartime*, 1945.

The structure of the U.S. accounts in their formative stage is discussed in Volume 10 of Studies in Income and Wealth, 1947. The framework underlying the U.S. National Income Accounts system is discussed in Jaszi's "The Conceptual Basis of the Accounts: A Re-examination" in *A Critique of the United States Income and Product Accounts*, Vol. 22 of Studies in Income and Wealth, 1958.

U.S. system of National Income Accounts (let us call them simply the "accounts") were never satisfactorily resolved but simply ceased to be discussed, and the conventions adopted by the Department of Commerce gradually came to be accepted by both producers and users of the data. But the early problems still remain, others that were not well understood then are better understood now, and still others that have always been widely recognized have become more important in a quantitative sense.

Our present system of accounts represents the application of two principal criteria to the measurement of economic activity: first, that output is best defined to include only goods and services bought and sold in the market; second, that a few selected nonmarket activities should be included in output because they are analytically indistinguishable from closely related market activities. The latter criterion is designed to prevent shifts of functionally identical activities from the market to the nonmarket sector, or vice versa, from changing measured ouput.[2] In short, the existing income and product accounts focus on the measurement of economic activity in the market, supplemented by imputed measurements for a few nonmarket activities with a close correspondence to market activities.

Sources of Dissatisfaction with GNP Accounts

National income statisticians have always expressed dissatisfaction with various aspects of the present system of accounts, but their discontent has not resulted in much change in practice—possibly because no one thought that the results would really look very different if the accounts were adjusted to reflect various suggested changes, and partly because many of the suggestions could not easily be implemented empirically. Both of these arguments have become less compelling in recent years, and there have been a number of studies aimed at providing the empirical groundwork for a restructured set of accounts that incorporate conceptual changes which many have long thought to be desirable.[3]

The current disaffection pertains to a number of specific areas: (1) the treatment of nonmarket activities; (2) the way in which output is classified between consumption and investment; (3) the widespread use of input costs

---

[2] To illustrate, homeowners do not actually pay rent to themselves for housing services, while renters buy housing services in the market. Thus the market criterion would count the services of rental housing as output, but not the services of owner-occupied housing. But such a treatment is so clearly incongruous that the builders of the accounts long ago decided in favor of imputing a value for the services of owner-occupied housing, using the rental price of equivalent housing to measure the flow of services. Over the years a substantial array of similarly motivated imputations have been included in the accounts as part of measured output. Imputations are made for the value of food consumed on farms, for the value of checking account services rendered by banks, etc.

[3] The recent study by Richard and Nancy Ruggles *(The Design of Economic Accounts)* suggests a number of alterations in the conceptual framework of the accounts, and provides some empirical estimates. Both John Kendrick and Robert Eisner have been directing NBER research projects designed to provide empirical estimates of economic activities that are presently excluded from the accounts. These range from the imputed cost of students' time and the value of free consumpion provided by business firms to employees, to the impact of capital gains on both aggregate income and income distribution.

to measure the amount of output; and (4) the adequacy of the accounts as a measure of social and economic welfare. In technical terms, these can be thought of as problems relating to the measurement of output in current prices (the first and to some extent the second), problems relating to the deflation of current price output (the third and in part the fourth), and problems relating to the analytical functions to be served by the accounts (the second and fourth).

For nonmarket activities, the problems cover income-producing activities that are omitted from the accounts as well as excluded activities that produce negative benefits. Use of the market criterion for defining output means that a secular shift in activity from the market to the nonmarket sector, or vice versa, will tend to produce a growth rate for measured output that is either too high or too low. For example, if an increasing fraction of housewives enter the labor force, the growth of measured output will tend to be biased upward because paid jobs constitute output but housewives' activities do not. If young people tend to stay longer in school and thus do not enter the labor force until they are older, and if, as a result, "student hours" grow more rapidly than labor force hours, the growth rate of measured output will contain a downward bias because student "work" is not considered to be output. And an increase in environmental deterioration over time would not show up as a decline in real output because the flow of benefits from the environment is not counted as output to begin with.[4]

The second area (the distribution of output between consumption and investment) has long been a source of concern to national income statisticians. The accounts do not even claim to measure total investment, since they count as investment only additions to the stocks of business capital assets and residential housing. All other output is either intermediate product (coal into steel) or consumption. Yet households possess a very large stock of durable goods (in addition to housing) which yield future services and thus constitute capital assets; governments possess an increasingly large stock of capital assets in the form of schools, highways, etc.; business firms accumulate assets in the form of knowledge acquired through research and development, an activity which has grown substantially in the postwar period and, if included, would now constitute an appreciable fraction of total business capital outlays; and investment in humans (schooling, to take the obvious case) is not only a rapidly growing form of capital outlay but one that probably represents the largest single component of total investment in the economy. Yet we continue to use a system of accounts that fails to recognize these forms of capital accumulation as investments.[5]

---

[4] Programs designed to reduce environmental deterioration—investment in pollution control, for example—are quite apt to show up as increased real output, as indeed they should if the benefits from the program exceed the costs. However, the level of output would still be overstated relative to the level in past years when there was no need for pollution control because there was less pollution.

[5] Some rough estimates of investment in knowledge, human capital, household durables, and public durables are contained in F. T. Juster, *Household Capital Formation and Financing, 1897-1962*, 1966. John Kendrick is currently engaged in an NBER study designed to provide comprehensive estimates of investment in the United States along the lines discussed above.

The third source of concern has more to do with deficiencies in the measurement of real output, given the present scope and structure of the accounts, than with concept or coverage. In significant areas of economic activity, what the accounts record as output is measured entirely by inputs or costs. For products like automobiles, steel, clothing, etc., the accounts measure the value of output directly using expenditures and an index of output prices. But for most publicly provided services, for the production of services like health and education, and for the production of goods and services where changes in the quality of output are important but difficult to estimate, output measures do not exist: instead, the quantity of inputs is used to measure the quantity of output.[6]

To illustrate: Most services rendered by governments are conventionally valued by the salaries paid to public employees plus the cost of any complementary inputs purchased in the market. Thus, the "output" of police services is measured by salaries paid to members of the police department, the cost of police cars, etc., not by the social and economic value of crimes prevented or violators apprehended; the value of education, whether public or private, is measured as the cost of teachers' salaries, teaching equipment purchased in the market, the cost of school buildings, etc., not by the value imputable to the gain in pupil knowledge; and the value of health services is measured by the cost of doctors' fees and drugs, not by the reduction in mortality rates, the reduction in time lost on account of illness, etc.

Although this class of problems is endemic in the service industries, it is by no means absent in the traditional goods industries. During wartime, for example, we usually measure the value of munitions output by adding up the cost of the inputs required to produce them: the reason is our inability to design a meaningful and independent measure of output prices. And in any product category where technological change is important and where the product has a multidimensional utility to users, the same difficulty tends to arise although in a somewhat disguised form. For example, measures of clothing output will be unaffected by changes in either durability or maintenance costs associated with changes in the mix of material inputs, *unless* the change adds to production costs. To the national income accountant, in effect, "a suit is a suit is a suit"—unless it costs more (or less) to make.

Finally, it has become apparent even to nonprofessionals that GNP is not an adequate measure of social or economic welfare. This will come as no surprise to the national income statistician: the accounts were quite consciously *not* designed to measure welfare. But most people, including economists, have always supposed that GNP and welfare were, in fact, closely enough related so that changes in the one could be identified by looking at

---

[6] The basic problem here is largely one of constructing an appropriate deflator for converting current-price output into real or constant-price output. For measuring current-price output, it makes no difference whether we use input costs or output values since the two must be identical. But for constant-price measures, it is clearly undesirable to infer changes in output from changes in input costs unless productivity change can be measured independently. In practice, moreover, even the current-price measures are apt to be distorted in the public sector, since not all the inputs are likely to be counted. In particular, because capital accounting in the public sector is notoriously poor and usually nonexistent, capital costs are likely to be understated.

changes in the other. It is increasingly clear that such an assumption is unwarranted.

Just to cite a few of the more dramatic specifics that cause GNP and welfare measures to diverge, virtually any type of disaster—personal or national—will cause the GNP to rise rather than fall. If a man's wife is killed in an automobile accident and he is thus forced to hire a housekeeper to care for his children, the GNP will rise because housekeepers' services are counted and housewives' services are not—and the stock of human capital is not reduced because it was not counted to begin with. A tornado that sweeps through Texas and destroys millions of dollars worth of capital assets will almost certainly cause the GNP to rise: workers must be hired to clean up the debris and rebuild the destroyed assets, and at least some of these resources would have preferred leisure (which is not measured) to market activity (which is). Moreover, the capital loss involved in destruction of property and lives does not explicitly enter the accounts at all, and is unlikely to have much if any influence even in subsequent years. Finally, social catastrophes like wars will often cause GNP to rise,[7] partly because work is substituted for leisure and partly because we have no way of measuring the loss in efficiency that usually results from shifting economic resources from peacetime to wartime uses.

Other manifestations of the GNP-welfare distortion are the treatment of time allocation, of "free" goods and services, and of by-products that yield negative benefits. Moreover, an aggregate measure like GNP cannot register the fact that welfare does not depend solely on aggregate performance but is sensitive to the way in which at least some of the aggregates are distributed among the population.

For time allocation, the problem is simply that only time spent at paid activity is counted as part of output. Hence, an increase in leisure or in time spent at unpaid (nonmarket) activities will not cause any direct increase in GNP, while time taken from leisure to sit in traffic jams or to wait for the appearance of the local commuter train will not make the GNP any less. Similarly, outputs that are "free goods," and therefore do not have to be produced in the market, are ignored in GNP despite the fact that these products are apt to have precise counterparts which *are* included in GNP in other economies precisely because they are *not* free and must be produced. For example, residents of the Virgin Islands need neither heating nor cooling equipment, since their fortunate location provides an unlimited supply of 70° weather for which Americans pay substantial sums every year; their requirements for clothing and shelter are reduced for the same reason. But this natural bounty is wholly ignored by the GNP statistician.

The problem of negative by-products has been discussed above: the basic difficulty is that no accounting is made for the decline in utility resulting from the unwanted side effects of economic activity—rivers that cannot be used for recreation, parks that are cluttered with disposable bottles, etc.[8]

---

[7] A really destructive event like a major earthquake or a war that devastates large parts of the country will probably show up as a decline even in measured real output.

[8] In the literature, the classic case of unwanted side effects was the rise in the costs of maintaining the exterior of a house because of soot emanating from neighboring factory smokestacks.

Finally, a perhaps inescapable shortcoming of the GNP accounts from a welfare viewpoint is the fact that they focus entirely on aggregates and pay no attention to the distribution of these aggregates. An economic system which generates conspicuously high incomes for some classes of its citizens and much lower incomes for other classes is unlikely to be as viable as one which provides a more even distribution of rewards. A system in which the distribution of the tax burden is widely regarded as unfair and inequitable is unlikely to have the same prospects for future performance as one in which the same burden is distributed with fewer perceived inequities. And a system in which the same total population is heavily concentrated in a small number of geographic areas is likely to generate a substantially higher level of negative social and economic by-products than one in which population is more widely dispersed.[9] These aspects of welfare are in principle much more difficult to quantify than many of the others discussed above, although it is conceptually feasible to quantify the costs of removing many of the outward manifestations of distributional distortions.

Framework of the Present Accounts

In examining the problem of social and economic measurement, it is useful to recall the origins of our present system of national accounts. This system was shaped and developed during the 1930's and 1940's when the most obvious forces affecting the level and movement of economic activity were initially cyclical, subsequently national defense. During major cyclical swings in the level of economic activity, focusing on market output produced a measure whose welfare implications were probably very similar to those that would have resulted from focusing on a much broader range of activities. And during a major war, the emphasis was naturally on productive capacity for military output, for which a measure like GNP is reasonably well suited. Hence, given the catastrophic decline in market activity during the Great Depression and the subsequent recovery with the eruption of World War II, many of the conceptual problems that had been extensively discussed during the formative period of the income accounts gradually came to be regarded as of little practical or analytical significance, and the accounts came to be largely a reflection of "activity" regardless of the purposes to which the activity was devoted.

Thus the present national income and product accounts of the U.S. are basically designed to measure cyclical changes in total activity. In such a framework, the focus is on flow of inputs and outputs; stocks of assets are important only insofar as they cause cyclical movements in the related flows.[10]

---

[9] This statement is not inconsistent with the observation that population shifts have historically been from sparsely populated rural areas towards densely populated urban areas, rather than the reverse: The balance of gains and losses can be positive even if the losses are substantial.

[10] The investment part of the accounts consists only of business plant and equipment and residential housing, which, during the 1930's, were the major sources of cyclical variability in investment activity. The relative unimportance of the assets themselves in the structure of the accounts, as distinct from the investment flows which add to assets, is underscored by the almost exclusive reliance in current usage on *gross* national product

Similar reasons explain the preoccupation of the present accounts with that portion of time allocated to market activities: If cyclical variability is the major concern, the critical labor–time variables are the amount of market employment and unemployment, not the amount of time that people choose to allocate to nonmarket activities, leisure, etc. Hence, the allocation of labor time has always been treated as a simple flow of inputs yielding market income, with no attention paid to the fact that time allocated to the market is only one of many possible uses.

Given this background, it was natural for the emphasis to be on a system of accounts designed to trace variations in output, employment, and productivity in the market sector, where performance during the 1930's had been so unsatisfactory. Moreover, it was entirely reasonable during this period to equate changes in output thus measured with changes in economic and social welfare, since changes in the one dominated changes in the other. But during the past few decades, the combination of sharply reduced cyclical movements in market output and the changing importance of nonmarket activities have made market output an increasingly poor measure of economic and social well being.[11]

An Alternative Framework

In general terms, economic and social output can be thought of as a flow of satisfactions or utilities generated by combining the services of various types of capital assets. A wide variety of such assets exist in the system, and these assets produce a number of different kinds of utilities. The assets themselves can be classified into five broad categories: (1) tangible capital assets (equipment and structures); (2) intangible capital assets (knowledge); (3) human capital assets (skills and talents); (4) physical environmental assets; (5) sociopolitical environmental assets.

Tangible capital assets comprise business assets, consumer assets divided into housing and durables, and government assets.[12] Intangible assets result

---

rather than *net* national product: the difference between GNP and NNP is, of course, simply the amount of capital stock estimated to be used up in the process of producing current output. Yet one rarely hears any mention of NNP (or its cousin, national income). One important reason is that most economists use the accounts to measure cyclical changes, and the capital consumption component of gross investment has little or no cyclical content.

[11] It is important to keep in mind that analysis of cyclical variability in output is still, and will presumably continue to be, a major use of any system of national accounts. Hence the emphasis should be on extension and refinement of the existing accounts to make them more useful for the analysis of trends in social and economic welfare, while at the same time insuring that a market subsector is retained to facilitate cyclical analysis.

In point of fact, a greatly expanded set of accounts with a "market activity" subsector might well be *more* useful for cyclical analysis than the present system. It is hard to believe that the quantitatively important collection of imputations now included in the accounts (e.g., housing services) adds anything to their usefulness for analysis of cyclical behavior.

[12] As noted above, only business tangible assets and housing are treated as capital assets in the present system of accounts. At some stages of economic development, defining capital assets in this way might have been appropriate and useful. But in a world where business firms spend upwards of $20 billion a year on research and development

from the application of human capital and other resources to research and development problems. This process results in the production of socially useful knowledge, a type of asset that is analytically distinct from the skills and talents of the people who produced that knowledge. Human skills and talents represent both innate ability and training, the latter ranging all the way from parental time spent with children through formal schooling and on to work experience designed to aid future productivity. Physical environmental assets can be thought of as comprising natural resources as traditionally viewed: mineral and agricultural wealth; other natural assets like temperature, precipitation, water, and air; and partly man-made assets like forest preserves and parks. The assets comprising the physical environment and the sociopolitical environment overlap to some degree. While welfare-producing assets like the amount and distribution of water resources and the quality of the atmosphere clearly belong in the physical environment category, environmental assets like population density are partly physical and partly social. The major assets in the sociopolitical category are difficult to define precisely, but are meant to cover such concepts as equity, security, freedom, social and economic mobility, privacy, and so forth.

Specifying a structure of economic and social accounts in which outputs (benefits) are derived from these assets seems both useful and possible, at least in principle. Empirical implementation is another matter; while clearly feasible in some cases, it is not possible at present for others and may not be realizable at all for some. Nonetheless, the exercise seems worthwhile, since the purpose of a system of accounts is to provide a conceptual framework for all meaningful and measurable aspects of social and economic performance.

Net economic and social output can be defined as the sum of direct consumption benefits yielded by this collection of assets, plus or minus net changes in the assets themselves. For most goods and services that pass through the marketplace, the suggested set of accounts would differ little if at all from the present accounts: net output would still consist of the flow of consumption goods and services plus net changes in the stock of capital assets used to produce the output.[13] However, there would be major differ-

---

(which clearly adds to the stock of useful knowledge and hence to future output); where the single most important capital asset in the economy is not business capital equipment but the stock of human skills and talents; where consumer and government capital assets in the form of roads, dams, automobiles, furniture, appliances, etc., are much larger than business-owned capital assets (the only difference being that consumers and governments use capital assets to produce services that are not bought and sold in the market); and where our natural resource and environmental assets are, in the view of many, being depleted and despoiled at a rapidly expanding rate; it seems just as incongruous now to exclude these facets of economic and social activity from being reflected in the national accounts as it must have seemed forty years ago to exclude residential housing.

[13] To produce market output, business firms combine the services of capital assets with material and labor inputs to produce goods and services which yield, directly or indirectly, a flow of utilities to consumers. In measuring results or performance, GNP represents the total value of all goods and services produced, depreciation represents the amount of capital equipment used up in producing these goods and services, and net national product is the total value of output less depreciation. The measurement of net output recognizes the fact that capital assets may be used up in producing a current

ences. First, a much wider range of outputs would be recognized as contributing to economic and social welfare, including some that are free for some countries or regions while only obtainable through the use of scarce resources for others. Second, changes in stocks for a much wider range of assets would be explicitly taken into account, with a resulting tendency to increase or reduce measured net output depending on whether assets were being augmented or reduced as a consequence of activity in the system. For example, deterioration of the physical environment because of various types of pollution—air, water, noise, waste—means that the flow of benefits from this asset has been reduced. Thus, where the process of economic growth deteriorates the physical environment, an augmented set of accounts would register the usual increases in net output resulting from growth in the market sector, but they would also record an offset consisting of the degree to which physical environmental assets had been depreciated, with a consequent reduction in the flow of future benefits.[14]

A Preliminary Look at Concepts

Empirical implementation of this suggested structure for economic and social accounts cannot be seriously explored here, but a few of the more far-reaching conceptual changes are worth examining in more detail. Before proceeding, it would be well to recognize the basic value structure ordinarily embedded in economic accounts. The implicit assumption underlying almost all measures of aggregate monetary output is that goods and services are worth their value "at the margin" as determined by the least anxious buyer—not, for example, what they are worth to the average buyer nor what buyers would pay if required. It is also assumed that marginal value is equal to marginal cost as measured by resource inputs. Thus, automobiles are valued at prices like $3,000 per unit and cans of tomato juice at prices like 30¢ per unit, reflecting an assumption that "at the margin" one automobile could be turned into 10,000 cans of tomato juice in terms of resources required to produce them and in terms of utility to consumers.

Time Allocation in the National Accounts

The valuation of costs and returns implicit in the accounts suggests that the total return to an extra hour of leisure time must, at the margin, be equal to the return from an extra hour of work, provided that consumers have a

---

flow of goods and services, with a consequent reduction in the capacity to produce future goods and services. If some of the goods produced are themselves capital assets, and if their value exceeds the wearing out of existing assets so that future production of goods and services is enhanced, net output will consist of consumption goods and services plus additions to the stock of assets.

[14] Alternatively, the community might choose to halt or reduce further deterioration, or to reduce accumulated deterioration, by diverting scarce resources to that end. In that case, the flow of benefits from the physical environment would either not be reduced as much as otherwise because environmental assets are more fully maintained or, if the level of accumulated deterioration were actually reduced, environmental assets and the consequent flow of future benefits would be increased because net environmental investment would have taken place.

continuous range of choice about the division of time between work and leisure. Time spent at earning income in the market yields an indirect flow of utilities in the form of purchased goods and services, while time spent at all other activities yields a direct flow of either present or future utilities that should be valued at the market wage rate. The same valuation would presumably apply to time spent in activities designed to maintain human capital (sleeping, eating, etc.), to activities that involve net investment in human capital (studying to increase one's future productivity, or spending time in training one's children so as to increase theirs), or to activities that involve direct consumption benefits (going to a baseball game or to the opera).[15]

In principle, we would want to count as output all of the services yielded by the application of human skills to welfare-producing activities. The total returns would constitute gross output, while net output would be the total less the amount of activity required to maintain the stock of human capital. Gross output could include either positive or negative net investment, depending on the extent to which activities added to the stock of skills through additional training or reduced skills because they failed to offset obsolescence and depreciation. At present, the accounts essentially specify that only the application of human skills to activities that result in money earnings are to be counted as output, and no adjustment is made for either positive or negative net investment in the stock of human capital. Hence, students, housewives, hospital volunteers, unpaid members of civic or social agencies, vacationers, and Wednesday afternoon golfers are all presumed to be engaged in nonproductive activity.

The possibilities for anomalies are boundless: we can get some insight into the appropriate treatment by noting some of the characteristics of the existing treatment which are clearly unsatisfactory. For example, according to the present system, output is increased if a woman stops putting in ten hours a week at a remedial reading clinic for ghetto youngsters and begins to work ten hours a week as a dental technician; output will be increased if a clinical health program manned by volunteers becomes funded through a government grant and the volunteers thus receive pay; output is increased if a man who ordinarily takes off one afternoon a week to relax is coerced into earning income during that afternoon; output is reduced if, to cite the traditional case, a man marries his housekeeper; and so on.

---

[15] Two points should be noted. First, it is not at all clear that the market wage rate is the appropriate measure of productivity in all (any?) nonmarket activities. If people allocate time rationally, however, there is much to be said for adopting that convention as a first approximation.

Second, it is interesting to speculate about the policy implications of the investment in human capital that takes the form of parental training of children. The total amount of this type of investment might well be appreciable compared with the investment in human capital that takes the form of regular schooling. If market wage rates measure the value of parental time inputs, there would necessarily be marked differentials in the amount of such investment by parents in different socioeconomic groups, given equal time inputs. Hence, there would be large differences in the estimated quantities of "capital" with which youngsters begin formal schooling, since they would have been exposed to a large amount of parental "investment" valued at markedly different imputed wage rates. The differential would be even wider if the amount of parental time invested in children were positively correlated with wage rates, as may well be the case. In short, compensatory education might have a very large differential to overcome, perhaps of the order of several years worth of investment in formal schooling.

Another aspect of the current treatment concerns the handling of depreciation and depletion of human skills. An implicit allowance for these factors enters the present accounts because all nonmarket allocations of time are ignored, including blocks of time used for the maintenance of human capital—time spent in sleeping and eating, as suggested above. While these types of activities could be considered as gross output, they are clearly not net output. But consider what would happen if a pill were invented that revitalized and restored the human body and mind in the same way that sleep does but without a time cost of seven or eight hours per day. Under the present system of accounts, this gain of 50 per cent in available time would not increase output except to the extent that the time was used to earn money income in the market. Otherwise, the present accounts would say that nothing has changed.

Finally, what of involuntary idleness? In some respects, the present convention of valuing only time spent at market employment is perfectly adequate: if someone is employed only part-time who would prefer to work full-time, or if someone is wholly unemployed, conventionally measured output is lower than it would otherwise be. Since time allocation is clearly suboptimal when unemployment exists, a welfare-oriented measure should indicate a decline in output. The appropriate treatment, in principle, would put a low or zero value on time spent in being involuntarily underemployed, given the market wage rate: being involuntarily idle is obviously different in a welfare context from choosing not to work on Saturday or on Wednesday afternoon (for pay) and to do something else instead.[16]

However, even the present conventions do not take full account of the effect on human capital of long periods of involuntary idleness. Surely one of the major costs of the depression of the 1930's was the erosion of human skills and talent due to prolonged and involuntary inability to use those talents in income-earning jobs. If human capital were recognized by the income accounts, prolonged and involuntary idleness that resulted in an acceleration of depreciation would reduce output to an even greater extent than the loss of currently produced goods and services, because of its effect on the stock of human capital and, in turn, on future output.

Physical and Sociopolitical Environmental Assets

One of the oldest questions troubling income theorists concerns the proper treatment of activities, mainly but not entirely governmental, designed primarily to prevent a reduction in social or economic welfare, e.g., the use of resources for national defense purposes. During the Second World War the United States devoted close to half of its total resources to military purposes: Should this have been considered net output in a welfare sense or a cost of maintaining the social environment? One suggested solution was that government-provided goods and services should be counted as net output to the extent that they were paid for by taxes, on the theory that willingness to pay

---

[16] Implementation of the "full output" notion thus requires much better information than we now have on the extent of involuntary idleness, defined to mean the difference between the amount of time people would prefer to work in the market, given the wage rate, and the amount they actually work.

taxes indicated a willingness to pay the price (foregone private goods and services) of these services. Hence, in the military output case, the community must place at least as much value on maintenance of the social environment as on the private consumption that could otherwise have been obtained. While this criterion correctly indicates that the community is better off using resources for national defense than not doing so, it does not register the simple fact that a deterioration of the sociopolitical environment will impose costs and thereby reduce welfare. This is to say, using resources for national defense may impose a lower welfare penalty than not doing so, but some welfare penalty cannot be avoided.

In principle, it is thus hard to see the objection to a criterion which says that the costs of maintaining a "given" social and political environment constitutes gross but not net output. A country which needs, or thinks it needs, to spend a quarter of its resources to maintain a military establishment for defense against actual or potential enemies is less well off than one which needs to spend only one-tenth or one-twentieth of its resources in this way, other things being equal. And a shift in the political stability of the world community which results in the need, real or imagined, for all nations to expand military expenditures from 10 to 20 per cent of total output has clearly diminished the social and economic well-being of the entire community.[17]

It is not of course only military outlays that fit this category. A community or world that needs to spend more resources on policemen, firemen, burglar alarms, safety locks, night watchmen, etc. is clearly worse off than a community or world in which these outlays can be kept to a minimum. No one buys police or fire protection, or hires night watchmen, because these services

---

[17] There is an interesting difference between the case in which real or imagined needs for defense cause a country to use x per cent of its resources for military purposes, and the case in which deterioration of the physical environment causes the country to use the same x per cent of resources to control pollution. In the latter case, there is a strong presumption that deterioration of the environment is a direct consequence of the normal functioning and growth of the economy: if so, the accounts clearly overstate the flow of benefits from economic growth unless they include an allowance for the negative by-products of growth.

In the former case, however, it is far from clear that deterioration of the sociopolitical environment, as manifested by the need to maintain a large defense establishment, is a direct consequence of the functioning and growth of the economic and social system. One could conceive of circumstances in which that might be the case; e.g., an aggressor nation that builds up its military strength in order to conquer other countries and thence derive future economic benefits. But in general the causality is unclear.

If the size of a defense establishment is basically unrelated to the functioning of the system but is simply an exogenous event, should one "penalize" the system by registering defense outlays as costs of maintaining the sociopolitical environment? If the objective is to measure social and economic welfare, it seems that the answer should be yes: resources used for defense cannot be used elsewhere, and I cannot see that it matters *for purposes of measurement* whether defense needs are a cause of one's own actions, are real but exogenous to one's actions, or are wholly imaginary. It does, however, make a great deal of difference *for purposes of policy decisions* whether or not the system has caused its own defense needs. If this is the case, there is a large hidden cost to a change in social policy that increases the optimum size of the defense establishment, just as there is a large hidden cost to a growth policy that produces deterioration in the physical environment as an inevitable concomitant of growth.

If defense needs are unrelated to economic and social policy, however, the appropriate analogy is to phenomena like earthquakes, floods, and other natural disasters: welfare is willy-nilly reduced, and there is nothing that can be done about it. But the reduction is real and needs to be registered in the accounts.

are desired per se: if there were no crime or fires, and no risk of either, there would be no expenditure on crime or fire prevention and everyone would be better off.[18]

It is interesting to contrast these preventive or environmental maintenance activities with those that involve the production of "positive" benefits. The two can be distinguished by asking whether society will always receive additional benefits from devoting additional resources to the activity. In the case of preventive activities, the answer is no: once resources are sufficient to reduce the level and risk of damage to zero (i.e., once we have hired enough policemen) no benefit accrues from hiring more. But this would not be true of resources devoted to producing houses or operas or baseball games: there is no natural limit to the amount of resources that will yield additional benefits in the aggregate for these activities, although there is of course a zero marginal utility point for any specific product and individual.

This analysis has quantitatively important implications for the measurement of net output. Not only do we in the United States spend a large fraction of total output on national defense and related activities, but it appears we have also been spending a growing proportion of output on public and private preventive activities of various sorts—policemen, firemen, private guards, weapons, safety locks, etc.

The analytically appropriate treatment is to view the social and political environment as an asset which yields direct consumption benefits in and of itself and also permits other productive activities to be carried on without interference. Like any asset, the social and political environment can deteriorate or depreciate, and it may do so for reasons having no causal association with activities designed to increase material well-being. Expenditures required to "maintain the asset intact" would thus constitute gross but not net output of the system. In the case discussed above, wars, crimes, and fires are some specific manifestations (costs) of environmental deterioration, while resources spent to suppress these manifestations must be presumed to have enabled environmental assets to be better maintained than in their absence. Thus, "depreciation" of the asset "sociopolitical environment" can be estimated as the *sum* of two components: first, costs imposed by the amount of deterioration that has been permitted to occur (as reflected by the damage resulting from crimes, fires, wars, etc.); second, costs incurred to maintain the asset at its present level (the resources represented by the services of policemen, firemen, members of the Armed Forces, etc.). In the absence of maintenance expenditures, or in the event of their reduction, it must be presumed that the asset would deteriorate further and that the costs represented by the specific manifestations of deterioration would thus increase. Optimum social policy, of course, consists of equating at the margin the cost functions associated with these two activities.

Before proceeding to examine similar problems relating to the physical environment—air and water pollution, waste accumulation, etc.—it is worth

---

[18] The relevant class of activities actually extends far beyond the national or personal security outlays discussed here. For example, resources used for medical care are largely in the same category: few people go to hospitals because they enjoy the rest and the good food!

noting that the distinction between gross and net output is a much more treacherous problem in social and economic accounts than is generally realized. To be precise, much of what economists have always considered to be output might be described more appropriately as intermediate product (a cost of producing output) rather than net output. As a simple illustration, take the treatment of laundry services—washing machines, clothes dryers, commercial laundromats, cleaning establishments, and so forth. Conventional income accounts treat outlays for these products and services as current consumption. But they really comprise a collection of inputs designed to maintain a stock of clothing at a given level of cleanliness and neatness. The real "net output" associated with these expenditures is not the expenditure itself but the flow of utility that comes from wearing clothes that are clean and pressed rather than soiled and rumpled. Evidently, if clean clothes could be obtained without the need to incur these costs, real output would not be reduced at all. Thus, the accounts should in principle treat the stock of clean clothes as an asset, the amount of dirt and other foreign matter introduced into clean clothes by the normal process of wearing them (or by living in a heavily polluted urban environment) as depreciation, and expenditures for laundries, dry cleaning, and washing machines as costs associated with maintaining the asset.

Physical Environment

By now the appropriate analytical treatment of the much-discussed subject of environmental pollution should be evident. A community starts off with some stock of environmental assets—air and water of a certain degree of purity, roads that are free of abandoned cars, playgrounds and streets free of discarded newspapers, broken bottles, and so forth. As a (perhaps inevitable) part of the process of industrialization and economic growth, these environmental assets tend to deteriorate or depreciate, thus reducing the flow of benefits from environmental assets. Expenditures designed to slow down or reduce deterioration are clearly costs associated with the maintenance of the asset rather than an output of the system. As with the sociopolitical environment discussed earlier, the full cost of deterioration is the sum of the reduced yield on the asset plus any costs incurred to prevent even greater deterioration.[19]

It is not easy to see how, in practice, one would measure the social and economic costs of environmental deterioration. One possibility is to estimate the cost of restoring the environment to some specified (previously attained?) level of purity, viewing these costs as a measure of the welfare loss from the actual level of deterioration. This procedure would almost certainly tend to overstate the true cost: The welfare loss from deterioration is likely to be an increasing function of the amount of deterioration, while the costs of prevent-

---

[19] Alternatively, one could view industrialization and economic growth as producing a series of dis-products and dis-services—various kinds of impurities and undesired products introduced into the physical environment and left there. In the absence of expenditures designed to reduce environmental deterioration, real net output is decreased by the negative value of these dis-products and dis-services.

ing deterioration are likely to rise sharply as the zero deterioration level is approached. That is, at very low levels of pollution, an increase in the amount of pollutant probably involves little or no welfare loss at the margin, but the loss is likely to rise rapidly as the pollution level increases to the point where discomfort, illness, or death begin to appear. And the marginal costs of removing the first 10 per cent of existing pollutants is likely to be small compared with the costs of getting rid of the last 10 per cent once 90 per cent has been removed. Hence, it might not be socially worthwhile to bring the environment back to some "100 per cent pure" state, given the probable high costs and modest benefits realized from removing the last small amount of impurity and the competing demands for resources.

Social and Physical Environment: Some Comparisons

As indicated above, the conceptually appropriate treatment for the contribution of sociopolitical and physical environmental assets is much the same. But there are some interesting differences in the problems associated with these two types of environments, and some of these differences can be usefully discussed even in the absence of quantitative information.

One of the differences can be illustrated by asking the question: What is the likely time-path of changes in real output, given that either of these environments has initially been permitted to deteriorate? That is, if the sociopolitical environment has deteriorated by x per cent (measured somehow), what will it take to restore that environment to its original state, and is the relationship different for the sociopolitical than for the physical environment?

It is more difficult to analyze the sociopolitical than the physical environment, since we know much less about the factors that influence or change it. It might be argued that deterioration of the sociopolitical environment, once permitted to begin, has a greater tendency to be cumulative and is more difficult to reverse. To illustrate, in recent years there appears to have been a marked increase both in the incidence of illegal activity and in air and water pollution.[20] Both are a manifestation of environmental deterioration—the first in the sociopolitical environment, the second in the physical environment. But the deterioration reflected by rising crime rates seems more likely to be self-reinforcing: Behavior that reflects an increasing irresponsibility toward persons or property is likely to encourage similar behavior on the part of others, simply because near-universal disapproval may be one of the major inhibiting forces to begin with. Thus one would argue that a rising rate of illegal activity will, in and of itself, produce a change in the social and political environment which will lead to a further rise, other things being equal. And to the extent that the basic sanction against illegal activity is widespread disapproval in the community, a reduction in the pervasiveness of disapproval will itself tend to increase the amount of disapproved activities. Moreover, if this change in environment is ignored by society, it is hard to see any reason

---

[20] The empirical facts are not entirely clear in either case, especially for the incidence of illegal activity. We are certainly more aware now of both types of deterioration, but that is a different proposition from knowing that the situation has objectively deteriorated.

for stabilization or reversal. Even if its basic causes were to be removed or alleviated, it might reasonably be expected that the sociopolitical environment would continue to deteriorate.

In the physical environment, in contrast, the same cumulative process may not be at work. An increased level of air pollution is a consequence of the fact that, in the absence of an appropriate penalty structure, various sorts of productive activities are conducted so as to expel waste materials into the atmosphere. Because productive activities tend to be concentrated geographically, the result is an atmosphere that is contaminated to a perceptible degree at selected (mainly urban) locations. But these concentrations of contaminants are continually in the process of being dispersed and diffused by natural forces. If contaminants were to be evenly spread over the entire atmosphere, the resulting contamination level would probably be so low that the welfare loss could safely be ignored. Assuming this to be the case at present (and foreseeable?) contamination levels, a worsening of the physical environment thus means that new contaminants are being injected into selected local areas at a greater rate than existing contaminants in these areas are being dispersed, a situation that might be remedied fairly easily and at moderate cost.

Suppose, for example, that a penalty structure were introduced which succeeded only in reducing the injection rate of new contaminants to the point where it was lower than the dispersal rate of existing ones. That change would be sufficient to reduce the contamination level, and the reduction would continue as long as more contaminants were being dispersed than were newly injected. If this analysis is correct, air pollution constitutes a self-liquidating rather than a self-perpetuating or cumulative type of deterioration.

Much the same argument applies to water pollution, where natural regenerative processes at work in most bodies of water have a persistent tendency to reduce pollution. The pollution level is increased only if more new pollutants are injected than are being removed through these natural processes. Thus, to reduce the pollution level, it may be sufficient to reduce the injection rate of new pollutants.[21]

It may thus be the case that the social and economic cost of a given amount of environmental deterioration is greater for the sociopolitical environment than for the physical environment. Not only might deterioration in the physical enviroment be arrested by simply cutting back on the amount of impurities being currently injected, but the methods of controlling deterioration are likely to be much better understood because they are essentially technical and scientific rather than behavioral. That is to say, society clearly has enough knowledge to reduce at least certain types of environmental deterioration to lower levels than at present: what is lacking is simply a political decision to

---

[21] This analysis, of necessity, greatly oversimplifies the problems of deterioration in the physical environment. For example, the dispersal rate of existing pollutants may be so slow that the injection rate of new pollutants might have to be reduced virtually to zero. Also, certain types of long-lived pollutants appear to move from one part of the physical environment to another and to produce cumulative effects that have not yet been fully registered: DDT seems to be a case in point. Finally, the "natural regenerative processes," which are clearly at work in many instances, can probably be rendered inoperative if pollution levels get to be sufficiently high. In that case, deterioration will either not be self-liquidating at all, or the process of regeneration will take so long that it will amount to the same thing for practical purposes.

incur the costs needed to realize that objective. But for the sociopolitical environment, not only do we probably need to do more than simply reduce new sources of social and political discontent below what they have been, but we may need to go a good deal further in order to overcome the cumulative effects of past social and political discontents. Moreover, we know much less about the relevant technology—the probable consequences of programs designed to change the sociopolitical environment—and thus we know less about how to use resources in order to achieve the desired objective.[22] Hence, the great public outcry over environmental pollution, and the interest and energy with which that problem is being attacked, may represent a misplaced emphasis. It might be much more important to concern ourselves with deterioration in the sociopolitical environment than in the physical environment.

---

[22] This proposition is discussed in F. Thomas Juster, "Microdata, Economic Research, and the Production of Economic Knowledge," in *Papers and Proceedings of the American Economic Association,* May 1970.

II

**Staff Reports
on Research
Under Way**

1. ECONOMIC GROWTH

Productivity, Employment, and Price Levels

Policies to attain "prosperity without inflation" are bound to be highly controversial. Opinions differ sharply, as each day's news makes clear, on the relative values of the several goals subsumed under the quoted catch phrase: rapid economic growth, low unemployment, and a stable general price level. And the differences extend also to the worth of these goals when balancing the short-run against the long. It would be too much to hope that scientific research, no matter what its auspices or scale, could quiet all controversy over these policies. Yet, to a significant degree, the differences of opinion do reflect inadequate knowledge of the facts and the relations among facts. We may reasonably expect that the differences can be narrowed by the work reported in this section, which groups together studies aided by a grant from the Alfred P. Sloan Foundation and studies on related topics. Included are an examination of the reliability of the available price and employment data, analyses of the historical behavior of prices and productivity, an effort to develop theoretical models of price formation, and the construction of econometric models of the determination of prices, costs, and productivity.

The first National Bureau publication in this group was *The Behavior of Industrial Prices*, by George J. Stigler and James K. Kindahl, which was recently published. Several related articles have appeared or will soon appear elsewhere. These include Nadiri and Rosen's "Interrelated Factor Demand Functions," in the *American Economic Review,* September 1969, and two articles by Fabricant: "Prices in the National Accounts Framework: A Case for Cost-Benefit Analysis," which will be published in the *Review of Income and Wealth,* and "Inflation and the Lag in Accounting Practice," which will be in a volume on "Contributions to Accounting by Other Disciplines," to be published under the auspices of the University of Kansas.

The individual studies still in progress are reported on in the following pages of this section.

Members of the National Bureau's Board of Directors have sometimes expressed the wish that, when an occasion offered itself, advantage should be taken of the opportunity to prepare and issue a Bureau volume, addressed to the public at large, on a broad theme of widespread interest. Such a volume should use the main findings of National Bureau studies, properly integrated and stripped of technical discussion and detail, regardless of the project under which they happened to be financed or the heading in the *Annual Report* under which the studies might be classified. The problem of inflation provides such a theme.

A report on the problem of inflation could help point up the relevance of the National Bureau's research, and—written in appropriate language—should help convey its results not only to specialist and nonspecialist economists, but also to other members of the concerned public, among whom are the National Bureau's supporters. I hope to use the next year to put such a volume together.

Over the next few years the National Bureau's studies in productivity, employment, and price levels will be aided by a new grant from the Walker Foundation.

Solomon Fabricant

Price Trends and Economic Growth

Several economists have recently attempted to measure the effects upon wages and price levels of the guidepost policy followed during 1962-66, and of its abandonment afterward. The planned paper on "Wage and Price Guideposts in a Growing Economy" is being extended in order to weigh and to compare the validity of the very different conclusions reached. To judge from the review so far, it is doubtful whether any of the econometric equations or other analyses that have been made public yield significant evidence on the degree of effectiveness of the guideposts. For one thing, the available statistical data are for this purpose simply too poor in quantity and quality. Consider, for example, the rather wide discrepancies between the list prices used in these analyses and the prices actually realized, that are reported by Stigler and Kindahl. Given these data, the factors affecting short-term changes in wages and prices are too numerous and too powerful to permit disentangling and determination—with even minimally acceptable confidence—of the separate effect of the application of the guidepost policy. That equations which give very different results are all accompanied by high coefficients of multiple correlation can merely reflect the fact that the equations are the end results of a trial and error search by different people. The paper on the guideposts will, of course, discuss in some detail the considerations—theoretical and empirical—that lead to these conclusions.

During the year, work continued on an aspect of another subject of great current interest. This is the connection among changes in monetary and fiscal policy, changes in business conditions, and changes in price levels. It was widely expected that the tightening of monetary and fiscal policy that began during the winter of 1968-69 would soon be reflected in a slowdown in general business and, as a result and more or less simultaneously, in a significant reduction, if not a complete halt, in the pace of price inflation. That the pace of inflation still shows little evidence of a slowdown has surprised and troubled many people, especially since signs of a decline in general business have been mounting for some time.

But even a cursory inspection of the historical facts indicates that the short-term behavior of prices cannot be characterized as simply as has been assumed. Several facts tend to be overlooked. First, price behavior is not the same throughout the price system. Second, the behavior in no part of the price system is always the same. Third, the response of prices to a tightening of monetary and fiscal policy may initially take the form, for a while, of an end to acceleration. And fourth, some groups of prices may continue to rise rapidly—sometimes even continue to accelerate—because of demand and supply factors peculiar to them.

To be more specific, the index of wholesale prices (or better, the index excluding farm and food prices, which conform poorly to business cycles) typically turns at about the same time as does general business. This is why the index is included in the National Bureau's list of "roughly coincident indicators." In contrast, the index of industrial material prices typically turns up or down before general business does; the index is a "leading indicator." In different contrast, retail prices and wage rates—the prices on which many people concentrate when worrying about inflation—tend if anything to lag behind turns in general business.

These uniformities are far from perfect, as Mitchell and the others who have worked on business cycles at the National Bureau have warned their readers. Departures from the usual behavior of the Wholesale Price Index, to continue with that example, have occurred in a significant proportion of business cycles. The departures sometimes ranged well outside the limits that one might infer from the term, "roughly coincident." And, as I have already hinted, the Consumer Price Index and the available indexes of wage rates, as well as indexes of prices in some other sections of the price system, have so infrequently been marked by downward movements that they could not properly be classified as "lagging indicators" —series that typically turn downward some time after a peak in business has been reached. The response of retail prices and wage rates to declines in business has often been visible only in a slowing down of their rates of growth.

Finally, the persistently rapid rises in the prices of health services and of construction costs, often cited as reflections of continued inflationary pressure, may instead be better examples of the importance of special demand and supply factors.

The country's experience with prices during the past year should be less surprising when viewed in the light of its broader experience, of which I have given just a few examples.

There are also other grounds for not expecting a rigid relationship between changes in prices and changes in business. The impact of a given monetary-fiscal policy is bound to vary from time to time, if only because what happens to business in general and to prices in particular is influenced also by the policy that came before and the policy that is expected to come later.

Various studies under way at the National Bureau, such as those by Friedman and Schwartz, deal with these complicated matters in one way or another. In the present study, attention is being focused on the behavior, and variation in the behavior, of the several categories of prices during different periods in our history.

Work has also begun on a topic that may be thought of as bearing on the competition among national goals. This is the question, in what direction, to what extent, and for how long may efforts to attain or maintain a stable economy be expected to influence the rate of growth of national output, or more particularly, the rate of growth of a major factor of output, namely, output per man-hour worked. It is a subject to which rather less attention has been paid than the trade-off between full employment and inflation, to which Gordon refers in his progress report below. The question necessarily involves a good deal of speculation. What I shall be doing is to set down some of the factual and theoretical considerations useful in guiding and disciplining this speculation. These include the factors determining the trend of labor productivity, on which Kendrick has been working, and the factors—not altogether different—that cause fluctuations around the trend during successive stages of the business cycle. The latter subject was studied by Hultgren some time ago. New data make it possible to extend and check some of his results. The Nadiri-Rosen study, reported below, also should be helpful.

Solomon Fabricant

Interrelated Factor Demand Functions

The purpose of this work is to integrate empirical investment and employment functions and to link both of these with capacity considerations, i.e., hours of work per man and utilization of capital equipment. Thus, we specify and estimate a complete dynamic model for all input demand functions, which allows interactions and feedbacks among these variables over time, and which integrates some existing empirical work into a unified structure.

The model has been fitted to aggregate manufacturing data, and the results are very good. Implied distributed lag responses show that physical capital is relatively fixed compared with other inputs. They also show that the primary role of variations in utilization rates is to adjust output levels rapidly in the face of the slow adjustment of capital stocks, as is predicted by our a priori hypotheses. These estimates are also capable of accounting for low estimates of the elasticity of employment with respect to output found in previous short-term employment function studies. In those studies, large short-run returns to inputs of labor seem to be due to the omission of input utilization rates, particularly that of capital.

The model has now been extended to include changes in inventories as another variable among the interrelated factors of production. We have completed the collection and processing of the quarterly time series data for seventeen two-digit manufacturing industries for the period 1947-68. The model has been re-estimated for these subindustries, and we are preparing to explore the interindustry differences in the estimates.

M. I. Nadiri
Sherwin Rosen

Problems in the Measurement of Nonresidential Fixed Capital

The purpose of the project is to revise existing capital input estimates to take better account of technological change in capital goods and of changes in service lives and utilization rates. The project is divided into six subtopics, on each of which considerable progress was made during 1969-70.

1. *Principles of Capital Measurement.* Analysis based on a theoretical model has suggested several principles. Deflators for investment spending should be adjusted for all changes in quality, whether or not they require a change in the base-year cost of production. But, in studies of economic growth, perpetual inventory capital stocks should be examined in accordance with three concepts of real investment. Using the first such concept, stock is corrected for all changes in quality; in the second, stock is corrected for changes in quality which increase the base-year cost of production of capital, and in the third, stock is completely uncorrected for changes in quality or productivity. Differences in the growth rates of the three stocks form the basis of studies of the sources of economic growth. This theoretical analysis has been set out in an article titled "The Advance of Knowledge and Measures of Total Factor Productivity."

2. *Techniques of Price Measurement.* In recent years considerable attention has been devoted in the literature to the possibility of adjusting price indexes for quality change through the use of the "hedonic" regression technique. The Census Bureau is now using the hedonic method in a new price index for single-family residential houses. A close analysis suggests that the Census price index and others may be biased upward, since the method cannot identify costless quality change in quality dimensions which are excluded (because of multicollinearity or data limitations) from the hedonic regressions. In the future more emphasis will have to be placed on detailed engineering studies to measure improvements in the ability of capital goods to produce output.

For the next few years, construction price indexes used to calculate capital stocks may have to be based on interim methods like those I proposed in the *Review of Economics and Statistics,* November 1968.[1]

3. *Revisions of Existing Price Deflators.* To supplement my earlier study of construction price deflators, I have done some work to assess the accuracy of the U.S. equipment price deflators. At present, most categories of equipment investment distinguished in the U.S. national accounts are deflated by product-class indexes of the Wholesale Price Index. A set of alternative data sources suggests that the WPI data contain a serious upward bias of as much as 2 per cent per annum during the period 1954-63. A National Bureau-type reference cycle analysis of cyclical fluctuations in the ratio of transactions to list prices suggests that the present official U.S. indexes understate cyclical fluctuations in equipment prices. While the information so far collected is not sufficient for a trustworthy estimate of the magnitude of this cyclical inaccuracy, government statistical agencies could sponsor research to extend my methodology. Such a study would be valuable not only in the study of capital stocks and economic growth, but also in revealing possible weaknesses in previous studies of the demand for investment goods, the results of which usually depend heavily on the cyclical path of real investment spending.

4. *Revisions of Investment Estimates.* Further Defense Department data have been collected. These will be used in future revisions and extensions of my original estimates of government-owned capital used by private contractors, as reported in the June 1969 *American Economic Review*.

5. *Utilization Estimates.* Detailed annual estimates of capacity and utilization in a large group of industries have been prepared from data for periods ranging back to 1910. The

---

[1] Robert J. Gordon, "A New View of Real Investment in Structures," *Review of Economics and Statistics,* November 1968.

data suggest that in many industries utilization rates in the late 1920's were low relative to the 1950's and 1960's. The time pattern of utilization rates in different industries is being examined in an attempt to determine the relative roles of aggregate demand and technical progress in causing the secular rise in utilization rates. Whatever the cause, changes in utilization rates were a major factor contributing to economic growth in the 1929-50 period and to the accompanying decline in the capital-output ratio.

6. *Changes in Service Lives.* Although data on changes in service lives are the most unsatisfactory of any used in this project, an attempt is being made to determine the rough order of magnitude of service-life changes in structures and equipment. Preliminary work suggests that service lives were stretched out during the 1929-50 period, contributing to an increase in the figure showing the ratio of actual capital stock to conventional capital stock. This figure was derived on the erroneous assumption of no change in service lives.

As the results of the six sections are completed, they are being written up in the form of a monograph, which it is hoped will be completed before the end of 1970.

Robert J. Gordon

Problems in Predicting the Rate of Inflation

How rapidly would the general price level increase if the U.S. unemployment rate were to remain forever at the low rates reached between 1966 and 1969? Widely diverse answers to this controversial problem have been proposed in recent research. The most common empirical approach, employed by Perry, Brechling, and others, fits a stable Phillips curve and predicts that at steady 1969-type rates of unemployment the rate of inflation would be stable at between 3 and 4.5 per cent. Diametrically opposed to this approach are recent papers by Friedman and Phelps, who argue that any attempt by policy makers to maintain forever the low 1969 unemployment rate would lead not to a stable but to an *accelerating* rate of inflation. In order to dampen and eliminate the accelerating rate of inflation, the unemployment rate must be raised to the "natural rate" at which there is no excess demand for labor. There is thus no permanent, stable trade-off between unemployment and inflation, as implied by the previous Phillips curve investigations. According to Friedman and Phelps, previous Phillips curve studies, like that of Perry, have fitted the wrong curve. Instead of attempting to estimate the Phillips curve relating the change in the *nominal* wage to the level of unemployment, previous studies should have used the change in the *expected real* wage as the dependent variable.

The present study is an attempt to appraise the two approaches by translating the implicit verbal argument of Friedman's 1967 Presidential Address to the American Economic Association into an econometrically testable model. Equations are derived which explain the growth of both wages and prices. The econometric equations are of the form:

(1) $g_{w/q'_t} = a_{10} + a_{11} m_t + a_{12} g_{m_t} + a_{13} g_{p^*_t} + e_{1t}$

(2) $g_{p_t} = a_{21} g_{w/q'_t} + a_{22} g_{w/q_t} + a_{23} g_{m_t} + a_{24} g_{s_t} + e_{2t}$

Here g means a proportional rate of growth, w/q' is "standard" unit labor cost, w/q is actual unit labor cost, m is the employment rate, p is the actual and p^* the expected price level, S is the ratio of new orders to shipments, and e is an error term. The first equation states that the rate of increase in standard unit labor cost is a function of the level and rate of change of the employment rate and of the rate of change of the expected price level; the second states that the rate of increase in the actual price level is a function of the rates of growth of standard and actual unit labor cost, the employment rate, and the ratio of new orders to shipments.

Considerable emphasis in the research is devoted to sensitivity tests of the results. Regressions are run with and without corrections for serial correlation, in levels and one- and four-quarter changes, for different subperiods of the postwar years, and for different methods of generating the expected price level (p^*). The sensitivity analysis demonstrates that the coefficients on some of the variables are much more stable than those on others. Among the innovations is a new "unemployment rate of man-hours" which corrects the more familiar published unemployment rate both for disguised unemployment and for partial unemployment. When it is substituted for the published unemployment rate, this new variable improves our explanation of postwar inflation. This unemployment rate was high relative to the published rate in 1962-64 and low in 1969. It therefore helps to explain the low rate of inflation in the former period and the high rate in the latter. Considerable attention is also devoted to correcting the wage (compensation) data for changes in the industrial mix of employment.

While, at the present time, the statistical results are tentative, they tend to confirm the Perry-Brechling view of the inflationary process. The coefficient on expected prices (a_{13}) in the wage equation is consistently .5 or less in all of the numerous regressions which employ several different methods of generating estimates of expected prices. Since the coefficients on standard and actual unit labor cost (a_{21} and a_{22}) add up to 1.0, the results for wages and prices together suggest a damped inflationary process in which workers fail to adjust completely to changes in expected prices but nevertheless maintain their share of the national income because there is a rigid relation of prices to wages, as indicated by the price equation.

A preliminary version of the theoretical discussion and empirical results has been written up in the form of a journal article. Subsequent stages of the research will involve dynamic simulations of the wage-price model under alternative economic policies and formal comparisons of the results with those of earlier investigators.

Robert J. Gordon

Postwar Productivity Trends in the United States

A manuscript of this monograph has been sent to a staff reading committee for review. A basic objective of the study was to update the estimates and analyses of productivity in the U.S. economy contained in *Productivity Trends in the United States* (NBER, 1961), with particular reference to the post-World War II period, 1948-66. Extensive use of the series contained in *Productivity Trends* indicated the desirability of extending them, particularly since governmental statistical agencies have not yet provided regular estimates of total real capital stocks for the economy, by sectors and major industries, nor the derived capital and total factor productivity estimates.

The concepts behind the estimates are essentially those introduced in *Productivity Trends,* with the addition of gross real capital stock, gross capital productivity, and gross factor productivity measures. The sources and methods underlying the estimates are described in detail in an appendix, which also contains more than eighty basic tables with time series of output, input, and productivity estimates for the U.S. economy by major industry divisions and groups. The estimates were prepared with major assistance from Maude R. Pech prior to her retirement from the National Bureau in early 1969.

Some of the main findings of the study may be summarized as follows:

The trend-rate of increase in total factor productivity in the private domestic economy does not appear to have accelerated since World War II. At 2.3 per cent a year in 1948-66, the trend-rate is the same as that which prevailed in 1916-29, and again in 1936-66 following a downward shift during the Great Depression. The 2.5 per cent rate between 1948 and 1966, obtained by the compound interest formula, reflects the fact that 1948 was somewhat below the trend, while 1966 was above. The slower average rate of growth from 1966 to 1969 at 1.2 per cent a year has brought total factor productivity back below the trend.

Output per man-hour and per unit of labor input (weighted man-hours) increased at average annual compound rates of 3.4 and 3.1 per cent, respectively, in 1948-66—an acceleration of 0.8 per cent in each compared with the 1919-48 rates. Over and above the trend considerations noted above, the acceleration reflected substantially higher rates of increase in capital per man-hour than in the 1919-48 period.

Real Net National Product increased at an average annual compound rate of 4.1 per cent between 1948 and 1966 (after a small upward adjustment to allow for a 1 per cent a year average increase in government productivity). Thus, the total factor productivity advance of 2.3 per cent a year accounted for well over half of economic growth as measured by real NNP.

Real average hourly labor compensation rose at an average annual rate of 3.3 per cent between 1948 and 1966—0.2 percentage points more than output per unit of labor input. The 0.2 per cent a year rate of increase in unit labor cost also indicates the rate of increase in the labor share of factor income originating in the business economy—from 69.7 per cent in 1948 to 72.5 per cent in 1966.

The relationship between the relative decline in labor input and the relative increase in the real price of labor indicates a historical elasticity of substitution of between .65 and .70. This is quite similar to the elasticities computed for earlier periods, when the labor share also increased mildly as the rate of relative increase in the real price of labor was proportionately greater than the rate of relative decline in the quantity of labor input.

There is a significant positive correlation between 1948-66 rates of change in output and in the productivity ratios for the thirty-two industry groups of the "industry" sector (excluding agriculture, finance, and services), and for the twenty-one manufacturing groups. There is also a significant positive correlation between rates of change in output and output per man-hour for 395 four-digit manufacturing industries, 1954-63. Fuchs also found a significant positive correlation for seventeen trade and service sector industries. Our results confirm Fuchs' finding that the relationship does not hold for the ten one-digit industry segments.

A major theoretical explanation of the output–productivity relationship is that rates of change in productivity and in (net) price of outputs are negatively correlated, as are those between rates of change in price and in output, assuming that the effects of price elasticities of demand are not outweighed by other demand elements.

For the manufacturing and broader industry groups, there is a significant negative correlation between rates of change in productivity (total and labor) and in output prices. This is reinforced by the associated finding that rates of change in productivity and in factor prices are not significantly correlated.

To complete the chain of relationships, we can note that industry rates of change in price and in output have a significant negative correlation for the period 1948-66.

The degree of positive correlation between relative industry changes in output and in productivity is higher than can be explained by the negative relationships between rates of change in productivity and price, and between price and output changes. This fact suggests that scale effects reinforce the positive relationship between rates of change in productivity and in output.

In the case of the nine one-digit industry segments, the chain of relationships breaks down with regard to relative changes in price and in output, which are not negatively correlated. It appears that price-elasticity effects are outweighed by income elasticities and shifts in tastes operating in the opposite direction. This is notably the case for the extractive and service segments; relative output of the former has declined despite relative price declines, while the opposite is true of services.

Our basic hypothesis as to the causal factors in productivity growth is that the rate of productivity advance is chiefly a function of the rate of growth of real intangible stocks of capital per unit of the tangible factors in which they are embodied, affecting their "quality" or productive efficiency.

Real intangible capital stocks grow as a result of net intangible investments designed to increase the output- and income-producing capacity of the tangible human and nonhuman factors. The chief types of intangible investment for which we developed estimates are research and development, education and training, health, and mobility.

Total intangible investment grew from 14.5 per cent of GNP in 1948 to 21.5 per cent in 1966. The relative upward movement represents a continuation of earlier trends. Real gross intangible stocks, obtained from the investment estimates, increased at an average annual rate 2.6 per cent higher than the growth rate of real tangible factor inputs in 1948-66—closely comparable to the rate of increase in total factor productivity.

Shorter-term productivity movements are closely related to the rates of utilization of productive capacity, and the ratio of employment to labor force.

The average age of tangible, reproducible fixed capital goods, as a proxy for the rate of diffusion of technological advance, also appears to be significantly related to productivity trends. The average age has declined between 1948 and 1966.

John W. Kendrick

Other Studies

A draft of Phillip Cagan's study on "The Flexibility of Prices," which examines the speed of adjustment of prices to changes in demand and supply conditions, was reviewed by a staff reading committee. It now awaits revisions by the author, who has been on leave to serve on the staff of the Council of Economic Advisers.

Public Finance

Introduction

Public finance is a field in which the potential for doing useful research has been broadened by recent technological progress to a greater degree than in many other fields of economics. This broadening has arisen from two sources. The increased availability of large-scale micro-data sets, consisting of sizable cross-sectional samples of individuals and/or firms with data on a large number of characteristics of these decision units, has resulted in increased opportunity for detailed microeconomic studies of behavioral adjustments to tax differentials. The development of solution procedures to deal with large nonlinear models, such as the Brookings-SSRC model, has made feasible the development of complex general-equilibrium tax policy models which can potentially be used to measure the many interacting effects of changes in the structure of taxes, transfer payments, and certain types of public expenditures.

These advances in technology are of course attributable to the rapid rate of technological progress in computer hardware and software. Even in the very recent past, it was not technologically possible to measure all of the relevant effects of policy changes, such as the restructuring of the income tax system, the reform of unemployment insurance schemes, the introduction of a negative income tax, or the implementation of a substantial change in the mix of taxes collected by governments. It has been possible to predict some of these effects in an incomplete general-equilibrium context. Harberger, for example, has made important contributions to the measurement of welfare losses that are caused by the inefficient allocations resulting from tax distortions.[1] Until re-

---
[1] See Arnold C. Harberger, "The Incidence of the Corporation Income Tax," *Journal of Political Economy*, June 1962, pp. 215-240; Harberger, "The Measurement of Waste," *American Economic Review*, May 1964, pp. 58-76.

cently, however, it has not been feasible even to consider development of a general-equilibrium model in which redistributive effects, effects on allocative efficiency, and effects on aggregate savings and investment could all be incorporated. It has accordingly not been feasible for public finance economists to measure the trade-offs among effects on growth and redistributive effects which are at the heart of the crucial political issues involved in assessing structural reform of the tax/expenditure system.

The variety of effects that need to be analyzed and the nature of the analyses required have been described elsewhere.[2] From a policy viewpoint, the most relevant empirical question regarding any proposed structural change is normally the long-term effects of the change when accompanied by whatever compensating changes in monetary and fiscal policy are required to offset any effects of the proposed change upon the current level of aggregate demand or upon the current balance of payments. Measuring such compensated effects requires a complex general-equilibrium model that will not be easy to specify. The specification problems are compounded by the necessity of substantial disaggregation in analyzing many tax substitutions and by the usefulness of incorporating microeconometric models utilizing relatively large-scale microdata sets.

Much of the National Bureau's current research activity in public finance is concerned either with how to proceed in specifying a large-scale general-equilibrium tax policy model or with utilizing microdata sets to study the impact of changes in the structure of tax and transfer systems. The work on approaches to general-equilibrium model specification has been largely limited to analysis of the effects of substituting a value-added tax for all or part of the corporate profits tax, and is described below in separate reports by Bossons and Shoup and by Petersen.

Current analyses of the impact of structural changes in tax and transfer systems are largely focused on four topics: (1) the differential initial incidence of alternative income tax systems, (2) the differential secondary incidence of alternative transfer payment systems, including both negative income taxes and income maintenance programs, (3) analysis of the effect on labor effort of changes in the structure of the current income tax and unemployment insurance programs, and (4) an analysis of the impact of intergovernmental grants. Research on the first topic was begun last year and is described in a progress report by Bossons. The new research projects on the second topic are described in reports by Bossons, Hindle, and Robinson and by Bossons and Hosek. Current research on the third topic includes a continuing study by Holland on the effects of taxes on the work effort by managers and entrepreneurs in new businesses and an analysis by Bossons and Hosek of the work disincentive effects of unemployment insurance. The effects of intergovernmental grants have been analyzed in a study by Dresch and Struyk.

In addition to these projects, which are decribed below in separate reports, a previous study of corporate taxation and corporate growth by Challis Hall, interrupted by Hall's untimely death in September 1968, is being completed by Norman Ture.

John Bossons

Measuring the Effects of Tax Substitutions

Following the priorities suggested in the outline of research on tax substitutions which we proposed last year, we have concentrated our initial attention on attempting to organize and clarify the research that will be required in order to build a general-equilibrium tax policy model that is adequate for the analysis of the redistributive, allocative, and growth effects of substituting a value-added tax for a corporate

---

[2] John Bossons and Carl S. Shoup, "Analyzing the Effects of Large-Scale Changes in Fiscal Structure: A Proposed Systems Approach," in *New Challenges for Economic Research,* 49th Annual Report of the National Bureau of Economic Research, New York, 1969, pp. 11-26.

profits tax. In the course of this discussion, two papers have been written to clarify some of the issues involved:

> John Bossons, "Evaluating the Substitution of a Value-Added Tax for the Corporate Profits Tax."
>
> Stephen P. Dresch, "An Urban-Regional Component for the General Equilibrium Tax Policy Model: Preliminary Considerations."

In addition to work done on these papers, a new, more detailed proposal embodying the results of discussions on the appropriate staging and likely costs of the proposed research has now been prepared.

John Bossons
Carl S. Shoup

Industry Price/Output Effects of Substituting a Value-Added Tax for a Corporate Profits Tax

In my study of the economic effects of substituting a value-added tax for the U.S. corporate profits tax, I have altered the direction of my research from balance-of-trade effects in terms of a general-equilibrium model, as I reported in the last *Annual Report,* to a partial equilibrium analysis of the short-run price/output effects of the tax substitution for a single industry. The reasons for this shift in emphasis are twofold.

First, the refinements necessary to describe adequately the tax substitution for the United States in terms of a simple general-equilibrium trade model are too many to provide useful a priori estimates of the tax substitution's trade effects. Although this type of model has been employed by Harberger, Mieszkowski, and others to yield interesting propositions on the incidence of broad-based taxes, it does not seem well-suited to answer questions about the trade effects of these taxes. The more elaborate general-equilibrium analysis that is needed would require more resources than I have at my disposal.

A second related reason for my shift in emphasis is that such a large-scale general-equilibrium analysis has been proposed as a major research effort for the National Bureau. (See the *1969 Annual Report,* pages 11-26.) I have therefore decided to concentrate on one necessary input to this analysis: the short-run price and output effects of the value-added tax/profits tax substitution.

The necessity for examining such price and output responses to the tax substitution arises from the possibility that oligopolistic interdependence in an industry will result in differing pricing policies for different industries, and that pricing policies, together with industry demand and cost conditions, will produce a variety of price and output responses to the tax substitution. To undertake any aggregate analysis of the effects of such broad-based taxes as the value-added tax and the corporate profits tax, it is therefore necessary to examine price and output effects for specific industries.

To accomplish this task, I am constructing a three-equation model which will incorporate an industry's price policy, demand conditions, and cost conditions. Substantial work has been done by others on the specification and estimation of demand and cost functions for various industries, but the price function remains the subject of considerable controversy and requires the most work. In addition to the general exploration of work already done on each of these functions, I am in the process of selecting a particular industry for which the short-run price and output effects of the value-added tax/corporate profits tax substitution may be estimated.

Bruce L. Petersen

The Initial Differential Incidence of Alternative Income Tax Systems

Since this project was described in last year's *Annual Report,* only current work will be summarized here. Work on this project is proceeding in two areas: (1) the analysis of alternative income tax systems, and (2) the specification of a model of the joint distribution of income and wealth. The latter model will be used as the basis for a more accurate analysis of the differential impact incidence of a tax change, as well as for analysis of the effect of a tax change on asset prices.

Two papers on alternative income tax structures have been completed this year:

> "Integration versus Dividend Deductibility."
>
> "The Effect of Tax Rates on the Impact of Tax Reform: The White Paper vs. an Alternative."

The first of these papers discusses alternative means of overcoming the effects of the "double taxation" of corporate income under the corporation and personal income taxes; the second discusses the impact of a new set of tax reforms recommended by the Canadian government in its White Paper of November 1969. Another paper on the design of rate schedules under different tax reforms is in progress.

Work on specifying a model of the joint distribution of income and wealth is proceeding in two stages. An initial paper analyzing individual responses to a 1963 Federal Reserve Board survey, a sample of 100,000 1962 income tax returns, and 1962 state tax data is near completion. This work is in part supported by the study described in Section 6 of this report by Raymond Goldsmith. Subsequent research will focus on the patterns of individual ownership of different types of assets as well as on updating the model.

John Bossons

The Cost and Incidence of Transfer Payment Programs in Canada

The primary purpose of this work is to analyze the relationship between family income and the characteristics of families. Data on the composition of family income by intrafamily recipients and by income components is to be used to examine the sources of income as a family moves through its total life cycle. Among other things, this work should yield insight into the causes of income differentials and the incidence of socially perceived poverty. In addition, the results will be used to assess the costs and incidence of the net fiscal transfers resulting from alternative negative income tax schemes.

In all of the forgoing, "incidence" is defined to mean the differential secondary incidence of a change in the tax/transfer structure that leaves the existing government deficit unchanged but allows for changes in labor force participation rates. Both interregional and urban/rural incidence patterns are to be examined, as well as the incidence of a scheme for individuals in different income and family status classes. For all the analyses, the primary data source being used is a sample of approximately 18,000 families obtained in the 1968 Survey of Consumer Finances in Canada by the Dominion Bureau of Statistics. Work-effort, behavioral adjustment equations will in part be based on the results of the companion study by Bossons and Hosek.

Work to date has concentrated on designing efficient computation procedures and on specifying a model of the source of income differentials. In addition, a preliminary analyses of a smaller sample of Ontario families has been undertaken by Colin Hindle; this study is decribed in a separate report. It is expected that this project will soon be completed.

John Bossons
Colin J. Hindle
T. Russell Robinson

Negative Income Taxation and Poverty in Ontario

The objectives of this research are to determine the incidence of poverty in Ontario and to test the efficiency of alternative means of eliminating poverty. Poverty is measured as the amount by which adjusted disposable family income falls beneath the "poverty standard." In this case the poverty standard is set equal to existing provincial general welfare assistance rates. These rates provide benefits, differentiated according to family size and composition, for food, shelter, clothing and other living expenses. Adjusted disposable family income consists of net money income plus imputed house rent for owner-occupiers, minus personal income taxes.

The process of negative income taxation is modelled by employing essentially static, initial incidence theory. The substitution of one system of negative taxes for another is assumed to leave all behavior, except work effort, unchanged. Adjustments in work effort are assumed to occur instantaneously in response to the impact of changes in net taxes or transfers. In the absence of further work on labor force participation effects, behavioral equations for heads of households and for spouses, estimated separately by Leuthold, have been used.[1] Decreases in work effort, of course, have the effect of increasing the cost of a negative income tax scheme.

The extent of cost increases due to decreased work effort provides some gauge of the desirability of different schemes. Other measures of relative efficiency, such as the amount of total poverty eliminated and poverty eliminated per dollar of negative tax paid, are determined by the pattern of secondary incidence. Programs that make payments to the nonpoor are, of course, less efficient when judged in this manner. However, differences also occur among schemes that transfer an equal proportion of their total payments to the nonpoor. Some exhibit what may be termed "poverty overkill," providing more funds for a given family within the set of families classed as poor than are necessary to completely extinguish poverty.

The effects and efficiency of various hypothetical negative income tax schemes have been generated by means of a computer simulation utilizing microdata. These data are drawn from the 1966 Survey of Consumer Finances, Dominion Bureau of Statistics, and consist of a 1 per cent sample of Ontario "census families." The census family definition is a very close approximation of the nuclear family concept frequently mentioned as the most suitable negative tax unit. In addition, simulations have been carried out to measure the efficiency of existing Canadian programs—family allowances and old age security benefits. At the time of the survey, these schemes made payments to all children under sixteen years of age and all persons over sixty-nine years of age, respectively.

Preliminary results indicate that Ontario poverty is concentrated in urban areas and is most prevalent among unattached individuals, as is shown in Table II-1.

TABLE II-1

Distribution of Families Below "Poverty Standard," by Family Characteristics, Ontario, 1965
(per cent)

	Nonfarm	Farm	Total
Unattached individual	44.4	3.9	48.3
Married couple	7.0	2.3	9.3
Married couple with children	15.5	6.3	21.8
Male head (no spouse) with children	0.4	0.0	0.4
Female head (no spouse) with children	19.7	0.5	20.2
Total	87.0	13.0	100.0

Existing Canadian grant programs turn out to be a relatively inefficient means of eliminating poverty. More poverty could be eliminated by using equal-cost, universal negative income tax plans, as shown in Table II-2. In all cases, the poverty gap is defined as the difference between disposable income excluding the transfers being analyzed and the poverty standard previously defined. In the case of universal negative income taxes, each of the three negative income taxes analyzed is defined with

---

[1] Jane Leuthold, "Formula Income Transfers and the Work Decision of the Poor," unpublished Ph.D. dissertation, University of Wisconsin, 1968.

rates yielding a net cost after work-effort adjustments equal to the cost of the grants which it replaces. The ratio of total poverty eliminated (measured in terms of the dollar amount by which the aggregate poverty gap is reduced) to the aggregate cost of each program is a measure of program efficiency.

TABLE II-2

Efficiency of Alternative Transfers
(per cent)

	Ratio of Total Poverty Eliminated to Total Cost	Fraction of Poverty Gap Eliminated
Existing programs		
Family allowances	7.6	4.5
Old age security	43.6	36.5
Universal negative income taxes		
Replacing F.A.	63.5	59.6
Replacing OAS	77.4	56.2
Replacing F.A. and OAS	56.0	82.4

Among negative tax schemes proper, best results (in the sense of program efficiency) are achieved by utilizing proportional taxation as opposed to either progressive or regressive taxation.

Colin J. Hindle

Effect of Taxation on Personal Effort

The design and scope of this project have been described in earlier reports. A preliminary account of some of the findings was presented to the Annual Conference of the National Tax Association in October 1969. This paper, which is to be published in the *Proceedings* volume of that Conference, covers the main findings from the interviews with respect to four general points: (a) The "price" effects on executive effort exercised by the income tax; (b) The influence of taxation on engineers and scientists who have gone into business; (c) The time spent by executives on management of personal tax affairs; (d) The time demands of corporate tax management.

I expect to complete soon a first draft of the study.

Daniel M. Holland

The Effects of Alternative Unemployment Insurance Programs

Research on this project is to center on two topics: the disincentive effects of unemployment insurance schemes and the analysis of alternative unemployment insurance schemes. Research on the first topic would focus on how unemployment insurance payments affect the duration of unemployment, studies being done for several different labor groups. The second topic involves an extension of an existing model, developed for the Canadian Unemployment Insurance Commission in 1968-69 to permit analysis of alternative unemployment insurance schemes in Canada. The extended models would incorporate information gained from study of the first topic as well as from other supplementary investigations and, in addition, would be expanded to allow study of further alternative programs.

The research will be based primarily on analysis of a large sample of Canadian individuals for whom data on labor force participation, wages, income, age, and family characteristics have been obtained from Unemployment Insurance Commission records and from income tax returns. The data set, a 5 per cent sample of Canadian individuals in the labor force in 1965 and 1966, has been assembled by the Dominion Bureau of Statistics, the Unemployment Insurance Commission, and the Department of National Revenue in Canada. The project is partially supported by the Canadian Unemployment Insurance Commission.

One measure of the efficacy of an unemployment insurance program is the degree to which it affects the size of the employed labor force, both through its effects on the duration of unemployment and through its effects on labor force participation rates for various groups in the population. Surprisingly little work has been done on this subject. It is not clear whether the duration of unemployment is significantly affected by unemployment compensation, nor is it known whether different labor groups react differently to such payments.[1] Lack of adequate data has precluded empirical measurement of these effects and, at the same time, has blocked development of theories of behavior of the unemployed, particularly a theory of duration of unemployment. The data source developed by the Unemployment Insurance Commission is thus highly useful.

We propose initially to do a study concentrating on married men, ages 25-50. Since these men typically do not leave the labor force when unemployed, changes in their labor force participation rates will be minimal. Thus the participation decision will tend to be independent of decisions regarding job search and duration of unemployment. Also, by studying only married men we avoid the question of how the presence or absence of a wife affects the unemployment behavior of male participants; this question can be analyzed later. Subsequent studies will probably focus on elderly workers, teenagers, and married women.

Work on the second major research goal, development of a model to analyze alternative unemployment insurance programs, will profit from information gained in research on the effects of unemployment insurance on the labor force. We would like to use this information to construct an analytic model that goes beyond that developed to evaluate the present Unemployment Insurance Commission proposals. Our tentative plan is to retain parts of the computer program specifying the model in its present form, modifying other parts to allow for the analysis of other changes in unemployment insurance structure and to incorporate relevant information generated by the disincentives study and other supplemental studies.

The details of such modifications remain unsettled. We would like to capture three effects, namely, anticyclical effects, effects of differential incidence of costs and benefits across individuals and industries, and disincentive effects. An integrated analysis of these effects seems necessary before one can specify compensation schemes which are equitable yet also promote the efficient allocation of labor.

A number of preliminary tasks must be completed before much of the above research can be undertaken. These tasks range from additional data validation to problems associated with the extension of the current simulation model. We expect to begin work on analyzing the 1965 and 1966 data in the summer of 1970. We expect that data for 1967 and 1968 will also become available at that time. In the meantime, we are concentrating on developing a model of labor force behavior under unemployment, assuming individuals to be maximizing utility subject to a full wealth constraint.

John Bossons
James Hosek

Inter- and Intrastate Analyses of Grants-in-Aid and Local Fiscal Activity

These studies are currently undergoing revision and staff review preliminary to publication by the National Bureau. Struyk's study, outlined in the *1969 Annual Report,* is an analysis of state grant-in-aid programs to local governments in New Jersey; Dresch's analysis, presented to Yale University as a doctoral dissertation, utilizes an interstate sample of local governments in metropolitan areas to examine the impact of varying state-local fiscal structures.

The basic model which is used to reconcile the two analyses can be indicated in brief outline. First, an adequate model of local fiscal behavior as it is influenced by grants-in-aid must reflect the structure of the grant-in-aid

---
[1] For a review of previous research, see Charles Lininger, "The Effect of Weekly Unemployment Benefit Amounts on the Duration of Unemployment Benefits," unpublished Ph.D. dissertation, University of Chicago, 1962.

system. The conventional model implicitly employed in much of the literature on local government finance assumes that variations in grants are independent of local characteristics and fiscal behavior. An alternative formulation would treat the aid level as dependent on local characteristics, such as income, or the level of local expenditure, as when grants are provided on a matching basis. In that case there is a simultaneous determination of grant and expenditure levels. Secondly, aid programs differ in terms of the intralocal incidence of aid financing, varying from the complete absence of local incidence to total local incidence. The impact of aid programs on local activity, in terms of both income and substitution effects, can be expected to depend on the degree of local incidence. Thus, it is necessary to consider the determinants of aid grants and the relationship between levels of aid and levels of local income net of aid-financing taxes.

In the interstate analysis of urban fiscal activity by Dresch, it is assumed that grants-in-aid have a complete local incidence and hence have no influence on the local budget constraint. This assumption is justified on the ground that, across states, gross differences in levels of aid reflect differences in the distribution of responsibility for the provision of local revenue between the state and local governments. In this context, several alternative influences of grants are considered, most importantly possible differences in the *intralocal* incidence of state relative to local taxes and the imposition of state governmental controls over local activity accompanying increases in relative state revenue responsibility. Thus, the effect of grants is not through the level of payments but through the relative dependence of the locality on state financing. To measure this relative reliance, an aid rate (aid relative to expenditure) is utilized in the expenditure equations.

The effect of aid is quantified in the analysis of undeflated expenditures and local revenues; an increase in grants of one dollar is associated with an increase of $0.15 to $0.25 in total expenditures or revenue, and most of the coefficients measuring this association are not statistically significant. Alternative specifications of the aid variable are compared and these aid effects are attributed to the use of the aid rate; it is argued that conventional aid level variables vastly overstate the impact of grants.

Stephen P. Dresch
Raymond J. Struyk

2. NATIONAL INCOME, CONSUMPTION, AND CAPITAL FORMATION

Introduction

Two separate lines of research have been pursued during the past year. The household capital formation and savings project, under my direction, is concerned with the development of behavioral relations that underly the acquisition of both tangible and financial assets by households. These studies involve analysis of both time-series and cross-sectional relationships. The latter are based on a set of experimental survey data obtained by the U.S. Bureau of the Census, with which the National Bureau is collaborating on the over-all project.

The survey data will be used mainly for analysis of financial asset changes. In addition, the survey is designed to facilitate investigation of the potential uses of anticipatory data relating to changes in both tangible and financial assets.

A second research area, and the major one, concerns analysis of economic and social accounts. Here, Richard and Nancy Ruggles are studying disaggregation problems. They have been concentrating on the construction of subsector estimates, using existing data, and on the development and exploitation of microdata sets that would permit types of disaggregation not otherwise possible. John Kendrick and

Robert Eisner are directing studies that involve expansion or elaboration of the present system of national accounts. Kendrick's work is focused on constructing estimates of imputed value for selected nonmarket activities—unpaid household work, the opportunity cost of students, and volunteer labor. In addition, Kendrick is estimating both stocks and flows of "intangible" assets. Eisner is directing a series of studies concerned partly with activities not ordinarily included in national accounts and partly with refinement and improvement of the present accounts. Projects now under way range from analysis of capital gains to the valuation and allocation of time spent in the household. These projects are discussed in more detail below.

F. Thomas Juster

Household Capital Formation and Savings

The time-series analysis of demand for consumer durable goods is now close to completion. Virtually all parts of the study, including the specification, estimation, and analysis of durable goods demand models, are in manuscript form. An objective (nonanticipatory) model has been estimated and compared with models incorporating both objective and anticipatory data and with one incorporating only the latter. A paper comparing the objective and anticipatory models was presented at the CIRET conference held in Madrid last October.

The objective model has a tripartite structure based on the partial adjustment of actual to desired stocks of durables, the formation of expectations via response to past forecast errors, and different response mechanisms for transitory and permanent changes in financial variables. Thus the model explains observed changes in the stock of consumer durables as the sum of planned changes (those due to expected movements in the underlying behavioral variables) and unplanned changes (those due to unforeseen movements in behavioral variables). The model can be used to explain purchases, as distinguished from net investment, on the usual assumption that purchases are equal to net investment plus depreciation measured as some fraction of initial stock.

The first part of the objective model, i.e., expected or planned investment, can be compared with an anticipatory model that includes only subjective purchase expectations and a variable measuring consumer financial expectations. The complete objective model—expected (planned) plus unexpected (unplanned) changes in stocks of durables—can be compared with an anticipatory model which includes purchase expectations, expectations about financial variables, and unanticipated changes in financial variables.

The empirical results are striking. Over the period 1949-67 the objective model explains about 88 per cent of the variance of net investment in automobiles, and a little over 93 per cent of the variance of net investment in nonauto durables and in total durables. For gross investment (purchases), the objective model explains over 93 per cent of the variance in automobiles and about 99 per cent of the variance in both nonauto durables and the total. All of the substantive economic variables in the model have significant t ratios and reasonable regression coefficients, and the implied lag structures are plausible. The objective model implies a mean lag of under one year, with the peak response in the second and third quarters. These results, and the implied elasticities, are comparable to and generally a little better than those obtained by other investigators.

The anticipatory model cannot be estimated for the same time period because the basic data are unavailable; strict comparability can be achieved only for the period beginning in 1960, and only for net and gross investment in automobiles. A comparison of the objective and anticipatory models for this shorter period indicates that the much simpler (two variable) anticipatory model does just as well as the much more complex (seven variables, including a lagged dependent variable) objective model for planned investment, and slightly outperforms the objective model for total investment. Despite the fact that the anticipatory model does not strictly relate to total durables purchases, it does about as well as the objective model even with total durables as the variable to be explained.

Moreover, when the anticipatory variables are simply added to the fully specified objective model, both expected purchases and consumer expectations add significantly to the variance explained by the objective model; all but one of the substantive economic variables in the objective model are reduced to virtually random numbers This conclusion holds for both automobile and total durable goods purchases. The only objective variables that continue to exert a net influence on purchases, holding anticipatory variables constant, are relative prices and the unemployment rate. In both models, the latter variable represents unexpected changes in financial circumstances, hence it is predicted to be significant holding plans and expectations constant. A possible interpretation of the finding that relative prices have a significant influence net of expectations is that price movements are generally unforeseen by consumers and are thus not adequately accounted for in subjectively expressed plans and expectations. It is interesting that among those variables included in the objective model, relative price is the only one for which the state of consumer information might be substantially altered by actual investigation of a potential transaction; the other variables in the model are clearly known to the consumer unit at the time purchase and other expectations are measured.

Recent empirical work has suggested a slight modification of the anticipatory model which seems to provide better structural properties. The basic idea is that the variable used to measure consumer expectations (actually, the Index of Consumer Sentiment developed by the Survey Research Center at Michigan) is best interpreted as a measure of the state of consumer uncertainty. It can be argued that consumer uncertainty makes a net contribution to the explanation of purchase decisions only when it is changing systematically; otherwise the purchase expectations variable will reflect the full influence of the state of uncertainty. The model implied by this interpretation is a nonlinear version of the anticipatory model described above: purchases are specified to be a function of purchase expectations, current unemployment, and changes in the SRC Index of Consumer Sentiment multiplied by a dummy (1, 0) interaction variable. The interaction variable has a value of 1 if, and only if, consumer sentiment is changing systematically; otherwise, it has a value of 0.

We plan to complete two manuscripts within the next few months. The first will cover the analysis and interpretation of the objective model of durable goods demand, and will incorporate comparisons of objective and anticipatory models. The second will concentrate on the anticipatory models, focusing on the interpretation and proper specification of the uncertainty variable. This paper will also incorporate an analysis of optimal forecasting methods for the anticipations model, analyzing questions of useful forecast span, single-quarter forecasts versus the average of multiquarter forecasts, and so forth. Both of these papers are being written in conjunction with Paul Wachtel.

The experimental survey work being carried out in conjunction with the U.S. Bureau of the Census is now sufficiently far along so that we have begun to obtain substantive empirical results. At present the initial survey and a six-months reinterview are on tape, and a number of preliminary regressions have been estimated. The focus is on analysis of alternative ex ante durable goods expenditure variables; analysis of the ex ante savings data is being deferred, since savings during the available six-month span are likely to be seriously affected by seasonal factors. For durables, the preliminary results suggest that expected expenditure variables have less forecasting value than variables reflecting the probability of acquiring specific items like automobiles, houses, or appliances.

The results also suggest that the omission of probabilities for the purchase of multiple units within a given time span has a perceptible effect on forecast accuracy. That is, probabilities of buying "more than one," which were obtained in the experimental survey, appear to contribute to the explanation of total purchases.

Since the results of the second reinterview (conducted in May 1969) are now on hand and can be incorporated into the basic analysis tape, we expect to begin substantive analysis of the savings data within a few months. A wide range of questions will be investigated here: the contribution of various types of family income to an explanation of savings behavior, the association between durables purchase expectations, savings expectations, and the corresponding actuals; the question of what explains savings and durable goods expectations, as well as observed savings and durable goods purchases; and so on. Michael Landsberger, formerly at the University of Pennsylvania, joined the project staff in July and will be working mainly on the cross-section analysis of the experimental survey data.

The fourth wave of interviews on the experimental survey was completed as scheduled in November 1969; these data are now being edited and coded at the Census Bureau. The fifth and final wave, originally scheduled for May-June 1970, has been postponed for a few months because of budgetary constraints. It is now expected that we will obtain fifth-wave interviews in the late summer or early fall of 1970. The data set for this experimental survey will eventually comprise two full years of information for roughly 4,000 households, and will permit simultaneous analysis of differences over time and several sets of differences among families for the same time span. It will also be possible to relate differences in both expectations and actual behavior for identical families, a procedure which simulates the behavior of expectational variables in time series much more closely than the usual cross-section analysis.

Processing and preparation of the basic survey data for analysis is under the supervision of Avrohn Eisenstein. Teresita Rodriguez has joined the project as a research assistant, working mainly with data processing on the time-series analysis.

F. Thomas Juster

The Design and Use of Economic Accounts

Our recently published study, *The Design of Economic Accounts,* provides a framework within which the accounts can be disaggregated. Our current work is concerned with this question in two ways. First, in the tradition of national accounts estimation, a variety of sources of information are being drawn on to disaggregate major sectors and subsectors and to provide systematic and consistent data. Second, microdata sets are being created for specific subsectors of the economy to permit the use of simulation techniques and to provide for estimates which could not otherwise be constructed.

At present, research on the development and use of national economic accounts is focused on three separate segments of the system: (1) investigation of techniques for providing price indexes related to the national economic accounts, (2) subsector disaggregation of income and balance sheets for the household and enterprise sectors, and (3) the development of microdata sets with the objective of developing social as well as economic accounts.

In present practice, the price information on which the deflation of the national accounts is based derives in large part from the Cost of Living and Wholesale Price Indexes. Neither was designed primarily to fit into the national accounts. Moreover, the samples underlying these price indexes do not take into account the intercorrelation which normally exists among prices, and as a result considerable sampling inefficiency exists. Given suitable computer processing techniques, it is now possible to improve the specification of the price observations required for the development of price indexes that would deflate both the end-use and income-originating measures of gross national product. Preliminary analysis suggests that it would be possible to provide more valid information with substantially fewer observations than are now used in the Wholesale and Consumer Price Indexes.

The disaggregation of the household and enterprise sector has as its object the development (for one point in time) of more detailed income statements and balance sheets for specific subsectors. For the household sector, an attempt will be made to examine specific socioeconomic groups, such as the aged and those belonging to certain poverty classes. For the enterprise sector, attention will be focused on certain unincorporated enterprise subsectors, such as farm and professional. Other work is being undertaken regarding the microeconomic behavior of establishments in the manufacturing sector and the manner in which such behavior is related to productivity, wages, and price determination.

Finally, related research is concerned with developing microdata sets for the household and enterprise sectors. This work involves the addition of imputed information from a variety of sources to the basic information obtained from samples of households and establishments. This research has the dual function of using microdata sets on households and enterprises to assist in subsector disaggregation, and of developing techniques of integrating supplementary data into already existing microdata sets.

Nancy D. Ruggles
Richard Ruggles

Studies in the National Income Accounts

Most of my time in recent months has been devoted to writing the monograph on postwar productivity trends (reported on in Section 1), and the national income studies have moved slowly as a consequence. With regard to imputations for nonmarket economic activities, Elizabeth Wehle, Jennifer Rowley, and Harold Wolozin are planning early completion of monographs on unpaid household work, opportunity cost of students, and volunteer labor, respectively. When these monographs are finished, I plan to write a summary essay covering these and other imputations—chiefly rental values of nonbusiness capital goods and final goods and services charged to current expense by business.

With regard to the total investment and capital stock project, some preliminary findings about the intangibles are summarized in the report on productivity mentioned above. The estimates involved in this study are being revised and checked by my principal assistant, Jennifer Rowley. We then plan to design appendix tables and write up the sources and methods underlying the estimates. By 1971, I hope to start on the analysis and to make some headway in writing the text. This study has been supported by grants from the National Science Foundation and by the general funds of the National Bureau.

John W. Kendrick

Measurement and Analysis of National Income (Nonincome Income)

Work is under way on the following major topics: capital gains, the value of services and investment in education, the value of services and net investment in automobiles owned by households, depreciation of business capital stock, executive compensation (with particular focus on stock options), the valuation and allocation of household time, and the depletion of natural resources. The broad plan of research and some of the initial undertakings were described in last year's *Annual Report* (pp. 58-59).

At the American Statistical Association meetings in Detroit, December 1970, reports will be presented by Michael McElroy on "Capital Gains and the Concept of Income," by Allan Mendelowitz on "Measurement of Economic Depreciation," by Wolfhard Ramm on "Services of Household Durables: The Case of Automobiles," and, possibly, by Robert Eisner and Arthur B. Treadway on the general concept and aims of the project. McElroy's work consists of a careful theoretical analysis of the origins of capital gains and their status as income, estimates of capital gains on corporate stock from 1946 through 1968, estimates of capital gains of unincorporated business from 1946 to 1966, and other estimates from a variety of sources. Mendelowitz is applying accepted capital value theory to the estimation of economic depreciation, relating depreciation to exhaustion of an originally anticipated net revenue stream. After exploring relations among expected revenue streams, discount rates, asset service lives, and depreciation, Mendelowitz is estimating revenue stream profiles by relating actual revenue to prior gross investment rates. Initial results, based on data from McGraw-Hill capital expenditure surveys, have been promising.

Ramm is using highly disaggregated market data on auto prices, qualities, and quantities to estimate hedonic price deflators and ex post depreciation patterns. This will allow the construction of more rigorous estimates of stocks, income (including capital gains), and net investment flows for automobiles. This work promises to be the first comprehensive study of its kind, and will result in empirical estimates, for most of the postwar period, that utilize the major methodological suggestions in recent literature. The theoretical work has been completed, the laborious process of collecting information and transferring it to computer-usable formats is largely completed, and initial econometric results for several years have been obtained.

Robert Wallace has been working with Project Talent[1] data, relating information on a number of schooling inputs (aptitude, achievement and personality tests scores for successive years) to post-high-school income, education, and occupation. The statistical work controls for a number of sociological factors and attempts to identify school outputs by reference to the subsequent incomes that various human capital components appear to command in the market. Wallace's tentative findings suggest that output variables representing "technical training," as opposed to "verbal training" or personality characteristics, are most relevant in determining future incomes.

Among further studies recently begun, that of Peter McCabe on the valuation and allocation of household time concerns services of human capital not traded in the market but either consumed directly by the household or applied to the production of more human capital. Stephen Zabor is undertaking an analysis of executive compensation, with particular attention to stock options and other items of deferred compensation. John Soladay is beginning work on natural resource depletion, focused on the theoretical basis for the accounting of exploration costs, on investment in the exploitation of natural resources, and on the capital gains and depreciation on these investments.

Renewal of financial support from the National Science Foundation is under consideration. If obtained, it will permit extension of the study to several other areas as well as completion of the econometric re-estimation of key economic relations on the basis of revised accounts.

Robert Eisner

Capital Gains and the Theory and Measurement of Income

While considerable attention has been focused on the tax treatment of capital gains and losses and, in a predominantly theoretical way, their behavioral implications in individuals' consumption and portfolio decisions, there has

---

[1] A survey of 100,000 high school students conducted by the American Research Institute (Palo Alto) in 1960, with follow-ups in subsequent years.

been no systematic appraisal of their relevance to the theory and measurement of income. This project is a conceptual and statistical attempt to explore the role of capital gains and losses as a form of income.

Present practice is to exclude capital gains and losses, whether realized or not, from estimates of personal income. This results in a measure which, for purposes of assessing both the magnitude and the distribution of individuals' purchasing power, is considerably narrower than the theoretically appropriate Haig-Hicks concepts of individual income as consumption plus the change in net worth. Accrued gains and losses are large and highly variable: for the years 1947-64, annual gains on major asset groups—corporate stocks, residential real estate, and the physical capital of the unincorporated business sector (including farms)—range from minus $50 billion to over $100 billion, averaging $26.3 billion after adjustment for price level changes. By comparison, over the same period personal saving averaged $18.3 billion and in almost every year was exceeded in absolute amount by capital gains (or losses). These estimates are preliminary, and minor revisions will be undertaken in the near future.

At present I am attempting to distribute this expanded measure of income over income size classes. Not only is this measure likely to show greater inequality than the distribution of income as measured by the Office of Business Economics, but its trend over time may well be toward more inequality. Inequality in the size distribution of OBE personal income has remained virtually constant during the past twenty-five years.

A second phase of the study is analysis of the relevance of capital gains and losses to the measurement of current economic activity or output. It can be argued that major portions of accrued gains reflect "output" in a broad sense, and that they do not cancel out when the basic Haig-Hicks concept of income is summed over individuals. The problem, it is maintained here, is strictly one of measurement, a conclusion that runs counter to the conventional notion of capital gains and losses as "unproductive" increments to wealth. It is argued that the net result of including these gains and losses in national income is a reallocation of income over time precisely analogous to the treatment of tangible investment by the OBE. A set of consistent stock/flow accounts has been developed as an expository framework for this expanded concept of national income.

Michael B. McElroy

3. URBAN AND REGIONAL STUDIES

Introduction

The National Bureau's research program in urban economics has expanded dramatically during the past year. Studies started last year and the year before have begun to come to fruition, and a number of new staff members have joined the Bureau's urban studies group.

The major part of the ongoing research is related to the development of a large-scale, experimental computer simulation model for studying the processes of urban development.

We are carrying out concurrently the over-all design and programming of the computer simulation model and the empirical investigation of the behavioral relationships needed for the model. Although all members of the urban studies group have made important contributions to the model design, Greg Ingram has assumed principal responsibility for its over-all design and implementation. Special recognition should also be given to Royce Ginn, particularly for his help in solving the complex programming problems encountered in developing the simulation model. His contributions are not limited, however, to the computer simulation. All of the individual empirical studies involve the processing of large and complex data files; none would have proceeded very far without his tireless efforts.

The individual econometric studies emphasize one or more areas pertinent to the computer simulation and are expected to provide either specific parameter estimates or the theoretical understanding needed for some components of the simulation model. An exhaustive description of these linkages is not appropriate here. However, a few general examples are useful in illustrating the relationship between the individual econometric investigations and the simulation. The Brown-Kain study is designed to evaluate moving behavior and to determine how and why households modify their pattern of housing consumption. Dresch's study investigates the hypothesis that workplace location of the primary wage earner is a major determinant of both the location of the household's residence and the type of housing it consumes. This hypothesis is fundamental to our current model design. If his findings do not confirm this key hypothesis, we will have to re-examine our views about the processes of urban development and possibly make major modifications of our model design. Mayo's study tests this underlying hypothesis in a somewhat different manner and may provide an alternative means of modeling the household's choice of residential location, if his and Dresch's studies fail to support our working hypothesis.

None of the previous studies will provide much direct evidence about how the housing stock adjusts to changes in the demand for housing services by housing-type submarket and location. This is a serious problem that cannot be evaluated fully because of the lack of satisfactory time-series data on changes in the housing stock. Even so, Silver's study of stock adjustment during the decade 1950-60 should provide some guidance for our modeling efforts.

None of these studies involves original data collection. All of them except Silver's use large bodies of underanalyzed data on housing markets, residential choice, and urban travel collected from land-use transportation studies in a number of metropolitan areas. One of the advantages of our approach to the development of an experimental urban simulation model is that it permits us to use varied bodies of data from several cities. This creates a number of difficult problems in reconciling parameter estimates from different data sources. However, we believe that these difficulties can be overcome and that the model will be more general as a result of the diverse bodies of data employed.

A more practical reason for proceeding in this way is that several million dollars would be needed to reproduce the data sources in a more consistent way and for a single city. Our entire budget is but a small fraction of this. The distribution of money spent on research and data collection is already badly out of balance. Another expensive and large-scale data collection effort would make this balance still more unfavorable. Furthermore, we still lack the knowledge to design a comprehensive data collection scheme of the kind that would be needed to answer the interrelated set of questions incorporated in the simulation model. Such a data collection effort might be justified after we have analyzed more carefully the bodies of data presently available to us and after we have completed a prototype computer simulation, but not before. Without this experience, we will not know precisely what kinds of data are most needed.

The Kain-Quigley study of housing market discrimination, although somewhat peripheral to the central urban modeling effort, is giving us valuable information about the characteristics and operation of urban housing markets and the way in which these markets are affected by racial discrimination.

In a similar way, the Struyk-James study on changes in industry location will be of value in simulating changes in the distribution of employment. We expect that changes in the location of basic industry will be exogenous to the urban simulation model. This is unsatisfactory.

We have been trying for some time to obtain funding that would permit us to begin a large-scale analysis of the determinants of the intra-metropolitan location of manufacturing establishments. We have acquired from Dun and Bradstreet a valuable and most unusual body of data from which we could learn a great deal about this process, and we hope that we will be able to expand our research in this area in the coming year.

In addition to these studies, there are several others that are not so closely linked to the objective of developing an urban simulation model. David Gordon's research on employment problems in the ghetto, Joseph Persky's analysis of the growth and change in racial composition of Southern metropolitan areas, and Masanori Hashimoto's study of regional employment rates across states and cities fall into this latter category.

John F. Kain

Modeling the Urban Housing Market

This research effort seeks to represent two important components of urban change. It attempts, first, to model changes which occur in the housing stock through new construction, modification of existing structures, and quality change over time; and, second, to simulate the locational choice of new and moving households. Since these activities are fairly complex, they are being represented in a computer simulation model. While there are undoubtedly a myriad of approaches one could use to simulate changes in the housing stock and locational choice, I have decided to represent these activities in a market setting. Thus the model has three major components: a supply submodel, a demand allocation submodel, and a market or assignment submodel.

The supply submodel simulates stock adaptation, construction, and quality change in each of the several zones which comprise the metropolitan area. The level of each of the possible activities is a function of its expected profitability and several constraints. The profitability is derived from this period's expected prices and engineering cost estimates. The constraints reflect such limitations as zoning restrictions and input availability. The output of this submodel is the revised stock of housing available for occupancy subscripted by structure type and zone of location.

The demand allocation submodel assigns movers of various household classes and workplaces to housing types, by means of traditional demand functions whose arguments are relative prices and incomes. The relative prices incorporate location in a general way in that they include not only the expected housing price but also the expected work-trip cost. This part of the model accommodates the cross elasticities of substitution between house types, since members of more than one household class can select a given house type. The output of this submodel is the number of mover households selecting each house type, subscripted by household class and workplace zone.

The market or assignment submodel matches up the movers with the available units. This will be done with a linear programming algorithm which will produce shadow prices on the various types of units. These shadow prices will then be used to formulate the expected prices for the next period.

The supply submodel was programmed first and is an operating prototype that simulates stock alteration and new construction. This prototype is now being modified to better represent quality change, especially disinvestment. The demand allocation and assignment submodels have been designed and will be programmed next. It is expected that the over-all market model will soon be operational. I will then run sensitivity analyses to identify important model parameters and tentatively simulate the effects of various transport investment and housing policies.

This model uses synthetic data, but it should be fairly easy to adapt to an actual city when the model is perfected and real data are available. Meanwhile, by means of informal consultations with those doing econometric work in the area, I hope to keep the data requirements of the model realizable and the specified parameters realistic.

Gregory K. Ingram

The Detroit Housing Consumption-Residential Location Study

This study is best described in terms of the broader framework of the National Bureau's urban modeling effort, as outlined by Kain and Ingram. The household sector is of primary importance for three components of the NBER model: (1) the mover identification model, (2) the housing submarket assignment model, and (3) the location model (assigning movers by housing submarket, to residence location). The immediate function of the Detroit study is to estimate the housing submarket demand equations and to identify and assign households to the alternative submarkets. Analyses of other issues of relevance to the NBER model are being pursued simultaneously; particularly important questions relate to the housing consumption choices of "non-normal" households, with normal defined as single-worker, male-headed, white households. Information on the housing consumption and residential location patterns of most non-normal household types is singularly lacking. It is hoped that the present study, with its rich data source, will significantly improve the understanding of these choices.

Although not explicitly incorporated in most previous urban models, a key assumption of the Bureau model is that workplace location alters the relative prices of different types of housing and significantly influences the choice of housing submarket. In this context, housing prices must be defined to include structure supply price, location rent, the costs (if borne by the household) of public services, and transportation costs (direct and opportunity), specifically the cost of the journey to work. The initial objective of the study is to identify the effect of workplace location on housing consumption choices.

The basic data source for the study is the home interview survey of the Detroit Transportation and Land Use Study (TALUS). The first phase of the research has consisted of constructing a "household-workplace" file for the 41,243 sample households. This was accomplished by merging several TALUS files to produce a composite containing (1) summary household information (e.g., residence location by census tract and TALUS analysis zone, structure type, tenure type and duration, race, income, family composition, number of working family members), (2) additional detail for the household head (sex, age, marital status, education, occupation, and industry) and the wife of head (labor force status), and (3) details of the primary work trips of the head and wife (workplace location, mode of travel, and elapsed time). Construction and editing of this file is now complete. Of the 32,629 households with working heads, it was possible to identify workplace location for 27,244. The actual (1960 Census) and sample geographic employment and residential distributions seem to coincide quite closely. This correspondence between the population and the sample is also observed in the socioeconomic dimension.

Major effort is being devoted at this time to identifying bundles of residential services which define the housing submarkets. The first step in this process utilizes the TALUS structure types: (1) single-family, (2) duplex and row, (3) small multiple, and (4) large multiple. Housing types will be further identified by the physical characteristics of housing units within census tracts, by neighborhood prestige, and by public service quality. As indexes of the quality of public service, public school and crime statistics are being developed. Preliminary analysis utilizing only tract characteristics is now under way.

Having defined housing types, the objective is the econometric estimation of the submarket demand equations of the form:

$$(1) \quad H_i^{h'} = a^{h'} X_i + \sum_{h=1}^{n} b_h^{h'} p_{j(i)}^h, \quad h = 1, \ldots, n$$

where $H_i^{h'}$ = the probability that household i will choose submarket h'; X_i = characteristics (e.g., income, family size) of household i; $p_{j(i)}^h$ = the price of housing type h ($h = 1, \ldots, n$), relative to the price of housing type $n+1$, at workplace j (the workplace of the head of household i), where the prices include the structure supply price, location rent, public service cost, and the cost of the journey to work. Since the workplace-specific relative housing prices are not observed directly, they must be estimated from the mean within-workplace residuals. The test of the effect of workplace on housing consumption is whether these workplace-specific "incentive factors" differ significantly from zero.

Assuming that a significant workplace effect is observed, the analysis will then attempt to identify the sources of the price variations. This will involve examining the relationships between the incentive factors and such variables as travel time, transit availability, etc. Also, the changes in the incentive factors over time will be examined through information on length of residence. The observed changes in the geographic residential distribution over the various periods will be decomposed into changes resulting from (a) changing workplace locations, (b) changing prices at given workplaces, and (c) changing household characteristics.

It will also be possible at this stage to estimate quantitatively the effect of housing market discrimination on the housing consumption patterns of nonwhites. The estimation of the submarket demand equations will be restricted initially to whites. By predicting black housing consumption on the basis of the estimated white equations and comparing this with the observed black consumption patterns, the distortion in choice can be specified. An effort will also be made to estimate the reverse effect of housing market restrictions on employment opportunities.

Other specific areas of investigation include the housing consumption patterns of the retired, blacks, female-headed households, and households with multiple workers. Since sample sizes in excess of 4,000 are available for each of these groups, detailed analysis will be possible.

The primary output of the Detroit study, in terms of the Bureau model, will be the submarket demand equations. From the estimated equations it will be possible to specify consistent sets of workplace-specific prices, which can then be used in initializing the simulation model.

Stephen P. Dresch

Residential Location Decisions

This study is an econometric investigation of the determinants of the residential choices of households. Objectives of the study have been to ascertain those attributes of households which may be used to identify submarkets in the urban housing market and to determine the relative importance of each of a number of subsets of locational attributes within each submarket. At the heart of the theoretical model is a transportation cost–location-rent trade-off model which additionally considers the impact on residential choice of local public services, housing attributes, social amenities, property taxes, accessibility to shopping areas, and pre-existing land use and topography. The theoretical development of the model stresses integration of both the demand and supply sides of the market for urban housing. Empirical testing of the model is conducted by considering each of twelve stratified groups within the population as comprising distinct submarkets who compete for housing. The groups which are considered are stratified according to race and sex of the household head, household income, family size, and the number of contributors to family income. Households are further stratified by workplace in order to isolate workplace and residence interactions.

The form of the model which was tested was:

$$P_{ijk} = F_{jk}(X_i, t_{ji})$$

where P_{ijk} = the proportion of workers who work at workplace j, and who are in the kth socioeconomic category, and who live at residential location i; X_i = a vector of variables which characterizes residential location i according to the sets of variables mentioned above; t_{ji} = travel time from workplace location j to residential location i. The subscripts of F indicate that there is a different function for each combination of workplace location and socioeconomic category. The equation thus describes the pattern of residential locations for each combination of j and k as a function of the characteristics of residential locations and the characteristics of the transportation system.

The model was estimated using ordinary least squares with census tracts as the unit of observation. Predicted and actual values of P_{ijk} were grouped according to broader geographical areas than census tracts to evaluate the ability of the model to predict population distributions over larger than tract-size areas.

Estimation of the model at the census tract level resulted in corrected R² statistics which ranged from about 0.04 to 0.45. Grouping the predicted and actual observations resulted in proportions of explained variance almost uniformly on the order of 80 to 90 per cent. Major substantive conclusions are:

1. Increases in commuting costs appear to be traded for lower location rents in every socioeconomic group investigated. The relative importance of commuting time and location rent variables decreases with increasing income.
2. Workplace locations of secondary wage earners in households, as well as that of the primary wage earner, seem to have a significant effect on household locational choice.
3. Public services apparently have no significant unambiguous impact on residential choice.
4. School quality seems to affect the locations of only the higher-income groups.
5. Attributes of the housing stock greatly affect residential choices, though different attributes are important for different groups.
6. Land use externalities do not appear to influence residential choices significantly.
7. Property taxes seem to be capitalized almost entirely into property values and therefore have no pervasive effect on location.

Some of these conclusions are subject to qualification because of problems of multicollinearity and sampling errors in the data. The predictive equations do appear to be relatively sound, however, based on the ability to forecast residential distributions about one workplace using behavioral equations estimated on the basis of other workplaces.

This analysis indicates that, while residential location models based upon location rent—transport cost trade-offs are substantially realistic, there are other sets of variables which strongly influence locational decisions and which should be considered in further investigations of this sort. Stratification by socioeconomic categories appears to be absolutely necessary in models of residential choice; behavior is significantly different among practically all groups considered.

Stephen Mayo

Metropolitan Moving Behavior

This research is concerned with household decisions to move, to purchase particular bundles of housing services, and to choose particular locations within an urban area. We are examining two questions: (1) Given the characteristics and changes in the characteristics of family units and the characteristics of the current residence, can we predict which households will move? (2) For households that move, can we explain how the demand for dwelling unit quality, size, and structure type, neighborhood quality, and the quality of local public services enters into their choice of a new residence?

The principal body of data used for the study was obtained from the Bay Area Transportation Study (BATS). In addition to the usual origin and destination survey, BATS conducted a more extensive home interview of an additional 3,000 households. This supplemental survey provided ten-year employment and residential histories for each household. From this data we have created a "movers file," which for each move made during the ten-year period describes: (1) the location, dwelling-unit and neighborhood characteristics, and value or rent of each residence; (2) the head of household's occupation, industry, and workplace location before and after each move; and (3) the relationship, sex, and age of all household members before and after the move.

In addition, we are now working on a second file which will give the characteristics of each household and residence in each year and indicate whether it moved in that year. We will use this file to analyze the determinants of moving.

The bundles of housing services included in the analysis are described in terms of tenure (own vs. rent), value or rent, structure type, age of structure, number of rooms, location, neighborhood quality and prestige, school quality (average achievement scores), and tax rates. Many previous studies have emphasized the importance of school quality and tax rates on the location decisions of urban households. Dwelling unit characteristics were obtained from the home interview survey; measures of neighborhood quality and prestige, from census tract statistics; and school quality and tax data, from local governments.

We assume that, at any moment in time, households demand a particular collection of attributes of the bundle of housing services and a particular location. Household demands for particular housing services depend on family structure, income, and where family members are employed. Therefore, changes in household characteristics may change the demand for either particular attributes or a particular location. When these changes in demand are large enough, the household will change its residence. For example, the birth of a child may cause the family to demand more space, or an increase in income may cause a family of the same size to demand a higher-quality unit.

Changes in bundles of housing services may or may not be associated with a move from one part of the metropolitan area to another. Similarly, a major change in workplace location from one part of the region to another may cause the household to move while it consumes otherwise identical bundles of housing services. On the other hand, changes in workplace location may change the price of certain attributes of housing bundles, thereby changing the characteristics of the bundle. The empirical testing of these several hypotheses has great significance in the validation of alternative theories of residential location.

A variety of statistical methods will be used in estimating these relationships. We have yet to determine the exact nature of the equations needed to estimate these demand relationships. The individual equations are obviously interrelated, but we still have to determine how this interrelationship should be specified.

Besides being of general theoretical interest, we expect the findings of this research to be helpful in determining the demand equations for the simulation model.

John F. Kain
H. James Brown

Housing Consumption, Housing Demand Functions, and Market-Clearing Models

Analysis of variance tests reveal rather dramatic differences in housing consumption by family type, employment status, workplace, income, and race. These differences among households are attributable to differences in tastes, differences in prices in the housing market as determined by workplace location, and by racial segregation, which effectively creates a separate housing submarket for blacks in major urban areas. There may also be effects on the side of supply, such as market imperfections or long lags in changing the housing stock.

To date most empirical research on urban housing has been devoted to describing the housing market prices, quantities purchased, and the quality of the stock. Little attention has been given to specifying the underlying demand and supply functions or how the housing market operates (e.g., how the stock is utilized or altered). For example, regression analysis relating housing prices or rents to resident income, housing quality, neighborhood characteristics, and race is essentially a description of the current housing market as determined by both demand and supply considerations and market imperfections. That housing prices are closely related to resident income and stock quality is testimony to the workings of the housing market. However, the particulars of the causal structure remain obscure. High-income residents, high-quality housing, and high house prices in a geographic area are all endogenous variables, reflecting the spatial configuration of jobs and the current housing stock throughout the city, which determines who will outbid whom at a given site.

To disentangle the sources of variation in housing consumption and housing prices requires in the first instance a specification of housing demand functions. Household interview data are required for this analysis. Previous analysis based on aggregated data, e.g., census tracts, unfortunately obscures the role of the workplace, a fundamental determinant of the relative prices of housing and work-trip costs confronting the household. Housing demand functions for the complex set of residential services which can be considered "housing" are being estimated from household interview data; these include income elasticities and price elasticities as derived from the effects of workplace location on relative prices.

These demand estimates permit a determination of the separate effects on housing consumption of supply imperfections, or lags in supply adjustments to demand, relative to differences in tastes. They also can be employed in simulation models of the "market clearing" process, a specification of how households relocate and what price they pay for different housing bundles. Recourse to either a mathematical programming formulation or more ad hoc iterative schemes in such a simulation depend for their success on using realistic housing demand functions as inputs.

The output of these simulations would therefore be the assignment of households to the existing housing stock and a set of derived prices. These, in turn, are important inputs to models representing housing stock additions and improvements as well as changes in such neighborhood characteristics as the tax base and the need for education.

Mahlon R. Straszheim

The Demand for Housing

The objective of this research is to examine the demand for housing in the short run. The general model upon which the analysis is based is of the form:

$$E(Q_i) = f(x_{li}, \ldots, x_{ki}, x_m, \ldots, x_s)$$
$$g(Y_i, p, Q_{i, t-1}, H_i)$$

$f(*) = 0$ if no residential move
$ = 1$ if residential move

where $E(Q_i)$ = expected value of housing services demanded by household i in a transaction during the period; $x_{li}, \ldots, x_{ki}$ = a series of "status" or "change" variables specific to household i; $x_m, \ldots, x_s$ = a series of variables specific to the neighborhood; Y_i = income; p = price; $Q_{i, t-1}$ = level of housing services consumed at the beginning of the period; H_i = household characteristics

This model emphasizes two important aspects of housing demand behavior. First, a portion of all households adjust their housing consumption by moving. Second, out of the total population, those households which do move are more likely to display a long-run level of demand, as measured by the amount of housing services purchased or rented in the market, than are "sitting" owners or renters, whose consumption of housing is measured by the potential market value or existing rental level of the dwellings which they occupy.

The empirical work employs data from several thousand individual household records collected by the Southeastern Wisconsin Regional Planning Commission. These data include information over a period of up to thirteen years (eight points in time) prior to the year of interview, on places of work and residence, and on income and value of housing for years in which place of work or residence was changed.

The analysis falls into two principal parts:

1. For that portion of the population which moved in the period prior to the interview date, the parameters of a variety of demand equations have been estimated.[1] The principal findings are: that a measure of income which includes the influences of wealth is superior to income measures which do not; that the level of housing services consumed prior to the residential move adds significantly to the explanatory power of all of the income measures employed; and that aggregation leads to a severe upward bias on the coefficient of the income variable, whether this be current income or some representation of the permanent component of income. Extensions of this portion will include further experiments with the income variable and attempts to account for quality differences among housing units.

2. The second principal portion of the analysis involves a sample of households present at the beginning of the period, regardless of whether they moved their residence during the period. The object is to discover the determinants of the residential move. Those variables which will be emphasized are: the divergence between long-run and actual housing consumption levels, differences in individual and average neighborhood household characteristics, changes in family size, and changes in travel time from home to work. In addition, hypotheses about the differences in causality between workplace change and residence change are to be tested. Differences in behavior between white and nonwhite households will also be examined. Nearly all the work on this portion has been concerned with preparing the data for analysis. Some preliminary examination of the processed data file is being conducted to familiarize the investigator with distributions within the data, primarily by means of cross tabulations and hierarchical decision trees where sequential decisions are hypothesized, e.g., workplace move, residential move, tenure type in new housing, type of area of new housing, location of new housing.

Irving R. Silver

A Housing Market Model

While a series of studies concerning specific components of housing market behavior are being developed from an urban simulation model, a simpler model of the housing market has been formulated which can analyze actual changes in the housing stock of individual metropolitan areas. This model attempts to explain adjustments in the quality of the existing stock of housing units as a response to price. The model postulates a continuum of quality within the stock, which, for empirical simplification, is divided into a few discrete classes. It is hypothesized that, within each small and relatively homogeneous area of the metropolitan area, change in the quantity of housing services, by converting the housing unit for some level of demand, depends upon the vector of price changes in the various quality levels weighted by some a priori measure of interclass degree of substitutability, e.g., spatial separation. Conversion, by definition, includes deterioration and improvement in addition to actual alteration of dwellings.

The empirical work is based on census tract data for several metropolitan areas for 1950 and 1960. Data for the San Francisco-Oakland and the Washington, D.C., areas are being processed and are nearly ready for analysis.

---

[1] Results of this analysis are summarized in the paper, "A Model of Housing Demand in Metropolitan Areas," to be published with other papers presented at a Conference on Urban Land Economics, by the John C. Lincoln Institute.

Additional data for St. Louis are also being acquired. Since the data include separate figures for the nonwhite portions of those census tracts having a large percentage of nonwhite households, additional hypotheses may be tested about racial discrimination. The predictive accuracy of the model will be tested against the results of the 1970 Census.

Irving R. Silver

An Analysis of Ghetto Housing Markets

There is a growing recognition that housing market discrimination plays a central role in the nexus of problems facing urban areas. Yet, in spite of the far-reaching effects of housing market discrimination, there has been very little systematic investigation into its nature and consequences.

This study, an econometric analysis of the ghetto housing market in St. Louis, Missouri, should help fill this gap. The analysis is based on a sample of approximately 1,500 households in St. Louis in 1967. The sample contains detailed information on both the characteristics of households and their dwelling units. Particularly noteworthy are detailed data on the quality of each dwelling unit and the surrounding neighborhood. There have been many surveys of dwelling units and many surveys of households, but we know of no other large-scale effort to collect and merge comprehensive housing and household information in this way.

Although the study emphasizes the impact of discrimination on urban housing markets and the resulting distortions of Negro housing consumption, it is cast in the more general framework of an analysis of urban housing markets. Therefore, we consider the actual patterns of housing consumption by both black and white households in St. Louis and attempt to evaluate the racial discrimination in determining these "patterns." The study deals explicitly with the multidimensional character of housing services. Thus, it considers the physical characteristics of individual dwelling units (e.g., number of rooms, total floor area, number of baths, condition, and over-all quality), the quality of surrounding properties and the neighborhood as a whole, and the quality of local public services.

For the most part, research into housing market discrimination has been concerned with measuring the extent of segregation, evaluating the causes of current and historical patterns of racial segregation, and determining whether Negroes pay more than whites for comparable housing. Although the last question has been the focus of a large number of empirical studies, there is no completely persuasive evidence either way on the matter. Most researchers would accept the view that blacks pay more than whites for housing of comparable size and quality, but this view is by no means unanimous. Our own findings for St. Louis in 1967 indicate that equivalent housing is roughly 8 per cent more expensive in the ghetto than outside.[1]

In any case, price markups for comparable housing may be relatively less important than other consequences of housing market discrimination. A far more serious result, for example, may be a limitation on or a distortion of Negro housing patterns. Many kinds of housing services may be completely unavailable to blacks or available only at prices or under circumstances that virtually prohibit blacks from consuming them. Indeed, our research indicates that a much smaller proportion of Negroes purchase housing than whites, even after differences in income, family size and structure, and other determinants of homeownership are taken into account. Thirty-two per cent of the Negro households in our sample were homeowners in 1967. Our analysis suggests that 45 per cent would have been homeowners had they been white. The differences for home pur-

---

[1] Some preliminary findings including those pertaining to housing market discrimination are contained in John F. Kain and John M. Quigley, "Measuring the Value of Housing Quality," *Journal of the American Statistical Association,* June 1970.

chasers were larger still.[2] If nonwhites are systematically excluded from homeownership, the consequences may extend beyond housing consumption. For example, homeownership is by far the most important form of saving for low-income households. If nonwhite households are discouraged from owning their homes, they may be denied an important method of wealth accumulation.

John F. Kain
John M. Quigley

Industrial Location within Metropolitan Areas

The main thrust of the study during the past year has been developing data and more clearly defining the process of metropolitan industrial location. With respect to the latter, the importance of the marginal components—new firms, firms relocating within the area, firms going out of business or moving out of the area, and firms expanding their employment at present locations—in producing the observed locational pattern of industry and industrial employment is being examined for four metropolitan areas. These areas are Boston, Cleveland, Minneapolis-St. Paul, and Phoenix. A report of the preliminary findings for the Boston area was presented at the Fall 1969 Research Conference of the Committee on Urban Economics, and a report on the findings of all four areas will soon be given.

A considerable part of last year's efforts was also devoted to investigating the limitations and usefulness of the establishment-level Dun and Bradstreet data, which are serving as our primary data source. As a result of this work, the cost of carrying out similar work for other cities will be substantially reduced,

---

[2] These preliminary findings were included in a paper presented at the December 1969 meetings of the AEA. They may be found in John F. Kain and John M. Quigley, "Housing Market Discrimination, Homeownership, and Savings Behavior," Harvard University, Program on Regional and Urban Economics, Discussion Paper No. 58.

and the quality of the data will be generally improved.

The ultimate goal of the project since its initiation has been not only to understand the dimensions of the location process but also to determine which factors most strongly influence the intrametropolitan location decision of manufacturers and to quantify those influences using behavioral models. It is anticipated that one of the four metropolitan areas currently under study will be selected for this purpose and that modeling will begin in the second half of 1970. In addition, Robert Leone and Gordon Saussy of Yale University are using the data to study the influence of transportation facilities and other factors on the location decision of firms in the New York and New Orleans metropolitan areas.

Franklin James
Raymond J. Struyk

Ghetto Employment Problems

I have spent the past year trying to complete some exploratory research on ghetto employment problems. The data needed became available much later in the year than I had expected, and in thinking about my work I have reconsidered many of the underlying analytic assumptions.

In my own area of interest, conventional marginal analysis has been applied quite directly to the analysis of ghetto employment problems and discussions of manpower policy. Typically, an individual's "disadvantage" is presumed to vary more or less as the sum of a collection of individual handicaps. A person earns low wages, for instance, because he has had relatively little education, or because he has had little specific training, or because he has had little information about job opportunities. Policy conclusions have derived directly from that framework. Since disadvantage is presumed to vary as a continuous function of a variety of relatively independent variables, analysts assume that marginal improvement of any relevant labor market characteristic will automatically bring about an incremental improvement in the worker's labor market situation. Thus, if he receives one additional year's equivalent of education, his earnings will be expected to increase automatically by a certain amount, regardless of his other characteristics and regardless of the social structure.

An alternative hypothesis might be to presume that, at any point in history, the prevailing and constantly evolving system of social and economic institutions defines and maintains class distinctions. It might be further assumed that these class distinctions change in such a way as to maximize the advantage of those in control of the institutions. At the most general level, it would envisage that individual labor market outcomes are determined primarily by those characteristics along which class distinctions are made, and only secondarily by those characteristics to which economists usually attribute productivity. With reference to ghetto employment problems, it would assume that those who are "disadvantaged" remain so more because it serves the interests of those in control of institutions that a class of people is considered "disadvantaged," than because they are relatively unproductive.

This kind of analytic framework suggests several illustrative observations about ghetto employment problems, observations which ought to be subject to empirical test. For example, it implies that those with easily determined and conventionally accepted second-class characteristics (blacks and women, for instance) dominate those jobs at the bottom of the hierarchical ladder (lower-status clerical, laborer, and service jobs). It would also predict that training programs designed to increase a disadvantaged worker's productivity will not necessarily bring about improvements in his labor market status; institutions may continue to channel him into low-status jobs despite his apparent increase in skill.

To begin to test these alternative hypotheses, I have been working with what seemed to me the most useful available set of data about ghetto employment problems, the new Urban Employment Survey, sponsored by the Bureau of Labor Statistics and the Bureau of the Census. In its first year, fiscal 1969, it sampled large numbers from the ghetto populations of New York, Chicago, Los Angeles, Detroit, Houston, and Atlanta (and also, for control purposes, from the rest of Detroit and Atlanta). Its extensive questionnaires provide more detailed information about job histories and labor market problems than we have ever had before. Using these data, I am trying to test the differences between a "conventional" and "class" analysis of these labor markets in several ways.

First, I am trying to explore the explanatory power and interrelationships of different sets of variables that influence such labor market outcomes as wages and occupational status—on the one hand, variables like education and job experience, which we tend to assume are directly related to "productivity" and, on the other hand, variables like race and sex, which we assume are more distantly related to productivity. Second, I am trying to test for discontinuities in the structure of jobs in the labor market, looking for evidence that a certain subset of jobs (defined by both industry and occupation) comprise the secondary half of what some have called the "dual" labor market. Third, I am trying to use these empirically derived definitions of the secondary labor market to help explain the relative effectiveness of the first and second sets of explanatory variables in influencing labor market outcomes—to look for evidence, in short, that some people are channeled into certain jobs with little reference to their skills.

David Gordon

Migration and Employment in Southern Metropolitan Areas

Over the last year my research has focused on large southern metropolitan areas. This work is meant to complement the earlier work I did with John Kain on the nonmetropolitan South. The general purpose of the current research is to explore the relation of migration and growth of employment in determining the racial and skill composition of southern cities.

The heart of this effort is a migration model. This model includes four streams of migrants for the period 1955-60: white in-migrants from metropolitan areas, white in-migrants from nonmetropolitan areas, black in-migrants from metropolitan areas and black in-migrants from nonmetropolitan areas. Out-migration has been broken down into white and black streams. The most interesting (and still tentative) findings to date are: (1) the importance of the hinterland in determining white and black nonmetropolitan in-migration. Each SMSA in the sample has been assigned a hinterland as defined by Rand McNally trading areas. Thus two SMSA's close to one another have a smaller "supply pool" of nonmetropolitan migrants to draw upon. This effect comes up clearly in regression results. (2) The relative constancy of white and black out-migration rates once adjustments are made for military movement. Blacks, however, tend to out-migrate at a substantially lower rate than whites. Differences in employment growth have only minor effects on out-migration. This can be interpreted as a substitution effect of "cheaper" labor within each racial labor force or, alternatively, an indication that the city in question is a "stopping off" point for migration elsewhere (e.g., Memphis for migration to Chicago). (3) Other things being equal (in particular the rate of employment expansion), blacks tend to be more willing to move to and less willing to leave SMSA's with a low proportion of blacks. This may reflect a larger pool of "available" jobs in these cities.

My research effort is currently moving backward in time. The central question is whether a simple migration model as described above can be adapted to explain the changes in the racial and skill composition of southern cities since 1900. I am currently working on a "simulation model" which will attempt such an explanation.

Joseph J. Persky

Research on Regional Unemployment

The purpose of this study is to analyze unemployment rates across states and cities. The study so far deals only with state differences, but the analytical procedure would be the same for cities.

Observed differences in state unemployment rates at any point in time reflect both short-run and long-run components. The unemployment, u_{jt}, for the jth state at time t can be decomposed into the cyclical component, c_{jt}, the secular component, s_{jt}, and the residual, v_{jt}. Two alternative forms of the decomposition were attempted here. One assumes that the three components are additive and the other assumes a multiplicative relation:

(1) $$u_{jt} = c_{jt} + s_{jt} + v_{jt}$$

or

(2) $$u_{jt} = c_{jt} \cdot s_{jt} \cdot v_{jt}$$

To facilitate the empirical separation of these components, the following relationships for the cyclical and the secular components were assumed. For the cyclical component,

(1-a) $$c_{jt} = \beta_j u_{t+n_j}$$

or

(2-a) $$c_{jt} = u_{t+n_j}^{\beta_j},$$

where u_{t+n_j} is the U.S. unemployment rate at time $t+n_j$ and β_j is a measure of cyclical sensitivity.

For the secular component,

(1-b) $$s_{jt} = \alpha_j + \gamma_j t + \delta_j t^2$$

or

(2-b) $$s_{jt} = \alpha_j e^{(\gamma_j t + \delta_j t^2)}$$

Thus the cyclical component of unemployment in a given state is related to the aggregate level of economic activity as represented by the aggregate unemployment rate, while the secular component is represented by a constant plus a trend. Substituting into (1) and (2), we get:

(3) $u_{jt} = \alpha_j + \beta_j u_{t+n_j} + \gamma_j t + \delta_j t^2 + v_{jt}$

or

(4) $\log u_{jt} = \alpha'_j + \beta_j \log u_{t+n_j} + \gamma_j t + \delta_j t^2 + v'_{jt}$

The first task is to obtain meaningful measures of the parameters in the above relationships, while the second is to compare and analyze the differences in these measures among states. Finally, I hope to identify mechanisms by which labor markets adjust to changes in demand and supply conditions in both the short and the long run.

Using seasonally adjusted quarterly data on insured unemployment rates for states from 1950-I to 1968-IV, the parameters α_j, β_j, γ_j and δ_j were estimated for both linear and logarithmic equations. The best fit for both equations in every state was obtained when $n_j = 0$; apparently there are no quarterly leads or lags in state unemployment responses to aggregate economic activity.

The following table summarizes the distribution of the parameters across states.

	linear equation					log equation			
	α	β	100γ	1000δ		α'	β	100γ	1000δ
mean	0.144	0.906	1.013	−0.189		−0.155	0.980	0.505	−0.062
standard deviation	1.476	0.315	4.917	−0.535		0.670	0.249	1.230	0.165
coefficient of variation	10.25	0.35	4.85	2.83		4.32	0.25	2.44	2.66

The dispersion of the parameters as measured by both the standard deviation and the coefficient of variation is smaller in the log than in the linear equation. In the short and long run, state unemployment rates behave more alike relatively than absolutely.

An examination of the results suggests that β is higher in high-unemployment states than in low-unemployment states when the linear equation is used; there is no comparable relationship with the log equation. For the linear equation, there is a positive correlation between β and average unemployment between 1950 and 1968 ($r = 0.59$), but for the log equation there is a weaker and negative correlation ($r = -0.37$). Evidently, a given fall in the aggregate unemployment rate is associated with a greater absolute decline in unemployment rates in high-unemployment states than in low-unemployment states. But a given decline in aggregate unemployment tends to be associated with a proportionately smaller decline in unemployment rates in higher-unemployment states.

To explore the determinants of cyclical sensitivity, the following regressions were run across states: $\log \bar{u}$ is the logarithm of the average state unemployment rate between 1950 and 1968, SW represents the proportion of secondary labor force in the population, i.e., teenagers, women over 20, and men over 65, CD/RS is the ratio of employment in construction and durable manufacturing industries to employment in wholesale, retail, and service industries, and S is median years of schooling.

β (from equation 3) = 0.579 + 0.494 (log $\bar{u}$) −0.011 (SW) + 0.005 (CD/RS) −0.012 (S) $\bar{R}^2 = 0.522$
                          (0.811) (4.800)   (−0.821)   (4.358)   (−0.393)   n = 49

$$\beta \text{ (from equation 4)} = 2.309 - 0.333 \text{ (log } \bar{u}) - 0.026 \text{ } (SW) + 0.005 \text{ } (CD/RS) - 0.005 \text{ } (S) \quad \bar{R}^2 = 0.396$$
$$(3.647)\,(-3.653) \quad (-2.167) \quad (5.204) \quad (-0.199) \quad n = 49$$

t values are in the parentheses.

The negative coefficient of *SW* in these regressions suggests the predominance of the discouraged worker effect. The positive coefficients of the *CD/RS* variable suggest that unemployment in construction and durable manufacturing industries is more cyclically sensitive than in the retail and service industries. This result is to be expected since output and sales in the former groups of industries are cyclically more sensitive.

Human capital analysis predicts negative signs for the coefficients of the *S* variable, assuming that skill level is a positive function of schooling level and that the specificity of skills is also related positively to the total amount of skill. Short-run fluctuations in final demand cause immediate fluctuations in the demand for variable factors of production. The more specific the skill, the less variable a factor of production is the worker possessing the skill. The results are consistent with this analysis, although the *S* coefficients are quite weak.

A preliminary investigation of the secular component, s_{jt}, shows interesting patterns in change over time.

1. States whose secular component declined experienced a faster growth in per capita income and a faster growth in nonagricultural employment than states whose secular component tended to rise.

2. States with declining secular components experienced faster growth in population, a smaller decline in the male labor-force participation rate, and a smaller increase in the female labor-force participation rate than states with rising secular components.

3. States with declining secular components showed net in-migration, while those with rising secular components showed the reverse. This suggests that migration was largely job-oriented, in that most migrants were formerly in the labor force and moved simply to obtain new employment.

At any given time, what proportion of the observed variation across states in unemployment rates is cyclical and what proportion is secular? To answer this question, I examined the composition of the variance in unemployment rates across states during different cyclical periods. While the calculations are not yet complete, the results indicate that the contribution of the cyclical component of variance to the total variance is larger during cyclical troughs than during peaks. If this is so, depressed areas would be more accurately identified by unemployment rates during periods other than recessions.

My current plans call for refinement and extension of the analysis. A few areas in immediate need of development are:

1. Refinement of the analysis of factors influencing β_j.

2. Identification and analysis of economic variables that explain differences in s_{jt} at a given time.

3. Exploration of interactions of changes in the demand for and supply of labor associated with particular trend patterns.

4. Use of these findings to synthesize relevant economic factors into a more complete model that explains cyclical and secular features of the regional unemployment distribution.

Finally, a parallel study of the effects of minimum wages on the labor market is being carried out. Preliminary results suggest that federal minimum wages had a depressing effect on both the employment rate and the labor-force participation rates of low-skilled groups in the labor force. Thus unemployment alone may not be a good indicator of minimum wage effects, since labor-force participation may also be affected. A more thorough study, with special attention paid to the lagged patterns of response to minimum wages, is planned in the future.

Masanori Hashimoto

4. HUMAN RESOURCES AND SOCIAL INSTITUTIONS

Introduction

During the past year work has proceeded on three broad research programs: education, the economics of the legal system, and the economics of health.

Some ongoing programs in education are being directed by Gary S. Becker (personal income distribution, consumption-labor supply decisions), while others are under the direction of F. Thomas Juster (net returns to education, savings, obsolescence of educational capital, school production functions, and agricultural productivity). Becker is primarily responsible for the legal economics studies, and Victor R. Fuchs is directing studies in the health area, which are reported on in Section 7 of this report.

Education Studies. A volume with contributions by three authors on the effects of human capital on the personal distribution of income is almost ready for a staff reading committee. One essay, by Barry Chiswick, deals with the effects of differences in the distribution of schooling on differences between regions and countries in inequality and skewness in the distribution of income.[1] Jacob Mincer has almost completed his study of the influence of schooling and postschooling investment on the structure and age profile of earnings. Becker's study of the theory underlying the observed distribution of schooling and other human capital was published as a Woytinsky Lecture at the University of Michigan.[2]

Gilbert Ghez, Robert Michael, and Becker are examining the influence of education on consumption and labor supply decisions. Michael's study, which concerns the influence of education on a household's "efficiency" in utilizing goods and time, has been through a reading committee and is being revised for publication as an Occasional Paper. Ghez's study, based on the household production function model, is designed to explain variations in consumption with age. It emphasizes the interdependence over the life cycle between consumption decisions and labor supply decisions. Becker's companion study uses the household production function model to examine life-cycle patterns in the amount of time spent by males in the labor force.

Both the income distribution and consumption-labor supply studies are being financed with the aid of a grant from the Carnegie Corporation.

Considerable progress has been made during the past year on a series of education studies being conducted with the aid of a grant from the Carnegie Commission on Higher Education. Paul Taubman and Terence Wales, who are studying net returns to education, have completed a paper on the historical relation between mental ability (as measured by the usual test scores) and educational attainment. Their results are surprising in some respects: the data show that the average ability of those entering college has increased steadily during the past several decades—a period when the proportion of high school seniors entering college has also increased. Thus the widely expressed fear that expansion of college enrollments to accommodate a rising fraction of the high school population would inevitably lead

---

[1] See the *1969 Annual Report,* pp. 69-70, where Chiswick's work is discussed.

[2] See his *Human Capital and the Personal Distribution of Income,* Institute of Public Administration, University of Michigan, 1967.

to a deterioration in the average quality of college students seems, at least so far, to be without foundation.

Another part of the Taubman-Wales study, which deals with estimates of the financial return to higher education after adjustment for the influence of ability on earnings, is partly in manuscript form. Examination of one data set (Wolfle-Smith) indicates that, while ability has a significant influence on earnings, its exclusion from the education-earning relation has little effect on the net influence of education, because ability appears to have an approximately equal influence on all education levels. Other data sets are yet to be examined, including the NBER-Thorndike sample of Air Force veterans discussed below.

Sherwin Rosen, who is examining the depreciation and obsolescence of educational "capital," has completed the analytical part of the study and is now testing the model on various sets of earnings data. Rosen is using the one-in-a-thousand 1960 Census sample, and hopes to make extensive use of the National Science Foundation registry data on professional earnings. Rosen's model essentially specifies that both current income and "learning" (which yields future income) are purchased as an inseparable package, that different kinds of jobs have different proportions of income and learning, and that these job packages are bought and sold in the labor market with prices determined in the usual way.

The study of savings behavior as it relates to educational attainment, being carried out by Lewis Solmon, has been handicapped to some degree by data problems which now appear to have been resolved. Solmon's preliminary results suggest that, while more educated individuals save more than others, the difference may be fully explainable by factors like current and prospective income that are strongly influenced by educational attainments. Solmon is also examining the question of allocative efficiency in portfolio composition, where the net influence of educational attainment may be both easier to identify and of greater consequence.

Robert Michael is exploring the relation between education and family size, focusing on how educational attainment influences contraceptive knowledge and use. Technical changes in contraceptive methods might be expected to influence behavior differentially for those with different amounts of education, for the same reasons that efficiency in processing any type of new information might be related to educational level.

Other studies in the economics of education are being conducted by Finis Welch, John Hause, and V. K. Chetty, the last in conjunction with Roger Alcaly. Welch is looking at agricultural data with an eye toward determining whether the presumed greater efficiency in processing and using new information shows up as a return to more highly educated farm operators. Chetty and Alcaly are using data from the growth study originated by the Educational Testing Service at Princeton to examine school production functions—relating teaching and other inputs to various measures of student output (largely test scores). The growth study data have the unique advantage of permitting good estimates of the "value added" by schools, since the study contains standardized test scores for a number of successive years. Hause, who is an NBER Research Fellow for 1970, is also working on the problem of net returns to education and ability. He is using a collection of exceptionally good ability and earnings data from Sweden, and is also examining the Project Talent[3] data.

During the next year we hope to extend our analysis of data from the NBER-Thorndike sample, in addition to exploiting it for measurement of net returns. These data can be used to examine the influence of education and ability on the distribution of income, the influence of several different dimensions of ability on both financial returns and other aspects of behavior, the relation between "quality" of higher-education institutions and financial returns, and related topics.

Legal-Economic Studies. We have continued

---

[3] See footnote, Section 2, p. 45, for a description of Project Talent.

our analysis of some economic aspects of the legal system. William Landes' study of the courts, with emphasis on court delays, pretrial settlements, and the bail system, has been accepted for publication in the *Journal of Law and Economics*. Isaac Ehrlich is studying the rate of participation in illegal activities. His hypothesis is that the frequency of illegal behavior is determined by the relative gains and costs as visualized by potential participants.

Since we consider our initial investigations into the legal system to be highly rewarding, we plan to expand our work in this area. In particular we hope to begin a study of the effectiveness of various kinds of legislation. For example, how do the antitrust laws deter collusions, and how successful are they? We plan to add a lawyer to our staff to aid in this work.

F. Thomas Juster
Gary S. Becker

Education Studies

Human Capital Analysis of Personal Income Distribution

A first draft of my study of the effects of individual investments in human capital on the distribution of earnings was completed in May. The study separates components of earnings attributable to schooling from those resulting from postschool investments, such as training on the job and other forms of improvement. "Earnings profiles" of individuals are interpreted as growth curves produced by the staggering of investment over the working life. The familiar Gompertz growth function provides a good statistical fit to typical profiles.

The implications of individual differences in self-investments are differences in levels and slopes of the earning profiles. The study shows that these implications yield a consistent interpretation of the systematic differences in means, variances, and skewness parameters of earnings in different schooling and age groups of the labor force.

Beyond such qualitative or comparative analysis, the study contains attempts at econometric estimation of the proportion of earnings inequality attributable to individual differences in investment in human capital. A by-product of this analysis is a regression method for estimating rates of return and volumes of investment.

The bulk of the empirical analysis is based on the 1960 Census one-in-a-thousand sample and is confined to earnings of white urban males. However, the study concludes with some comparisons of earnings distribution of race and sex groups, as well as of persons and families.

One finding of particular interest in the quantitative analysis is that as much as two-thirds of the observed inequality in the 1959 earnings of urban males can be attributed to the distribution of investments in human capital. This result suggests that the return on human capital is already a more important explanation of income inequality in the United States today than the return on physical and financial capital.

Together with contributions by Becker and Chiswick, this study will be included in a monograph on the relation between human capital and the distribution of income. The monograph will represent a summing up of insights obtained from ongoing research in human capital at the National Bureau. This research is supported by grants from the Carnegie Corporation and from the Economic Development Administration of the U.S. Department of Commerce. Much of this research and some of the findings of the current study were reviewed in my survey paper "The Distribution of Labor Incomes: A Survey, With Special Reference to the Human Capital Approach." This paper was published in the March issue of the *Journal of Economic Literature*.

Jacob Mincer

A Theory of Life-Cycle Consumption

A model of life-cycle consumption is developed which carries markedly different implications than the standard Fisher-Modigliani-Brumberg model. In this new view of consumption, not only permanent income but also the price of time plays a major role. The model specifies that households achieve their consumption aims by combining the services of market goods and their own time. The demand for market goods (as well as the demand for consumption time) thus appears as a derived demand for a factor of production: it therefore depends not only on real wealth, but also on the price of time.

The equilibrium conditions of the model explain why consumption and earnings are correlated over a life cycle, even in the absence of unexpected changes in income. This dependence arises because temporal variations in the price of time generate substitution effects (1) between market goods and consumption time, and (2) between nonmarket activities at different points in time.

By contrast, under the Modigliani-Brumberg life-cycle hypothesis, whether consumption rises or falls with age is completely independent of the actual shape of the earnings profile, provided that income expectations are fulfilled. Earnings there are important only in determining the level of wealth.

The implications of the model were tested with data from the BLS 1960-61 Survey of Consumer Expenditures and the one-in-a-thousand sample taken from the 1960 Census of Population. Households were grouped by year of age of the family head because no measure of real wealth is available and because it is reasonable to assume that, although each household's income expectations may be disappointed, cohort income expectations are likely to be unbiased. For each year of age of the family head, average family consumption, average earnings, and average family size were computed. Average family consumption by age of head was then regressed on average earnings by age of head, family size, and age itself (all variables in logarithms except age). Under the assumption of constant and age-neutral growth, the cross-sectional estimate of the wage rate effect is an unbiased estimate of the life-cycle substitution effect.

The results show that the wage rate effect is significantly positive (a point estimate of .23 with a standard error of .02), thereby throwing considerable doubt on the Modigliani-Brumberg life-cycle hypothesis. Furthermore, the wage rate effect is generally stable across education classes, i.e., across groups differing in permanent income, as the model predicts.

The variable "age of family head" was introduced into the regressions to capture the stimulating effect of positive interest rates on future consumption, as well as the effect of the upward trend in earnings over time. The implied estimate of the elasticity of substitution between nonmarket activities at different points in time is relatively small, less than .3.

The elasticity of substitution between time and goods is considerably higher, a point estimate of about .6, thereby accounting for the positive correlation between consumption and earnings over a life cycle. These results can also explain the procyclical sensitivity of both consumption and labor supply, without the necessity of resorting to models of biased group-income expectations.

Gilbert R. Ghez

Education and Consumption Patterns

Since last year's report on this project, which analyzes the effect of education on efficiency in nonmarket consumption, additional empirical work has been completed. The 1960 BLS Consumer Expenditure Survey data were analyzed for some fifty detailed consumption categories, thus disaggregating the dozen or so items previously studied. The new results are not easily summarized except for the observation that the neutrality model (which assumes that education has a technologically neutral productivity effect on all nonmarket production functions) appears to be much more consistent with the expenditure pattern for nondurable goods and services than for durable goods. One explanation for this finding is suggested. From the nondurables alone the implied effect of education on real, full income through nonmarket efficiency is approximately three times as great as previously estimated for all goods: a 1 per cent increase in the education level raises income by about one-third of 1 per cent, aside from its effect through market earnings.

The manuscript is currently in the hands of a reading committee.

Robert T. Michael

Time Spent In and Out of the Labor Force by Males

This study is a companion to that reported on by Ghez, and concentrates on the implications of the same model for time spent in and out of the labor force by males. The percentage increase or decrease in nonworking time with respect to a 1 per cent rise (or decline) in the wage rate would be a weighted average of the elasticities of factor and commodity substitution discussed in Ghez's report. This weighted average is estimated at about +0.25.

If we combine this figure with our estimate of the effect of a positive interest rate and with Ghez's estimates, we can conclude that the elasticity of substitution between goods and time is about .5 or .6, while the elasticity of substitution between commodities over time is much smaller, say, less than .25. The share of time in the total cost of producing commodities is substantial, on the order of one-half. The interest rate has a large effect on the growth of nonworking time over the life cycle: it explains a growth of about 1 per cent per annum.

Although these estimates have been entirely derived from life-cycle data, we have been examining their implications for secular, seasonal, and cyclical changes in the working and nonworking time of males. Preliminary calculations suggest that they can predict the secular changes in working time (and in the consumption of goods) remarkably well.

Gary S. Becker

Economic Growth and the Distribution of Labor Income

I am studying some of the determinants of personal income distribution, on both a national and a statewide level. In particular, the study investigates the effects of economic growth on a number of key parameters (mean, variance, and skewness) of the distribution of labor income.

The theoretical model, based on the human capital approach to the distribution of earnings as formulated by Mincer (*JPE,* Aug. 1958) and Becker and Chiswick *(AER Proceedings,* May 1965), has now been completed. This approach can be summarized by two equations. The first states that the earnings of an individual at a moment in time are a return to untrained ability and a series of productivity-improving investments in human capital. The second states that the inequality of earnings among individuals is a function of the average level of investment in human capital, the average rate of return to this investment, and the variance of both these magnitudes.

My analysis concentrates on schooling, which is only one form of investment in human capital. I examine how the growth process, i.e., changes in factor ratios and technology, developments in the capital markets, and increased demand for output, may affect the costs and returns to investment in education. Empirical work will attempt to explain changes in the distribution of earnings over time by three variables: the average level of schooling, the average rate of return to schooling, and the variance in years of schooling. All the necessary data are contained either in published Census statistics for the period 1940-60, or in Census tapes in the possession of the National Bureau. The procedure will also enable me to make some projections of the future distribution of labor income.

I am now devoting most of my time to fitting the model to data for the United States and for the individual states and regions. I intend to further disaggregate according to age, sex, race, and urban-rural residence, where possible.

Michael Tannen

Net Returns to Education

The primary purpose of the study is to investigate the relationships among education, mental ability, and income. The following aspects of the study have been completed.

First, we have traced the relationship between mental ability and education over time, where education is the fraction of high school graduates entering college, and ability is percentile rank on IQ tests. In regressions of ability on education, we find a significant monotonic decline over time in the education coefficient. We find also that the average ability level of high school graduates entering college was higher in the late 1950's and early 1960's than it was in the 1920's and 1930's. This results from a significant increase in the fraction of high school graduates continuing to college at high-ability levels, with little or no increase at low-ability levels.

These results have important implications. The change over time in average ability for high school graduates entering (or not entering) college means that age-income profiles for a given education level, drawn from a cross-section sample that spans various cohorts, will reflect ability differences. Next, since the ability-education relation has changed over time, the bias in the education coefficient estimated from cross-section regressions of income on education must also have changed. And the fact that the ability-education relation has shifted over time may allow us to estimate and thus correct for the bias.

Second, we have analyzed previously unpublished details of data collected by D. Wolfle and J. Smith. Their sample consists of graduates of Minnesota high schools (1938) for whom ACE test scores and 1953 income data are available. We find that both education and the ACE test score measure of mental ability contribute significantly to income, and that the combination of high scores and high education is particularly important. On the other hand, mental ability as measured by rank in class performs very poorly in explaining income differences. When income-education relations are estimated, both including and excluding an ability variable, the difference in the education coefficient is very small—less than 4 per cent. This finding is of particular importance, since we also find that the coefficient on education in the regression of ability on education is higher in the Wolfle-Smith sample than in almost all others. Thus, the bias in the income-education relation due to the omission of ability should be larger in the Wolfle-Smith sample than in most others, suggesting that this bias may be negligible in general.

Third, we have studied the income-education relation for a group of top corporate executives over the period 1940-63. The sample was first drawn by W. G. Lewellen in an effort to obtain good estimates of after-tax income for high-ranking executives. We find that those with one or more degrees generally earn significantly more income than high school graduates in the years 1950 to 1958. After 1958 there is no significant relation between income and education.

A major part of the study currently under way is the analysis of the NBER-Thorndike sample. The original sample was drawn from a group of volunteers who took the air cadet qualifying examinations in 1943. In the mid-fifties, Thorndike obtained income and subsequent education data for nearly 10,000 of these individuals. The National Bureau has recently completed a follow-up survey, which contains, among other variables, individual earnings data at various points in time, including 1969 and the first year of full-time work.

One of the major purposes of our study is to determine the extent to which education is used as a licensing or screening device by firms. We demonstrate that screening—defined as restricted entry into high-paying occupations, where the restrictions vary with education—does not affect the social or private return to educating one individual, but may greatly affect the return to educating many. A test for screening has been developed, along with a method of estimating the social returns to a policy designed to increase the educational attainment of large numbers of people. The Wolfle-Smith data suggest that screening does exist, and that it may be important.

Paul Taubman
Terence Wales

Learning and Knowledge in the Labor Market

The ultimate objective of this research is to estimate rates of obsolescence and depreciation on human capital among various professions and across broad educational groups. These calculations may be useful for several important problems. For example: (1) It has been argued that higher education makes its recipients more "flexible" in adapting to new situations. If so, higher-education capital should depreciate at a lower rate than that of other levels. (2) On some assumptions, obsolescence rates can be interpreted as approximate measures of rates of change of knowledge. The extent to which it is sensible to standardize labor inputs in terms of years of schooling in time-series production studies depends on how the content of education changes over time. If the rate of change of knowledge is sufficiently rapid, the standardization criterion is not invariant over the sample period; hence, productivity calculations and imputations may be biased and misleading. (3) Cross-specialty comparisons should be extraordinarily interesting in and of themselves. For example, has the rate of advance of knowledge in medicine outstripped that in mathematics? Can these differences be explained largely in terms of different research support among fields?

Knowledge cannot be measured directly, and human capital assets are not traded in markets. But for some purposes, the labor market can be interpreted as a rental market for human capital. Thus, almost all available information is contained in observed age-income data, and obsolescence-depreciation parameters must be inferred from them. My approach is to specify a "vintage" human capital investment model and estimate a function related to hedonic price indexes. To make an analogy with automobiles, one has information on market rentals (equivalent to asset prices), school of graduation and specialty (make and model number), year of graduation ("vintage") and age (depreciation).

The analogy with tangible goods is far from complete, however, and major conceptual difficulties remain. Most important, education is not produced only in school and does not cease after graduation. In other words, individuals can "retool" or invest in more than one vintage, and have incentives to do so in order to maintain their capital intact. Evidently, there is insufficient information in age-income data to solve this problem in full, and certain outside restrictions must be imposed.

Most of my efforts to date have been concerned with attempting to specify reasonable a priori restrictions on rates of learning over an individual's lifetime. What is the optimum path for the accumulation of knowledge or human capital? The logical basis for the model rests on the assumption that *learning is a joint product of working experience*. Firms can be thought of as producing not only marketable output sold to the public at large but also learning opportunities sold to their own employees.

Workers are willing to purchase these opportunities in order to increase their marketable knowledge and subsequent income. Payments take the form of equalizing differences among jobs offering different investment values (at varying cost), and the market provides a wide range of choice to workers, depending on what job they choose. Given this market determined trade-off between current income and learning, lifetime incomes can be maximized by choosing among work activities in the optimal way. The solution to this problem yields optimum rates of investment over the worker's lifetime. Under fairly general conditions, it has been shown that the age-investment function can be well approximated by four or five parameters (instead of the original forty or fifty).

This particular learning model has some interesting properties, quite independent of the depreciation-obsolescence problem. In essence it is an analysis of "markets" for lifetime income opportunities, in which market equilibrium conditions determine entire age-income profiles. As usual, the rate of change of income with respect to age is explained in terms of supply and demand—costs of providing various learning opportunities and distributions of worker characteristics such as "ability" and motivation, as well as capital market imperfections and labor market restrictions.

As an example, consider the effects of a minimum wage. The difference between the market rental value of a worker's existing skill and his actual wage is the price he pays for new knowledge. But this difference is also the return to the firm for providing the worker with an investment opportunity. A minimum wage puts a ceiling on the worker's demand price for investment opportunities. Thus, a worker coming to the labor market with a sufficiently small endowment of knowledge and skill will be literally priced out of the market for learning opportunities. This may be part of the explanation for the observed high concentration of nonwhite workers in low-skilled occupations, even apart from discrimination. This phenomenon may also explain why so few nonwhites have gone through formal or informal job training programs. If this is so, a program such as the "wage subsidy" would raise the ceiling on investment opportunities and allow more knowledge to be bought, thus increasing the upward occupational mobility of disadvantaged groups.

After the model is fully constructed, I intend to estimate the relevant parameters for various academic fields, using income data available from the National Science Foundation Registry. For medicine, there are data from other sources; and for general education classes, data are available from U.S. Census sources. To date I have drafted one paper entitled "Learning by Experience and Joint Production," concerning optimum accumulation of a firm-specific capital good (knowledge about its production function) produced jointly with marketable output. It is shown that various learning phenomena can be specified empirically in terms of "progress functions," using cumulated output or inputs. The rate of learning is endogenously determined, given the parameters of the system.

Sherwin Rosen

Education and Savings Behavior

This study examines the influence of education on observed savings behavior for individuals and families. Educational differences might be associated with differences in the amount saved as a fraction of income, and also with differences in the composition of any size savings portfolio. People save in order to accumulate financial assets and to purchase consumer durables, which will provide service flows in the future. Moreover, people may choose an income stream which involves the acquisition of postschool human capital in the form of on-the-job training, and this is also a form of saving.

The principal data for the inquiry are from the Consumers Union questionnaires answered between 1958 and 1960. These surveyed attitudes, expectations, expenditures, and savings patterns of families who were members of this national organization. In addition to providing information on several current income measures, earnings of various family members, expenditures, and the amount of various types of savings (both financial assets and consumer durables), the survey furnished income data over a period of years, beginning in the first year of full-time employment of the family head. Moreover, the data set contains a collection of attitudinal questions which might provide clues about time preference, taste for risk, goals for saving, and ability to accomplish these goals. Data on education, age, family size, and occupation are also available.

Since the respondents are members of Consumers Union, the quantitative data are probably more accurate than for most such surveys. In addition, a number of consistency checks have been built into the empirical analysis; because there are over 6,000 observations for families answering four successive questionnaires, it is possible to eliminate seemingly irregular observations which do not pass these tests without seriously worrying about degrees of freedom.

The first part of the study has considered whether educational differences result in different savings/income ratios; that is, at a given point in the life cycle, do more-educated people save more or less than less-educated people? One underlying cause of differential aggregate savings patterns by education might be that the educational process alters individual time preference. Responses to several of the attitude questions may throw some light on the association between time preference and education. If saving is a function of time preference, and if people with low time preference also choose to obtain more schooling, then an observation that more educated groups save more, *ceteris paribus,* need imply nothing about the effect of education on saving. The educated (low time preference) individuals would have been relatively large savers even without education, due to their inherent low time preference.

Differences in education also appear to result in differences in the *nature* of subsequent income. Various aspects of income might differ because of education or because of the type of occupation entered after education; these include level, time path, variance over time, source (whether from physical or human capital), and split between wages and fringe benefits. Many of these characteristics have been thought to influence the proportion of income saved. For example, consumption theory leads to the conclusion that savings will be a larger part of income when reliance is on human (versus nonhuman or physical) capital to earn income.

Aspects of both consumption theory and human capital theory suggest that savings as a fraction of income will tend to increase as education increases, and, other things being equal, as age increases up to retirement. To test this hypothesis, I divided the Consumers Union Survey respondents into education-experience cells, and estimated consumption functions for those in each cell. The expectation was that marginal and average propensities to consume would be negatively correlated with both level of education and labor force experience. The latter conclusion was generally confirmed, but there did not appear to be a strong pattern across schooling groups. However, saving in this test was defined to include only saving in the form of financial assets.

According to Mincer's theory and evidence, saving in the form of on-the-job training rises with formal education and declines with age. Since younger and more educated members of the labor force save more of their incomes in the form of on-the-job training, they will save correspondingly less in the form of financial and durable assets to attain any total amount of saving. Since older workers invest less in on-the-job training, they should invest more in other forms of saving to result in the equivalent amount of total savings. If we expect the savings/income ratio to rise with labor force experience, there should be a positive relationship between age and financial saving. On the other hand, although it might be expected that more educated people save more in total, they also invest more in on-the-job training (at the same age). Hence, it is unclear which way the relationship between financial saving and education will go. Estimates of actual investment in on-the-job training by members of the sample will be constructed, using Mincer's definition, and "full" savings functions will be estimated.

Currently I am looking at responses to attitude and behavior questions to find clues as to how time preference and investment efficiency vary with schooling. The data should indicate whether there is a systematic relationship between education and savings portfolio decisions. Some of these questions concern ways in which purchase of services of durables differ from purchase of the durables themselves; that is, the holding of durable versus financial assets, the holding of long-run versus short-run securities, and the holding of variable versus fixed price assets. This part of the study is in a preliminary stage.

In addition to the savings study, I am working on several other projects during my year as a Research Fellow. Papers entitled "On Equality of Educational Opportunity" and "Opportunity Costs and Models of Schooling in the Nineteenth Century" have been completed and are to be published in the *American Economic Review* and the *Southern Economic Journal,* respectively. I have analyzed measures of quality of colleges and expect that these results can be used in conjunction with the NBER-Thorndike data sample. I have also begun a study of the effects of compulsory schooling laws on nineteenth century education.

Lewis C. Solmon

Education and Family Size

Empirical research has shown that the effect of education on productivity in the labor market is positive, and the theory of human capital has tended to focus upon those incentives to invest in education that result from a positive net return. Thus relatively little work has been done on the manner in which education enhances productivity. Little attention has been paid to the question, "How or why does education affect productivity?" One hypothesis is that education has an "allocative" or cognitive effect, whereby it fosters an awareness of alternative methods of production or increases the capability of the more highly educated to adopt new production techniques.

What little evidence there is on education's effect on productivity in the nonmarket sector also indicates a positive relation. The objective of this study is to analyze, within the context of a set of household production functions, how this cognitive effect of education might operate within the nonmarket sector to alter commodity prices and real income, and thereby affect behavior. The specific productive process examined is the use of contraceptives in limiting family size. The approach is to view the derived demand for children as a joint-products problem involving nonmarket commodity production.

Empirically the effect of education on family size may reflect several factors, principally the higher permanent money income level (with its corresponding shift in demand toward higher-priced units or "quality"), the higher time value of family members, and the effect of education on contraceptive knowledge and use. The fact that previous studies have observed conflicting net effects of education on family size may simply be the result of a dominance of one or the other of these separate factors. The empirical analysis in this project will attempt to isolate these three effects, with the emphasis on the net influence of education.

The first set of data to be analyzed will be the 1968 NBER-Census Bureau Consumer Anticipations Survey of some 4,500 households. These data should permit separate estimates of the partial effects of income and time value and the residual education effect. In addition, recent empirical findings by demographers are being reviewed to provide further direct evidence of education's effect on the desired family size and on the use of contraceptives.

Robert T. Michael

NBER-Thorndike Sample

Analysis of several important and interesting questions will be greatly facilitated by the forthcoming availability of the NBER-Thorndike sample of Air Force veterans. With the assistance of Dr. Robert Thorndike (Columbia University), the Veterans Administration, and the U.S. Air Force we have managed to obtain a data set that promises to be of exceptional value for research in the economics of education.

We have now completed and processed four separate mailings to the roughly 9,700 men in the original Thorndike sample. After the first two mailings, which yielded approximately 2,500 returns, we were able to obtain updated addresses for close to 4,000 of approximately 7,000 nonresponse cases (roughly 300 of the original sample proved to be deceased). Subsequent mailings to these new addresses yielded another 2,000 returns, hence our current total is about 4,500. We have now successfully updated another 1,000 or more addresses, using public telephone directories, and plan a fifth and final mailing to these new addresses as well as to all remaining nonrespondents. On the basis of experience to date, it appears that the sample of returns will eventually reach between 5,500 and 6,000 cases.

Not only have response rates been exceptionally high, given the usual standards for mail surveys of this type, but the quality of the information appears to be well above average. Virtually all respondents have provided an estimate of current earnings in dollars, and well over 90 per cent have provided earnings on the first job held after termination of formal schooling. There are a substantial number of income reports for the years between initial job and the present. The survey contains information on schools attended, years of attendance, and degrees received. For about three-quarters of the higher-education institutions attended by sample respondents, we have been able to obtain a measure of college "quality." Thus, it will be possible to analyze the returns to different qualities of higher education.

In addition to the basic earnings and schooling data, information was obtained on nonearning activities of sample respondents: these data indicate type of organization, kind of activities, and amount of time involved. We also have extensive data on demographic and family characteristics variables, as well as on socio-economic attitudes, family background, etc. Some limited data were obtained on total holdings of financial and other types of assets, as well as on savings; this information is of unknown completeness and reliability, although it appears to be less extensive than the basic earnings and schooling data.

The basic ability data were obtained from a series of twenty tests administered to all sample respondents by the U.S. Air Force in 1943. Factor analysis of these test scores suggests the presence of at least four, and possibly five, identifiable dimensions of "ability": one factor apparently represents general reasoning ability, another quantitative aptitude, another spatial perception, another general physical dexterity, and the last may represent taste for risk. The spatial perception and physical dexterity measures are, of course, a consequence of the interest of the tester (the U.S. Air Force) in identifying individuals with an aptitude for pilot training. The availability of this collection of ability dimensions will make it possible to estimate the economic returns to several dimensions of ability, and possibly to explore whether or not the returns to these ability dimensions have changed over the years. It will also permit investigation of the particular dimensions of ability associated with financial success in any given occupation.

F. Thomas Juster

The Use Value of Education

This study is a continuation of a series of studies concerning the nature—in production and consumption—of education. The fundamental idea is that a large part of the return to education may have its roots in the decision process. If education facilitates the collection, evaluation, and storing of information, then increased education should be associated with propensities toward correct choice. For static analysis it is not informative to distinguish between education as a factor contributing to allocative efficiency and education as an ordinary good which directly increases either utility or physical production. But in a dynamic setting, where abilities to learn and adjust are important, the distinction is relevant.

The theoretical analysis is concerned with identifying the value of information, where learning is defined as the erosion of ignorance and ignorance refers to either subjective or objective uncertainty as reflected in error variance. The role of scale economies associated with the collection and application of information is stressed, as are such factors as the rate of technical change and product differentiation, which increase both the rate of obsolescence of knowledge and the value of learning.

The empirical analysis concentrates on U.S. agriculture, where a rapid rate of technological change has lent value to discretionary capacities. The major questions asked are: To what extent has the interaction between agricultural research and farm operator education "created" the returns to scale commonly found in empirical estimates? And, is there evidence that federal extension activities and increasing farmer education have speeded the diffusion of the products of agricultural research? Data are now available to address these questions. The 1964 Census of U.S. Agriculture provides output and input data, including farm operator education, which is cross classified by value of sales, age of operator, tenancy (full or part owner, managers, and tenants), and type of farm. This detail, previously unavailable, permits an analysis of questions concerning the rate of appreciation or obsolescence of abilities associated with schooling (the age cross classification), returns to scale (value classes), incentive structures (tenancy), and an analysis of the differential impact of research activity by type of farm. The results of several models will be compared, ranging from full income, in which appreciation of land values and income from off-farm work are included as output, to the now standard gross revenue and value-added models.

Finis Welch

Aptitude, Education, and Earnings Differentials

A major problem arising in the empirical analysis of costs of and returns from formal education is the isolation of the earnings increment that can be attributed to an increment of formal education. The imputation of the return from the investment is usually made by controlling for several demographic variables, such as sex, race, age, and geographic location, and then attributing the differences in the earnings' streams of individuals with various levels of formal schooling to differences in the amount of schooling. Most studies have been based on information with two important limitations. First, there is usually no independent measure of individual ability, and this leads to an unknown bias in the apparent returns from schooling. Second, the earnings profile plays an important role in analyzing the returns from investments in formal education. Since most studies are based on cross-sectional data at a single point in time, some assumptions are made to generate pseudo-earnings profiles. Cohort (longitudinal) data would enable one to avoid these somewhat arbitrary assumptions about secular growth and its effect on individual earnings.

Two samples are being studied which contain information usually not available for the analysis of return from education. The first is a sample of all Swedish third graders from Malmö, who were given a four-part intelligence test in 1938. Information on school grades, formal education, social class, measured intelligence ten years later (for some), and follow-up information including taxable income was obtained in 1963 for the cohort. The basic data tape was made available by Professor T. Husén of the Pedagogisk-Psykologiska Institution at the University of Stockholm's School of Education. In addition, data were gathered from individual tax records in the Swedish archives on earnings, income from capital, taxable income, and income of wife for males in the sample. These data cover 1949-68, at five-year intervals. The original sample size was 835; earnings profile information was obtained on 500 to 600.

The second source of data is a sample of 10,500 respondents to a Project Talent[1] follow-up survey, carried out with the aid of a grant from the National Science Foundation. The original survey provides 130 background items from the time when respondents were in the 11th grade, including various aptitude test scores, family background, high school attitudes, and high school information. The follow-up survey made six years later includes information on earnings, weeks worked, weeks unemployed, and additional formal training.

These two unique samples will make it possible to test directly a number of hypotheses

---

[1] See footnote, Section 2, p. 45, for a description of Project Talent.

about the way measured intelligence, family background, and attitudes affect the returns from schooling, as well as their direct influence on earnings.

Initial calculations with the Project Talent high school graduates who had no additional formal training suggest that differential measured aptitude has a small but positive effect on earnings five years after graduation. Some people had conjectured that higher-aptitude individuals might well have obtained significantly higher incomes even without college education. The conjecture, if it had been correct, would have implied an understatement of the opportunity costs of acquiring more education.

John C. Hause

Comparison of Measures of the Growth in Educational Output

As a first step in our analysis of so-called educational production functions, we compare various alternative measures of the growth in educational output during a particular period of schooling. The specific output measures we are concerned with are:

(1) $$T_{ij+1} - T_{ij}$$
(2) $$T_{ij+1} - \hat{T}_{ij+1}$$
(3) $$D_{ij+1} - D_{ij},$$

where T_{ij} = the actual score on the ith test in the jth period, $\hat{T}_{ij}$ = the predicted score in the ith test in the jth period, D_{ij} = the percentile achieved on the ith test in the jth period.

The first measure, raw differences in test scores, is probably the most commonly used growth index, yet it is clearly far from ideal. Its principal shortcoming is the failure to adjust for the arbitrary scaling of test scores.[1] The second procedure, on the other hand, attempts to make such an adjustment by removing the arbitrarily determined growth in the mean test scores (the trend in test scores) from one period to the next. Thus each individual's test score is assumed to grow in the same (linear) fashion as the mean score, yielding a predicted or expected test score for each individual. The "true" growth in test scores is then the difference between actual and expected test scores. Even this procedure is inadequate, however, if the variances in the distributions of test scores are changing over time, or if the distributions are not normal and other moments are allowed to vary.

The final measure to be considered, the change in the percentile in which a given student's test scores fall, is truly ordinal but is strongly related to the second measure, if test scores are normally distributed with constant variance. In this case, the relationship between the second and third measures depends directly only on the "fineness" with which the third measure is specified; for example, changes in percentiles, deciles, or quintiles. If the variances of other properties of the distribution are changing over time, the third measure is clearly superior to the second.

The primary concern of the present phase of our investigation is not, however, with a theoretical comparison of measures of output growth. We are interested in the *actual* relationships among these growth indexes.

We have been exploring data obtained by the Educational Testing Service at Princeton in connection with their "Growth Study." Approximately 34,000 school children were given a battery of tests requiring about ten hours of testing time. The sample included approximately 9,000 public school students in the fifth grade, 9,000 in the seventh grade, 9,000 in the ninth grade, and about 5,000 in the eleventh grade. In independent schools, the sample included 1,000 ninth-grade and 1,000 eleventh-grade students. These students were enrolled in 140 elementary feeder schools and 33 secondary schools. Samples of the original 34,000 students were retested at two-year intervals during the eight-year course of the study. There

---

[1] All these problems arise because the measures of education are ordinal rather than cardinal, that is, there is neither a zero point nor a well-defined unit of measurement for educational achievement (or ability). See Samuel Bowles, "Towards an Educational Production Function," in *Education, Income, and Human Capital*, W. Lee Hansen, editor, Income and Wealth Conference 35, New York, NBER, 1970.

are thus five sets of data describing the educational achievements of those students who were in the fifth grade in 1961.

The analysis of these data could be begun by calculating these measures for the tests administered in September-October 1961 and September-October 1963 (January-February 1963 for those who were in the eleventh grade initially). In the case of the third measure we intend to try several alternatives: (a) standard deviation units, two on each side of the mean, yielding four classes; (b) half-standard deviation units, four on each side of the mean, yielding eight classes; and (c) deciles, yielding ten classes.

Roger E. Alcaly
V. K. Chetty

Economics of the Legal System

An Economic Analysis of the Courts

In the folklore of criminal justice a popular belief is that a person arrested for a crime will have his case decided in a trial. Empirical evidence does not support this belief. Most cases are disposed of without a trial through negotiations between the prosecutor and the defendant, resulting in either a guilty plea or a decision not to charge the suspect. What factors determine the choice between a pretrial settlement (hereafter denoted by PTS) and a trial? What accounts for the large proportion of PTS's compared with trials? In particular, how are certain aspects of the criminal justice process, such as the bail system and court delay, related to the decision to settle or to go to trial? The main purpose of this study is to answer these questions by means of a theoretical and empirical analysis of the criminal justice system, using standard tools of economic theory and statistics.

A theoretical model has been developed to identify the variables relevant to the choice between a PTS and a trial. The model's basic assumption is that both the prosecutor and the defendant maximize their utility, appropriately defined, subject to a constraint on their resources. It is shown that the PTS-trial decision depends on estimates of the probability of conviction by trial, the severity of the crime, the availability and productivity of the prosecutor's and defendant's resources, trial versus PTS costs, and attitudes toward risk. The model is then used to analyze the existing bail system and court delay, and to predict the effects of a variety of proposals designed to improve the bail system and reduce court delay. These proposals include "preventive detention," monetary compensation to defendants not released on bail, and the imposition of a money price for the use of the courts.

An additional feature of the model is its usefulness in analyzing the frequently expressed belief that the criminal justice system discriminates against low-income suspects. This proposition is analyzed by relating a defendant's income or wealth to his decision to settle or go to trial, the probability of his conviction, and his sentence if convicted. The interactions of these factors with the bail system and court delay are also examined. Finally, the model is applied, with some modifications, to civil cases.

The second major part of this study is an empirical analysis using data from two main sources: (1) a survey conducted for the American Bar Foundation on the disposition of felony cases in state courts in 1962, and (2) yearly data on criminal and civil cases in federal courts contained in the *Annual Report of the Director of the Administrative Office of the U.S. Courts*. Multiple regression techniques are used to test a number of important hypotheses derived from the model. These include the effects on the demand for trials (or conversely PTS's) and on the probability of conviction of the following variables: (1) the bail system; (2) court queues; (3) the size of the potential sentence; (4) judicial expenditures; (5) subsidization of defendants' legal fees; and (6) demographic variables, such as population size, region, county income, per cent nonwhite, and urbanization.

Some of the empirical findings are that:
1. The propensity to go to trial in state

courts was larger for defendants released on bail than for other defendants, holding constant the average sentence and several demographic variables. This is predicted by the model, since the opportunity cost of a trial compared to a PTS is greater for a defendant not released on bail than for one released as a result of court delays. Moreover, differences in wealth among defendants had no observable effect on trial demand.

2. Trial demand was negatively related to trial delay, and positively related to PTS delay, across U.S. district courts for 1960, 1967, and 1968. Thus, a widening differential between trial delay and PTS delay will tend to reduce the demand for trials, as the model predicts.

3. The subsidization of defendant's legal fees in the U.S. district courts increased the demand for trials. This is consistent with the hypothesis that a reduction in the cost differential between a trial and a PTS will increase the demand for trials.

4. Regression analysis of civil cases across U.S. district courts for the 1957-61 period indicated that the demand for civil trials was also a negative function of court delay.

5. The probability of conviction in state courts, as measured by the proportion of defendants sentenced to prison, was greater for defendants not released on bail than for those released. Regressions using the proportion of defendants acquitted and dismissed as the dependent variable supported the finding that defendants not released on bail were more likely to be convicted.

6. Convictions leading to prison sentences were *lower* in U.S. district courts where defendants had relatively high average wealth, while convictions resulting in monetary fines were *greater* in the same districts. These results are consistent with the model's prediction that a wealthier defendant has a stronger incentive to invest financial resources in his case if the penalty is a jail sentence, and a lesser incentive if the penalty is a fine.

In addition to a more intensive analysis of the above results, further work is planned along three lines.

1. The American Bar Foundation data used in the preliminary analysis were limited to data published in two volumes. However, the basic data (available on IBM cards) on the characteristics of over 11,000 felony defendants in state courts are still in existence. These data indicate sex, age, race, years of school completed, amount of bail, type of offense, time from arrest to disposition, sentence received, and type of legal service provided—a set of characteristics that can be incorporated into the empirical analysis to determine their relation to the frequency of trials, the likelihood of conviction, and the sentences received if convicted.

2. Data on the disposition of defendants in other countries, for example, England and Canada, are available from selected samples. A comparison of the workings of court systems in these countries with the United States will provide us with additional empirical tests of the model.

3. Widespread criticism of the existing bail system and proposals for bail reform play an important role in current policy debates over effective law enforcement. Proposals for bail reform generally focus on eliminating the traditional reliance on income as an indirect criterion of pretrial release. When these policy considerations are added to the findings described above (that pretrial detention is an important determinant of the trial versus settlement decision and the probability of conviction), a thorough analysis of the present bail system and proposed alternatives seems justified. This project consists of three parts. First, a theoretical model is developed to determine the optimal amount of bail and the optimal number of defendants released for various offenses in order to minimize the community's losses from a bail system. Such factors as the direct costs of detention (e.g., costs of maintaining persons in prison), the reduction in expected losses from crime, the losses to defendants, and the degree of uncertainty in predicting which defendants will commit additional crimes during pretrial release are relevant in determining the optimal bail system. Second, the present bail system and various reforms will be compared

with an optimal system. Third, an empirical analysis is planned to explain the factors that give rise to variations among defendants, both in the amount of bail charged and in the likelihood of their release.

William M. Landes

Participation in Illegitimate Activities and the Effectiveness of Law Enforcement

The President's Commission on Law Enforcement and the Administration of Justice estimated the economic costs of reported crime in the United States in 1965 at $21 billion (about 4 per cent of the national income), which is more than the estimated economic cost of unemployment in that year. In the same year, public expenditure on police, criminal courts, defense council, and "corrections" at the federal, state, and local levels amounted to $4.2 billion. In view of the economic and social significance of crime, it is important to determine whether the public's scarce resources are being wisely allocated to law enforcement. Is there at present "too much" or "too little" enforcement of existing laws?

The answer to these questions can be obtained by investigating two related issues. First, what is likely to be the effect, on the level and severity of criminal activity, of an increase in the probability of apprehending and convicting offenders, in the punishment imposed on those convicted, and in other measures for combating crime? Second, to what extent would additional public expenditure on law enforcement agencies increase their effectiveness in apprehending and convicting offenders?

1. My study on participation in illegitimate activity has attempted to investigate the first issue by setting up an economic model of the decision to engage in unlawful activities and testing it against the empirical evidence. The novelty of this approach, as distinguished from traditional sociological approaches, lies in its attempt to separate "taste for crime" from objective opportunities and other environmental factors, both analytically and empirically, and to investigate the extent to which illegal behavior could be explained by the effect of opportunities, given "taste." This framework is used, for example, to explain why many offenders allocate their "working time" to both legitimate and illegitimate activities, rather than to criminal activity alone, and why many offenders tend to repeat their crimes even after being apprehended and punished, without resorting to assumptions regarding unique motivation. It is also used to explain why those with specific legitimate skills have relatively little incentive to engage in offenses punishable by imprisonment, and those with higher nonwage income may have a greater incentive to commit offenses punishable by fines. More importantly, the analysis offers behavioral implications regarding the effect of some measurable factors on the frequency of illegal behavior. The main testable hypotheses are that, on the one hand, crime is deterred by an increase in the probability of apprehension and conviction, in the rate of punishment if convicted, and in the returns from alternative legal activity, and, on the other, is enhanced by an increase in the probability of (legal) unemployment and in the size of illegal payoffs. Attitudes toward risk are expected to play an important role in determining the relative effect of probability and severity of punishment. It is shown that a 1 per cent increase in the probability of apprehension and conviction has a greater, a smaller, or the same deterrent effect in comparison with a 1 per cent increase in severity of punishment as offenders are risk preferrers, risk avoiders, or risk neutral, respectively. Moreover, it is shown that if offenders were risk preferrers, the effect of punishment might be negligible in absolute magnitude. The observation that punishment has little deterrent effect on some offenders need not, therefore, be interpreted as evidence of irrationality; it can be explained by preference for risk. The analysis also shows that the degree of response of "full time" and "professional" offenders to changes in variables reflecting deterrents and gains is likely to be lower than that of "part time" offenders. Law enforcement may therefore be less effective in

the case of "hard core" criminals relative to occasional offenders.

The hypotheses regarding the deterrent effect of law enforcement on crime follow from the basic thesis that offenders behave rationally. However, in the case of crimes punishable by imprisonment, an increase in the probability and severity of punishment would reduce the frequency of illegal behavior even if offenders were irrational, for those imprisoned are prevented from committing further crimes, at least temporarily. While both deterrence and prevention may equally well serve the basic purpose of law enforcement (i.e., to reduce total crime), it is important to establish the independent deterrent effect of imprisonment, both to verify the validity of our approach with respect to crimes punishable by imprisonment and to determine the effectiveness of punishment by imprisonment relative to alternative penal modes (probation and fines) which are expected to have only a deterrent effect.

By considering a model in which offenders are assumed a distinct subpopulation, unaffected by deterrents and gains, we are able to estimate an upper bound for the preventive effect of imprisonment on the frequency of specific crime categories. The elasticity of this latter effect is shown to be the same for probability and severity of punishment and necessarily lower than unity (in practice it has been generally estimated to be lower than 0.1). Since some of our empirical estimates of the elasticity of offenses with respect to probability and severity of punishment exceed the magnitude attributable to a preventive effect (some exceeding unity), and since the elasticities are significantly different in relative magnitude (e.g., the elasticity of burglaries and larcenies with respect to a change in severity of punishment exceeds that with respect to probability of punishment), the existence of an independent deterrent effect of law enforcement is clearly confirmed.

The empirical investigation employs a cross-state regression analysis of the seven felony crimes reported by the F.B.I.'s Uniform Crime Reports. Since my last report, the empirical work has extended along three lines. First, a simple multiple regression framework was employed in the analysis of data from 1950 and 1940. The results proved consistent with those obtained from 1960 data, reported in last year's *Annual Report*. Second, a two-stage least squares regression analysis was employed in the investigation of specific offenses and broad crime categories. The results confirmed the significant deterrent effect of the probability and severity of punishment on all offenses and the significant positive effect of income inequality and unemployment on the incidence of crimes against property. Finally, a three-stage least squares technique was employed to estimate simultaneously the "seemingly unrelated equations" of specific offenses. The results proved to be consistent with those obtained by using the two-stage least squares technique. It should be noted that our emphasis on simultaneous equation estimation techniques has been due not only to the presumed simultaneity relations between the frequency of reported offenses and the probability of apprehension and conviction but also to errors of measurement in the estimates of these variables. The fact that the results are consistent with the hypotheses and confirm our initial results is quite encouraging.

2. Some preliminary work has been done to determine the "productivity" of public expenditure on law enforcement. A simultaneous equation model of law enforcement and crime has been developed. The frequency of offenses, the probability of apprehension and conviction, and per capita expenditure on law enforcement are treated as endogenous variables, jointly determined by the system of equations. The model was then tested against data on total felonies in 1960. The results show a positive and significant effect of expenditure on police on the probability of apprehending and convicting felons. These results, combined with estimates of the effect of probability of punishment on total felonies, make it possible to estimate the effectiveness of law enforcement in reducing crime and the resulting social losses.

Isaac Ehrlich

5. BUSINESS CYCLES

Introduction

During the past year the Bureau's business cycles research program has focused on new methods of analyzing cyclical episodes using selected series of economic indicators, analysis of the influence of money on secular and cyclical changes in real and nominal output, and evaluation of the structure and performance of large-scale econometric models.

Ilse Mintz has been working on what might be termed "growth" cycles. In most European countries absolute declines in the level of economic activity have been rare during the postwar period, and analysis of cyclical episodes using an absolute change framework would have yielded virtually no observations. Yet there have clearly been marked differences in the growth rate of economic activity, differences which can be translated into a cyclical framework of expansions and contractions in rates of change rather than in absolute magnitudes. Mrs. Mintz has been applying this technique to United States experience during the postwar period, and is preparing a paper to be presented at the Business Cycle Colloquium in September.

The work on money being conducted by Milton Friedman and Anna Schwartz has been concerned with the division of changes in income between prices and real output, a problem which has long been troublesome to economists. Details of their recent work are reported below.

The analysis of econometric models has yielded interesting, and sometimes disturbing, conclusions. In particular, the findings of Haitovsky, Evans, and Treyz suggest that econometric models per se have very limited ability to forecast aggregate economic activity. Zarnowitz, Boschan, and Moore have been trying to determine whether econometric models can simulate the observed cyclical behavior of economic time series, not only within the sample periods of the respective models but for lengthy extrapolation periods in which the exogenous variables in the models are subjected to specified types of shocks. These findings are reported in papers prepared for the Conference on Econometric Models of Cyclical Behavior, held in November 1969 under the joint sponsorship of the National Bureau's Conference on Research in Income and Wealth and the Social Science Research Council (see Part III of this report).

Other current studies in business cycles include Gregory C. Chow's work on econometric models, begun originally in collaboration with Geoffrey H. Moore and Arthur F. Burns, Philip Klein's study of consumer credit, about to be reviewed by the Directors, Robert Eisner's work on determinants of investment using McGraw-Hill data, and Benoit Mandelbrot's methodological work on the cyclical properties of time-series data, discussed under "R/S Analysis" in Section 9 of this report.

It is expected that the Bureau's work on econometric model analysis and evaluation will be expanded during the coming year. We have applied for a grant from the National Science Foundation to study short-term forecasting methods: subprojects in this proposal include work on large-scale model simulation, evaluation of forecast effectiveness, and developmental work on two formal models—one designed to incorporate the National Bureau's traditional view of the cyclical process, the other designed to exploit expectational and anticipatory data sets that are often neglected in existing models.

In addition to the research programs outlined above, we have devoted some attention to monitoring the current business situation. Statistical procedures that have been developed over the years in the Bureau's business cycles research program have begun to be applied to the analysis of current conditions. These procedures are designed to facilitate the comparison of current conditions with those prevailing during cyclical episodes that were eventually classified as business cycle contractions, as well as with episodes that eventually were best classified as periods of retardation but not contraction.

F. Thomas Juster

Business Cycle Turning Points

My Occasional Paper on German business cycles has been published. This year I have interrupted the study of foreign business cycles in order to apply the experience gained so far to the dating of cycles in the United States. Only a small proportion of the period since World War II has been designated as a recession by traditional standards, and, as of early 1970, no turning point has been recognized in more than eight years. The U.S. experience in the 1960's has, therefore, resembled that of European economies, where practically no absolute declines in activity, and thus no classical recessions, have occurred. This suggests the desirability of supplementing the traditional U.S. business cycle chronology by a chronology of growth cycles, i.e., cycles in rates of growth or in trend-adjusted data.

In dating U.S. growth cycles we are also pursuing a secondary aim: to study the possibility of replacing the traditional NBER practice of handpicking business cycle turns by computerized, objective, reproducible methods.

The first task required for mechanical cycle dating is the selection of the indicators to be used. Herein lies one of the main differences between subjective and objective procedures. In the former, the analyst is free to select and weigh indicators according to the requirements of the specific situation under review. Thus, in setting cycle turns, the NBER has not relied on any fixed list of series, although certain series were, of course, regularly taken into consideration. With mechanical methods—and this is one of their main disadvantages—a fixed selection of indicator series must be used. Decisions about the contents of such a list then become a crucial step in the dating of reference cycles.

Our first criteria in choosing indicators are the usual ones: economic significance, comprehensiveness, regularity of timing, etc. In addition, however, we tried to identify a group of indicator series that would yield turns coinciding with, or at least very close to, traditional NBER reference turns. Duplication of these handpicked turns is desirable for two reasons. First, it argues for the appropriateness of substituting objective methods for subjective ones. Second, use of an indicator list which reproduces classical turns will enable us to attribute differences between growth cycles and classical business cycles to differences in concepts rather than to differences in data.

After several experiments we have, for the time being, settled on a list of seventeen indicators. When combined into indexes, these indicators yield turning dates over the 1948-61 period that are either coincident with or close to months traditionally regarded as U.S. business cycle turns.

Growth cycle turning points have been determined on the basis of these seventeen series. As expected, they are much more numerous than classical turning points from 1948 to 1969 (fourteen rather than eight turns). Also as expected, downturns in growth cycles tend to precede, and upturns to lag behind, their classical counterparts.

A detailed description of these findings will be presented and discussed at the NBER Business Cycle Colloquium in September 1970.

Ilse Mintz

Money

Because preparation of our *Monetary Statistics of the United States* for publication was inordinately time-consuming, we made less progress than planned in revising the draft of "Monetary Trends in the United States and the United Kingdom: Their Relation to Income, Prices, and Interest Rates." In this study we analyze the characteristic behavior of the quantity of money over long periods in relation to other economic magnitudes. Our purpose is to test some general propositions in monetary theory, and to test some of the empirical generalizations suggested by our study of U.S. monetary history. A framework for the analysis, developed by Milton Friedman, appeared in the *Journal of Political Economy* (March-April 1970) and has been proposed for publication as an NBER Occasional Paper.

The study of trends was originally designed to exploit the availability of reasonably accurate monetary data for the United States covering an entire century, paralleled by data on national income, prices, and interest rates. After we had completed our analysis of United States data for the period 1869 to 1961, it seemed both desirable and possible to check the results with data for other periods and countries. For the United States, we added data through 1969. The most readily available monetary data for other countries were for the United Kingdom, covering 1880-1968. Accordingly, we extended our analysis, supplementing these monetary data with readily available income, price, and interest rate data.

To isolate longer-term relations, we attempt to remove from the data the effects of shorter-term (business cycle) movements. Though brief in duration, cyclical fluctuations are often large relative to the more gradual long-period changes. Hence comparisons between dates separated even by decades can be seriously distorted if the initial and terminal dates refer to different stages of the business cycle.

We eliminate cyclical fluctuations from the data by averaging over cycle phases—that is, our basic observation is either the average of an expansion (cyclical trough to peak), or a contraction (cyclical peak to trough); these periods are sometimes referred to as half-cycles. For the United States, we adopted the NBER's historical reference cycle chronology, which ends with the trough in 1961. For our purposes, we designated subsequent turns in 1966 (peak), 1967 (trough), and 1969 (peak). For the United Kingdom, we decided to revise some of the turns listed in the reference chronology available through 1938[1] and extended it

---
[1] See Arthur F. Burns and Wesley C. Mitchell, *Measuring Business Cycles,* New York, NBER, 1946, p. 79.

through 1968. A brief description of the issues we deal with follows.

The long-term trends in money and income can be defined as comprising three elements: changes in population, in prices, and in real income per capita. We present this decomposition for trends as well as fluctuations about trends, and for levels of the series as well as rates of change. One striking feature of our empirical results is the extraordinary parallelism in the movements of money and income, both nominal and real. This parallelism is to be expected from the general theoretical framework that underlies our analysis but not necessarily from the income-expenditure framework that has been so widely accepted in recent years.

Neither the quantity theory nor the income-expenditure theory provides a satisfactory explanation of the division of changes in income between prices and output. We test a number of hypotheses that might explain it. The evidence leads us to reject some beliefs that, judging from the literature, seem to be widely held, but provides no simple and satisfactory alternative. The evidence suggests, however, that a correct hypothesis will give considerable weight to expectations about prices.

Our evidence is also inconsistent with the simple interpretation relating the quantity of desired money balances to the interest return on alternative assets. While the liquidity preference relation does play an important role, it is but one element in a much more complex pattern. We also revive the earlier work of Irving Fisher, redoing and extending some of his calculations. Fisher's conclusions and results hold up remarkably well for the period subsequent to the one he covered.

The central element in the quantity theory of money is the existence of a stable function relating the real quantity of money demanded to a small number of other economic variables. The evidence from our analysis of secular changes is highly encouraging, though not conclusive, for validation of the hypothesis.

We also examine the view that there have been long swings in growth rates for the U.S.

economy and other economies. Our emphasis is not on whether long swings exist, but on whether they are best interpreted as episodic or as reflecting an underlying cyclical mechanism. The monetary data support the episodic interpretation.

We hope to complete the revised draft of the monograph by the end of 1970.

Milton Friedman
Anna J. Schwartz

Study of Short-Term Economic Forecasting

A collection of essays by Rosanne Cole, Stanley Diller, F. Thomas Juster, Jacob Mincer, and Victor Zarnowitz was published in 1969. The volume, titled *Economic Forecasts and Expectations: Analysis of Forecasting Behavior and Performance,* was edited by Mincer. An Occasional Paper by Cole, *Errors in Estimates of Gross National Product,* was published in 1970.

Plans have been drawn up for a new, related but more comprehensive, research project on evaluating different types and aspects of economic forcasts and the relation between forecasting accuracy and methodology (see the report by Juster above).

Since December 1968, quarterly surveys have been conducted (in February, May, August, and December) of forecasts by those members of the Business and Economics Statistics Section of the American Statistical Association who are professionally engaged in a continuing analysis of the business outlook. The surveys were designed in cooperation with the National Bureau, which has assumed responsibility for the evaluation of their results. The analysis is processed on the Bureau's computer under the supervision of Charlotte Boschan. I have presented a description of the new survey and the press releases giving each quarter's figures in successive issues of *The American Statistician* since February 1969.

A report on the results of the first four surveys was presented at the annual meeting of the American Statistical Association in August 1969 and published as "The ASA-NBER Quarterly Survey of Economic Outlook: An Early Appraisal" in the *Proceedings of the Business and Economic Statistics Section,* A.S.A., 1969. The forecasters have, on the average, underestimated the strong increases that occurred at the time in the national aggregates of output, income, and spending—a common error of predicting too little growth and too little inflation. They have attempted, with partial success, to correct such errors through upward revisions; with the reduction of predictive spans and the use of additional information, forecasts for a given target period have generally improved in successive surveys. The revisions, however, have on the whole been insufficient, so that the short predictions, although typically more accurate than the longer ones, still understated the rise in the comprehensive economic indicators. As a rule, the dispersion of errors among the forecasts of individual participants increased with the length of the predictive span, both within and between the surveys.

Analysis of the surveys as more become available should help to answer problems concerning (a) the relation between forecast methodology and accuracy; (b) the informational value of participants' statements about the probabilities attached to their forecasts; (c) the dependence of predictions upon the underlying specified assumptions about economic policy changes and other exogenous events; (d) the structure and internal consistency of multiperiod predictions for groups of interdependent variables; and (e) the implications of the varying degree of consensus among the forecasters. In each survey, questions are asked to elicit replies that bear upon these various aspects of forecasting. Periodic assessments of the results are planned.

At the NBER Fiftieth Anniversary Business Cycle Colloquium, to be held on September 24, 1970, in New York, there will be a session devoted to a comparative analysis of short-term macroeconomic forecasts of various types, and simulations produced by econometric models. On forecasts, I plan to prepare a report summarizing, bringing up to date, and extending the findings of the NBER studies in this area. Ex ante forecasts based on econometric models, informal models and judgment, and anticipatory data would be compared with each other as well as with a variety of predictive benchmark measures; the results should add to our knowledge of the relative accuracy, properties, and determinants of economic forecasts. On simulations, I shall draw upon the recent work for the Conference on Econometric Models of Cyclical Behavior and attempt to extend it along the lines suggested elsewhere in this report (see "Business Cycle Analysis of Econometric Model Simulations" below).

Victor Zarnowitz

An Analysis of the Forecasting Properties of U.S. Econometric Models

Our analysis of Wharton Econometric Forecasts from 1963 to 1968 and of OBE Econometric Forecasts from 1967-II through 1968-IV suggests the following:

1. For both models, the first two quarters of forecast are significantly improved by including mechanical constant adjustments based on single-equation residuals of previous periods. This finding is consistent with the proposition that constant adjustments will improve forecasts if models are misspecified and have autocorrelated residuals. Specifically, when the Wharton model is used without adjustment the first two-quarter-forecast errors for GNP and its major components are almost twice as large as the comparable simulation error, measuring the latter as root mean square (RMS) per cent error or RMS error divided by the RMS of a no-change forecast. This difference disappears in longer forecasts. When constant adjustments are used, in contrast, the error for sample period simulations and ex post forecasts is always of the same order of magnitude.

2. The true ex ante forecasts are significantly better than other ex ante forecasts for virtually all variables and all time periods in the Wharton models and for most of the variables and time periods in the OBE models. True ex ante forecasts use the constant adjustments actually made by the forecaster; the other ex ante forecasts use either no constant adjustment or a mechanical adjustment based on previous single-equation residuals. Thus the actual adjustment methods differed from other adjustment methods in that they were based partly on judgment. In turn, judgments were based on information that would affect endogenous variables, although it was not included in the specification of individual equations, as well as on the forecaster's a priori expectations of what constituted a "reasonable" prediction. The results indicate that the use of judgment appreciably improved the Wharton forecasts and noticeably improved the OBE forecasts. Finally, actual (judgmental) adjustments are better than any mechanical adjustment for the Wharton model when the realized (ex post) values of the exogenous variables are used, but are not usually superior to mechanical adjustments in ex post forecasts for the OBE model.

3. Not only are the true ex ante forecasts better than ex post forecasts using the same constant adjustments, but ex ante forecasts with mechanical constant adjustments are better than similarly adjusted ex post forecasts in almost half of the cases. The superiority of true ex ante forecasts over ex post forecasts that use the true ex ante constant adjustments is surprising. One would expect that the substitution of realized values of exogenous variables for "guessed" values should improve the forecast, if the structure of the model is correct.

The observed superiority of the true ex ante forecasts might be explained along the following lines. After the forecaster had selected the "guessed" values of exogenous variables, the preliminary forecast generated by the model may not have been consistent with his a priori expectations for the current quarter and for the next quarter. The forecaster might then reconsider some of the constant adustments in order to make his forecasts accord more with a priori notions. If the realized values of exogenous variables are then substituted for guessed values, the resulting forecast would not be in line with either a forecast based on the model or one based entirely on a priori notions.

This hypothesis cannot explain the finding that mechanically adjusted ex ante forecasts are superior to comparably adjusted ex post forecasts in almost half of the cases. This could be due to random occurrences in a small sample or to some systematic factor. It is possible that it results from a fortuitous offsetting of underestimated government spending changes and excessively large fiscal multipliers, or from the fact that forecasters subconsciously guessed exogenous values that resulted in forecasts conforming with their good a priori idea of "reasonable," or it could be due to some other reason.

4. Most of the ex post forecast error generated with mechanical constant adjustments is due to imperfect covariation rather than imperfect central tendency or unequal variation: Thus, forecast errors are due primarily to unsystematic fluctuations rather than consistent errors in forecasting trends or cyclical fluctuations. In addition, the annual forecast error for GNP is substantially smaller than the sum of the absolute value of errors in the four component quarters. This finding suggests that these models may be better suited for predicting annual rather than quarterly movements, despite their quarterly nature.

5. Closer analysis of both the sample period simulations and ex ante and ex post forecast errors suggests that errors might have been lower if the fiscal multipliers implied by the models were smaller and if the monetary multipliers were larger. Since fiscal variables tend to enter these models as simultaneous determinants of GNP while monetary variables enter through the lagged structure, the degree of simultaneity in the economy may be overstated by the models and the contribution of lagged variables understated. This hypothesis is strengthened by the finding that there is substantial propagation of error in the system: the mean square error of total GNP is much larger than the mean square error of the sum of the individual aggregate demand components. In part, this problem may be the result of faulty estimation techniques, a conclusion consistent with recent findings that the results obtained by using two-stage least squares are virtually indistinguishable from those obtained with ordinary least squares for macromodels of the size examined here.

6. Some of these difficulties might be mitigated by a method of estimation that we call ROS (regression on simulated values). The method involves, first, initial estimation of the complete model by the usual methods, then second, use of the *complete system solution* values rather than observed values of the endogenous variables to re-estimate the coefficients. Our results indicate that this method reduces the average forecast error for the first two quarters, and also reduces the size of the fiscal multipliers, the degree of simultaneity, and the propagation of error for the first few periods. However, errors using ROS coefficients are slightly larger than ordinary methods for later quarters, suggesting that ROS coefficients will be most useful if they are estimated with complete system solution values for lagged as well as current values.

We are currently updating and extending our paper for the Conference on Econometric Models of Cyclical Behavior. We plan to contrast econometric forecasts with the results of other forecasting methods (including autoregressive models), to expand our analysis of the causes of forecast error, and to examine the basic question whether a different strategy should be used to build forecasting models than to build structural models. Poor econometric forecasts in late 1968 and early 1969 have confirmed our previous observation that the econometric forecasting record through 1968 was better than an analysis of the econometric models would have led us to anticipate. While we feel that econometric forecasting models may improve for a number of reasons, there is nothing in the recent record to justify reliance on the accuracy of forecasts made with these models.

Michael K. Evans
Yoel Haitovsky
George I. Treyz

Business Cycle Analysis of Econometric Model Simulations

A comprehensive report under the above title has been completed and will be published in the proceedings of the Conference on Econometric Models of Cyclical Behavior. The completed work covers three quarterly models of the U.S. economy, one prepared by the Wharton School, another by the Office of Business Economics (OBE), and the third prepared jointly by the Federal Reserve Board, the Massachusetts Institute of Technology, and the University of Pennsylvania (FMP). Simulated series for a variety of important national aggregates and cyclical indicators were examined for each of these models, including GNP in current and constant dollars, employment, real expenditures on consumption and types of investment, personal income, corporate profits, price and wage levels, the unemployment rate, new and unfilled orders, interest rates, etc. The analysis includes complete-model simulations for (a) selected six-quarter periods around recent business cycle turns; (b) sample periods of varying length between 1948 and 1968; and (c) hundred-quarter periods starting in 1966 or later and extending into the future. One set of nonstochastic simulations of a given type was required for each model, but for the stochastic simulations, which relate to (c) only, as many as fifty computer runs per model were made. The purpose was to gain information on the variability of responses to different configurations of shocks, and to avoid excessive reliance on any particular, and possibly idiosyncratic, shock distribution.

The following are some of the main conclusions of the study.

1. For the nonstochastic sample-period simulations, there is evidence that the calculated values tend to drift away from the actual values, though in varying degree and not necessarily continuously. In simulated series for trend-dominated variables, such as GNP, the drift appears as an increasing underestimation of growth. The discrepancies between the levels of the simulated and actual series are generally much greater than those between the corresponding quarterly changes. Simultaneous estimation over long periods of time, with model-generated values of lagged endogenous variables, is liable to produce autocorrelated errors which cumulate, thus throwing off-base the affected multiperiod predictions. Since the chance for such error cumulation is greater, *ceteris paribus,* the longer the distance from initial conditions, models with longer sample periods are at a relative disadvantage in this test.

2. Simulations of this type also indicate that models such as Wharton and OBE produce a progressively more heavily damped time-path of aggregate output. Only the first one or two recessions covered have been reflected to some degree in the declines of the simulated real GNP for these models. The FMP series are too short to allow a test of whether this model would have simulated another contraction beyond the two included in the sample period.

3. Each of the six-quarter simulations covers only one business cycle turn and starts from new (correctly measured) initial conditions: hence any one of these episodes has an approximately equal chance to be replicated, and no systematic changes over time are observed in these data. The simulations are not significantly better when they start one quarter ahead of the reference turn than when they start two or three quarters ahead: small shifts in the base have minor and unsystematic effects.

4. About one-quarter and one-third of the recorded turns are not matched by the short and long sample-period simulations, respectively. Missed turns, large discrepancies in timing, and drastically reduced amplitudes of fluctuation are all major sources of error in the

simulated series, which are associated with turning points in the actuals. For the more cyclical and volatile variables, such timing and amplitude discrepancies result in especially large errors.

5. The simulated series are for the most part classifiable according to their timing at business cycle turns, but some of them are not because they have too few turning points. These are mainly series for comprehensive aggregates of income and employment, which should have shown good cyclical conformity and typically coincident timing. Although the simulations do differentiate broadly between the groups of leading, coincident, and lagging indicators, these distinctions are much less sharp in simulations of all types than in the actual data.

6. Nonstochastic simulations for future periods, unlike those for sample periods, produce smooth trend-dominated series for the comprehensive indicators of over-all economic activity, rather than series with recurrent, if damped, fluctuations. Thus the models examined here (Wharton and OBE; the evidence for FMP is incomplete) do not generate cyclical movements endogenously. It is important to note that, in these "control solutions," the projections for the exogenous variables are essentially growth trends, without the fluctuations or disturbances that are often pronounced in the corresponding historical series. (The sample-period simulations, on the other hand, fully incorporate all these exogenous movements.)

7. In the ex ante, hundred-quarter simulations with random shocks applied to the extrapolated model equations, fluctuations are frequent but in large part too short to qualify as cyclical movements. When autocorrelated shocks are used (to reflect the serial correlations among the residuals in the sample-period equations), the result is much smoother series whose upward trends are interrupted less frequently by longer but also smaller declines. This procedure is often helpful, but mainly with the more volatile series. In general, the simulated series have considerably weaker cyclical elements, and relatively stronger elements of long trends and short erratic variations, than the historical data for the same variables.

8. Since the shocks used may not be adequately scaled, ratios of the stochastically simulated to the control series were also analyzed, in the expectation that they would show greater cyclical sensitivity. The expectation was confirmed, but the ratio series are also much more erratic than the shocked series proper.

9. Cumulated diffusion indexes constructed from the ratio series display specific cycles whose average duration is similar to that of cycles in trend-adjusted GNP, as recorded in the postwar period; the turning points in these index movements provide reference dates on which to base measures of conformity and relative timing for this set of stochastic simulations. The results for several sample runs agree with the general conclusion expressed in the last sentence of point 5 above.

Further work in this area should include more standardized simulations (notably a common sample period for the different models) for the sake of comparing the results. It should cover some other models as well: the more diverse the models, the greater the potential gains from such studies (provided that the systems are generally reasonable by the criteria of economic and statistical theory). Still another promising extension of the analysis would be to impose shocks or fluctuations on the projections of the exogenous variables and study the effects of such disturbances on the ex ante simulations of the economic system.

This study would not have been possible without the active cooperation of the builders of the models included. It also owes very much to the work of Josephine Su, our research assistant.

Victor Zarnowitz
Charlotte Boschan
Geoffrey H. Moore

Econometric Model of Business Cycles

A progress report, "An Econometric Model of Business Cycles," was completed and presented at the Conference on Econometric Models of Cyclical Behavior in November 1969. The paper, prepared by Geoffrey H. Moore and myself with the assistance of An-loh Lin, is a simplified, aggregative version of the model. The introduction summarizes the main theoretical ingredients explaining the cyclical process. Twenty-five structural equations are formulated in section 2, including five identities. Statistical estimates of the structural parameters are given in section 3, using quarterly data on the U.S. economy from 1949 to 1967. Some aspects of the errors of the model are analyzed in the last section. Also included is our reply to comments from R. A. Gordon and M. S. Feldstein, which discusses relevant issues and should be treated as a part of this paper.

Additional empirical tests are currently being performed and, depending on the outcome, a revised version of the model may be prepared.

Gregory C. Chow

Determinants of Investment

Collection of McGraw-Hill data relating to capital expenditures of 1967 and 1968 has now been completed. Checking and processing are under way. The body of individual firm data will thus extend for fourteen years, from 1955 through 1968. Further computer analysis and an extensive report along lines indicated previously are in prospect.

A paper on "Investment Anticipations and Realizations: Cross Sections and Time Series of Data of McGraw-Hill Surveys, 1955-66" was completed and presented to the CIRET Conference in Madrid in September 1969. The exchange with Jorgenson and Stephenson and Hall and Jorgenson was continued in "Once More on that 'Neo-Classical Theory of Investment Behavior'" (with M. I. Nadiri), *Review of Economics and Statistics,* May 1970, and "Tax Policy and Investment Behavior: Further Comment," *American Economic Review,* September 1970.

Robert Eisner

6. FINANCIAL INSTITUTIONS AND PROCESSES

Interest Rates

The study of interest rates, undertaken with the aid of grants from the Life Insurance Association of America, is concerned with the behavior, determinants, and effects of interest rates. Publications to date include *The Behavior of Interest Rates: A Progress Report,* by Joseph Conard; *The Cyclical Behavior of the Term Structure of Interest Rates,* by Reuben A. Kessel; *Changes in the Cyclical Behavior of Interest Rates,* by Phillip Cagan; *Yields on Corporate Debt Directly Placed,* by Avery Cohan; *The Seasonal Variation of Interest Rates,* by Stanley Diller; and *Essays on Interest Rates,* Volume I, edited by Jack Guttentag and Phillip Cagan. The study "New Series on Home Mortgage Yields Since 1951," by Jack Guttentag and Morris Beck, is in press.

In addition, Volume II of "Essays on Interest Rates" is undergoing Board review. It contains (in addition to reprints of the Diller study and parts of the Cagan and Kessel studies mentioned above) the following papers: Jack Guttentag, "Introduction"; Mark Frankena, "The Influence of Call Provisions and Coupon Rate on the Yields of Corporate Bonds"; E. Bruce Fredrikson, "The Geographic Structure of Residential Mortgage Yields"; Avery Cohan, "The Ex Ante Quality of Direct Placements, 1951-61"; Thomas J. Sargent, "Expectations at the Short End of the Yield Curve; An Application of Macaulay's Test."

Phillip Cagan's manuscript on "A Theory of Monetary Effects on Interest Rates" is still being revised. Royal Shipp, Robert Fisher, and Barbara Opper report below on their work on income property mortgage characteristics.

Jack M. Guttentag

Interest Rates and Other Characteristics of Income Property Mortgage Loans

This study examines secular and cyclical movements from 1951 to 1968 in interest rates and other terms of mortgage loan commitments on multifamily and nonresidential properties (hereafter called income properties). For the period through mid-1965, data from fifteen large life insurance companies have been collected, under the direction of Jack M. Guttentag with the cooperation of the Life Insurance Association of America. The data from July 1965 through December 1968 were made available by the LIAA, which has been collecting comparable data from the same fifteen companies on a current basis.

In addition to a description and analysis of the data, the study will include a comprehensive statistical appendix showing monthly, quarterly, and annual averages of interest rates and other loan terms, cross classified by location, property type, and other criteria.

Interest Rates. The study of variations in interest rates will include a cross-sectional multiple regression analysis of yield determinants and an examination of cyclical and secular movements in interest rates. To date, only the cross-sectional analysis has been completed. It covers those four quarters for which more information is available than for other periods (1954 III, 1959 IV, 1963 III, and 1965 I). Coefficients of multiple determination (R^2) ranged from .415 to .510 for three of the quarters, when interest rates were relatively stable. In the fourth quarter of 1959, however, when large month-to-month increases in average interest rates were occurring, the R^2 dropped to .238.

Loan and property characteristics that had consistent and highly significant relationships to interest rates in each of the four periods were capitalization rate, property type, geographic location, and lending company. Capitalization rates appear to serve as a proxy variable for a number of risk-determining loan or property characteristics for which survey data were not available (e.g., local market considerations). Loan amount, loan-to-value ratio, and maturity were not consistently related to interest rates.

Nonrate Terms. The nonrate terms covered are loan amount, maturity, loan-to-value ratio, capitalization rates, and per cent constant, which is the annual level payment, including interest and amortization, per $100 of debt. These average nonrate terms on mortgage commitments of $100,000 and over trended upward between 1951 and 1968. Accompanying the construction booms that emerged during this period, there was a particularly marked expansion in the total number, the total dollar amount, and the average dollar amount of new commitments approved. Despite a substantial upward trend in interest rates, the per cent constant increased only slightly, because there was a marked lengthening in the average loan maturity. Meanwhile, there was a slight decline in the average debt coverage ratio (net operating income as a multiple of debt service), largely a reflection of increases in the average loan-to-value ratio and in the average capitalization rate.

One of the most striking findings of the study is the lack of strong cyclical variability in most nonrate terms. Nevertheless, average loan maturities and average loan-to-value ratios did tend to increase more slowly during periods of rising interest rates than they did when interest rates were falling. The same behavior is noted in the Guttentag-Beck study of home mortgages.

Royal Shipp
Robert Moore Fisher
Barbara Opper

A Study of the Gibson Paradox

Over long periods of time, interest rates have been highly correlated with the level of prices, rather than with the rate of change of prices as predicted by classical monetary theory. Irving Fisher's[1] famous explanation of this paradox—called the Gibson paradox—was that the pertinent expected rate of change of prices, π_t, is a distributed lag function of the actual rate of change of prices:

$$(1) \quad \pi_t = \sum_{i=0}^{m} v_i \Delta p_{t-i} / p_{t-i-1},$$

where p_t is the price level at t and where the v_i's and m are parameters. Fisher maintained that the distributed lag function (1) is characterized by a long mean lag, and that this explains the Gibson paradox. He implemented his explanation by calculating regressions of the form

$$(2) \quad r_t = \sum_{i=0}^{\hat{m}} w_i \Delta p_{t-i} / p_{t-i-1} + e_t,$$

where $\hat{m}$ and the w_i's are estimates of parameters, r_t is the nominal interest rate at time t, and e_t is a statistical residual. Fisher estimated (2) using the distributed lag estimator which he had invented. Without exception, he found that $\hat{m}$ was large and that the estimated lag weights w_i were positive, dropping off slowly with increases in i. Thus, expectations seemed to adjust so slowly that the expected rate of inflation typically resembles the level of prices more closely than it does the current rate of inflation.

However, Fisher's work seems to constitute less of an explanation of the Gibson paradox than simply a redefinition for it. For, as Phillip Cagan[2] has pointed out, the estimated mean lags in (2), which typically range from ten to thirty years, seem implausibly long on the maintained hypothesis that the w_i's principally reflect the lag in the formation of expectations. The problem, then, is to explain why the lag is so incredibly long.

As a preface to addressing that main problem, it seems necessary to supplement Cagan's argument, which is the starting point of our work, with a careful statement of the criterion of plausibility. To say that the w_i's assume an implausible pattern presumably means that they do not resemble the v_i's, which seem to characterize the way people form expectations in equation 1. To substantiate that claim requires that we have some independent information about the v_i's. To obtain that information, we invoke John F. Muth's hypothesis[3] that the expectations of the market can fruitfully be hypothesized to be the optimal (minimum mean squared error) forecasts of statistical theory. Furthermore, we posit that the actual rate of inflation can be approximated by a mixed autoregressive, moving-average error process. This implies that the v_i's of the optimal forecasting scheme are members of Jorgenson's[4] class of rational distributed lag functions. It is possible to calculate the v_i's from knowledge of the parameters of the mixed autoregressive, moving-average error process in the actual rate of inflation. The v_i's supply a standard against which we can judge the plausibility of the w_i's of (2). Preliminary results obtained through this procedure confirm Cagan's doubts about Fisher's results: the estimated v_i's associated with the optimal forecasting schemes are characterized by very short mean lags, in marked contrast to Fisher's direct estimates of equation 2. Hence it appears very doubtful that long lags in the adjustment of expectations could explain the Gibson paradox, since those lags deviate so radically from the ones implied by optimal forecasting.

The main purpose of this study is to provide

---

[1] Irving Fisher, *The Theory of Interest*, New York, 1930, pp. 399-451.

[2] Phillip Cagan, *Determinants and Effects of Changes in the Stock of Money, 1875-1960*, New York, NBER, 1965, pp. 252-259.

[3] John F. Muth, "Rational Expectations and the Theory of Price Movements," *Econometrica*, July 1961, pp. 315-335.

[4] Dale W. Jorgenson, "Rational Distributed Lag Functions," *Econometrica*, January 1966, pp. 135-149.

an alternative explanation of the Gibson paradox. With a dynamic macroeconomic model, an attempt is made to determine under what conditions direct estimation of equation 2 is likely to enable one to obtain good estimates of the v_i's of (1). It turns out that, unless the interest elasticity of the demand for money is very small, direct estimation of (2) can be expected to produce very poor estimates of the v_i's. Moreover, for plausible values of the parameters of the model, the mean lag characterizing the estimated w_i's of equation 2 will be very much longer than the mean lag of the v_i's. The mean lag in (2) depends on many of the parameters of the model, not only the v_i's of (1). Hence, the long lags obtained by Fisher contain some important general implications about the values of those parameters. In addition, the results of our study help explain why the lags characterizing estimates of equation 2 are so much shorter for the post-World War II period.[5]

Thomas J. Sargent

Institutional Investors and the Stock Market

At the request of the Securities and Exchange Commission, the National Bureau is preparing a background report for the Commission's study of institutional investors and the stock market. This report is slated to be included in one form or another in the Commission's own report to the Congress.

In the preparation of this report, the staff, in cooperation with the Flow-of-Funds Section of the Federal Reserve Board, is revising the national balance sheet for the United States (see R. W. Goldsmith, R. E. Lipsey, and M. Mendelson, *Studies in the National Balance Sheet of the United States,* 1963) for the years 1952 through 1958 and extending it through 1968. The staff of the study is also making some additions to the Federal Reserve Board's flow-of-funds statistics, including, in particular, (1) separation of personal trust funds and nonprofit organizations from the household sector and (2) a rough subdivision of the flow-of-funds accounts for the more narrowly defined household sector and for nonfinancial corporations into about half a dozen subsectors. The sectoring will be by wealth in the case of households and by industry in the case of nonfinancial corporations.

The report, to be submitted to the Securities and Exchange Commission by June 15, 1970, is expected to consist of five chapters and a number of statistical appendixes. The chapters are to deal with:

1. Basic considerations.
2. Institutional investors and the stock market before 1952.
3. The position of institutional investors and corporate stock in the national balance sheet and the flow-of-funds accounts, 1952-68.
4. The determinants of the supply of corporate stock, 1952-68.
5. The demand for corporate stock by financial institutions and households, 1952-68.

The project is under my general direction. Most of the statistical work is being done or supervised by Helen Tice. Reports on specific features of the national balance sheet or of the flow-of-funds accounts are being contributed by Grace Milgram (land); John McGowan, Mahlon Straszheim and Peter Eilbott (supply of, demand for and value of corporate stock); John Bossons (subsectors of the household sector); Ralph Nelson (nonprofit organizations); and Leo Troy (labor unions), described below.

Raymond W. Goldsmith

Unions as Financial Institutions

My project deals with the finances of local, intermediate, national, and international unions in the United States. Special attention will be paid to certain items in the unions' accounts. Among the asset items are: investments in

---
[5] William P. Yohe and Denis S. Karnosky, "Interest Rates and Price Level Changes, 1952-69," Federal Reserve Bank of St. Louis *Review,* December 1969.

mortgages, U.S. Treasury securities, and equities. Among receipts and disbursements are: dues, interest, dividends, payments to officers and employees, and the purchase of investments.

Selected financial totals for the union movement as a whole are expected to become part of the flow-of-funds accounts of the Federal Reserve Board, as part of the project reported on above by Raymond W. Goldsmith.

Detailed data will be available for the years 1962-68, and estimates of the main items will be prepared for the period 1948-61. Detailed information is supplied by tapes of the U.S. Department of Labor. The tapes have been edited to add organizations omitted from the Department's records and to identify all reporting unions.

Preliminary results show that total union assets climbed from about $1.8 billion at the end of 1962 to over $2.1 billion at the end of 1966. By far the largest component of union assets was cash on hand and in banks, about 28 per cent of the total in 1962 and one-third in 1966.

Leo Troy

Performance of Banking Markets

The two projects described below are studies of the relation between the structure of banking markets and the performance of the banking industry. The American Bankers Association has provided financial support for the study and has also assisted in securing the cooperation of banks in the provision of data.

Performance of Banking Markets in the Provision of Services to Business

The purpose of this study is to determine whether the prices paid by businesses for bank services are related to such characteristics of the structure of banking markets as the concentration of control over bank deposits and the degree of branching restrictions. The model of bank pricing developed here implies that, because of regulatory constraints and long-run profit-maximizing criteria, banks attempt to maximize profits on the entire package of services supplied to a customer, rather than on each service separately. Observed prices of particular services provided by banks are, therefore, influenced by the composition of the package of services purchased by individual customers. Banks are compensated in three distinct ways: through interest on loans, through deposit balances, and, to a minor extent, through fees. To estimate the parameters of the relationship between price and market structure, data which describe the entire bank-customer relationship are required, rather than interest rates on loans, which have been used in all previous attempts at empirical estimation of this relationship.

Data on the total relationship between banks and their business customers were compiled from a questionnaire. The banks were requested to supply data for individual business customers on the package of services provided and the remuneration received.

The parameters of the bank pricing model, augmented by the inclusion of variables to represent demand and size variations between markets and the two structure variables, have been estimated for the two main bank prices: interest rates and deposit balances. The general findings indicate that loan rates are positively associated with both concentration and the degree of branching restriction; that is, interest rates on loans are higher as market concentration is greater and/or as branching restrictions tighten. However, the parameter estimates imply very small absolute differences in interest rates even for major differences in market concentration and branching restrictions. The parameter estimates of the regressions on deposit balances imply no association between the size of these balances and either concentration or branching restrictions.

Our conclusion is, therefore, that market structure affects the price paid for the package of services provided business but the magnitude of the impact is extremely small.

A manuscript of the complete report has

been reviewed by a staff reading committee and is being revised in the light of criticisms received. A manuscript of an Occasional Paper which presents a major portion of the empirical work has been submitted for review by a staff reading committee.

Donald P. Jacobs

Banking Structure and Performance in Consumer Credit Markets

The initial tabulations of data collected on the performance of commercial banks in their consumer lending activities revealed measurable differences in various indexes of performance (such as finance charges, services, and lending policies) among banks operating under different types of banking laws. Most recent work has been devoted to developing an over-all index of performance that combines the individual indexes. Preliminary tests have not produced very strong evidence of significant differences in these over-all measures by type of banking law.

Related work on the price elasticity of demand for personal loans at commercial banks suggests a considerable amount of price competition among banks and between banks and other types of lenders. There is also evidence that bank charges and lending policies are significantly influenced by nonbank competition in these markets. This, in turn, suggests that some of the differences in performance that might be expected to develop under different types of banking structures may be offset by other stronger forces in local markets. Some tests of this hypothesis are being developed.

Paul F. Smith

Behavior of the Commercial Banking Industry, 1965-67: A Microeconometric Study

At present, much of the information concerning the operation of the commercial banking system is rather fragmentary, and most of the quantitative analysis tends to be highly aggregative. Yet one of the very clear lessons gained from recent experience is that the impact of monetary policy is not necessarily distributed evenly throughout the banking system. For example, it is apparent that the use of alternative policy instruments can significantly alter the distribution of reserves among the individual banks in the system. Interest rate ceilings, in particular, seem to have a major impact on the allocation of funds. These distributional aspects take on added importance because of the fact that the different types of banks are likely to respond quite differently to any given set of financial conditions. Thus, in order to predict the banking system's response to monetary policy, it is necessary to provide estimates of two distinct effects: first, the impact on the distribution of available funds and, second, the response by individual banks to the change in financial conditions.

This research project is studying the above aspects of banking operations during the period 1965 through 1967—a period marked by some very sharp changes in monetary policy and by some pronounced responses within the banking system. In order to analyze bank behavior on a disaggregated basis, the study employs call-report data for each of the nearly 14,000 commercial banks in the country. This information shows the composition of the banks' portfolios at the end of June and December for the years 1965, 1966, and 1967. For those dates, about 150 pieces of portfolio information are provided for each bank. Although some of the breakdowns are not as complete as might be desirable, the data provide considerably more detailed information than that now available even on an aggregate basis.

The content of the study can be divided into two major components: (1) descriptive analysis and (2) regression analysis of bank portfolio behavior patterns. Because of the enormous quantity of data involved, both components of the research have thus far been confined to intensive exploratory analysis, using only a portion of the available data. For example, the descriptive analysis compares just two types of banks: the very small banks and the large banks with numerous branches. Similarly, the regression analysis is restricted to the relatively small group of banks with deposits in excess of $500 million. The results of the exploratory analysis have proven most useful, and the analysis is now being extended to encompass the entire body of data.

David T. Kresge

Other Studies

Benoit Mandelbrot is investigating the influence of rational anticipation on the variability of prices in competitive markets. This study follows the lines of his earlier work, which indicated that, as anticipation of the variables that influence price is improved, and therefore price is made increasingly "rational," the variability of prices is increased.

Richard Selden is revising his study "Financial Intermediaries and the Effectiveness of Monetary Policy: The Case of Finance Companies" preparatory to staff review, and Robert Shay is planning the final summary report on the Consumer Credit Study.

The program of studies on the quality of credit in booms and depressions is also nearing its final stages. The report on *Home Mortgage Delinquency and Foreclosures,* by James Earley and John Herzog, has been published. George Hempel's manuscript on "The Postwar Quality of State and Local Debt" and Edgar Fiedler's "Statistical Compendium on Credit Quality" have been submitted to the Board of Directors.

7. STUDIES IN INDUSTRIAL ORGANIZATION

Economics of Health

Since the last *Annual Report,* the following papers have appeared:

>Richard Auster, Irving Leveson, Deborah Sarachek, "The Production of Health, An Exploratory Study," *The Journal of Human Resources,* Fall 1969.
>Victor R. Fuchs, "Can The Traditional Practice of Medicine Survive?", *Archives of Internal Medicine,* January 1970.
>Victor R. Fuchs, Elizabeth Rand, Bonnie Garrett, "Health Manpower Gap Reexamined," *New England Journal of Medicine,* February 5, 1970.
>K. K. Ro, "Patient Characteristics, Hospital Characteristics and Hospital Use," *Medical Care,* July-August 1969.

A paper by Victor R. Fuchs, Elizabeth Rand, and Bonnie Garrett, "The Distribution of Earnings in Health and Other Industries," has been accepted for publication by *The Journal of Human Resources.*

A volume entitled "Essays in the Economics of Health and Medical Care" is now in preparation. It will incorporate most of the work completed during the past few years.

The advisory committee for the program is chaired by Dr. George James, Dean of the Mount Sinai School of Medicine, and includes the following members: Gary S. Becker, Columbia University and NBER; James Brindle, Health Insurance Plan of Greater New York; Norton Brown, M.D.; Eveline Burns, New York University Graduate School of Social Work; Philip E. Enterline, University of Pittsburgh; Marion B. Folsom; Eli Ginzberg, Columbia University; William Gorham, Urban Institute; David Lyall, M.D.; Melvin Reder, Stanford University; Peter Rogatz, M.D., State University of New York.

The program is supported by grants from the Commonwealth Fund and the National Center for Health Services Research and Development. Reports concerning individual studies follow.

An Econometric Analysis of Spatial Variations in Mortality Rates by Race and Sex

The primary objective of the study is to measure the effects of income, schooling, and other economic variables upon health, and to isolate their role in explaining the well-known discrepancy in the health status of whites and Negroes in the United States.

The study makes use of spatial data (census divisions, states, and standard metropolitan statistical areas—SMSA's) for the United States in the 1959-61 period. The statistical techniques employed are ordinary least squares (OLS) and two-stage least squares (2SLS). Health is measured by 1959-61 age-adjusted mortality rates for whites and Negroes (or nonwhites) by sex. A tentative and partial summary of findings follows.

1. In multiple regressions that do not take account of schooling the coefficients of family income are usually negative and often approach or achieve statistical significance at conventional levels. Income elasticities of the mortality rate from OLS regressions for SMSA's vary from −.06 for white males to −.31 for Negro males.

2. The results when family income is decomposed into a labor and a nonlabor component suggest that, in the case of white males, the observed coefficient of family income represents a compromise between the favorable health effects of increases in nonlabor income and the unfavorable (or less favorable) health effects of increases in earnings. Estimated nonlabor income elasticities of the mortality rate for white males vary from −.13 to −.37.

3. The OLS regression coefficients for a measure of schooling are negative and usually achieve statistical significance. The existence of an inverse relationship is also supported by the results for 2SLS. Schooling elasticities of the mortality rate (OLS) vary between −.24 for white males to −.67 for Negro males. The high correlation between income and schooling makes it difficult to determine whether income improves health through schooling or schooling has an independent effect on health.

4. Both the OLS and 2SLS results suggest the existence of a strong inverse relationship between the mortality rate and the per cent married with spouse present. This effect seems especially strong for Negro males.

5. Per capita state and local public welfare expenditures are found to be inversely correlated with the mortality rate. The elasticities are −.05 for white females and −.10 for Negro females.

6. The mortality rate is positively correlated with a measure of psychological tensions (the death rate from ulcers of the stomach).

7. The results for a regional dummy variable suggest that residing in the South reduces the mortality rate for white females while it increases the rate for Negro females.

The estimated regression equations are being used to "explain" the observed race and sex differentials in mortality rates.

Morris Silver

The Demand for Health: A Theoretical and Empirical Investigation

The aim of this study is to construct and estimate a model of the demand for the commodity "good health." This is, of course, what consumers demand when they purchase medical services. As economists, we are interested in health—measured here by rates of mortality and morbidity—because of its influences on the amount and productivity of labor.

My model takes as its point of departure the view that health is a durable item. This view is adopted because "health capital" is one component of human capital, and the latter has been treated as a stock in the literature on investment in human beings. Consequently, it is assumed that individuals inherit an initial stock of health that depreciates over time—at an increasing rate, at least after some stage in the life cycle—and can be increased by investment. Gross investments in the stock of health are said to be produced by household production functions, whose direct inputs include the time of the consumer and such market goods as medical care, diet, exercise, recreation, and housing. The production function also depends on certain "environmental variables" that influence the efficiency of the production process.

93

The most important of these variables is the level of education of the producer.

It should be realized that in this model the level of health of an individual is *not* exogenous but depends, at least in part, on the resources allocated to its production. Health is demanded by consumers for two reasons. As a consumption commodity it directly enters their preference functions, or, put differently, sick days are a source of disutility. As an investment commodity it determines the total amount of time available for market and nonmarket activities; that is, an increase in the stock of health reduces the time lost from these activities, and the monetary value of this reduction is an index of the return to an investment in health.

Figure II-1 illustrates the determination of the optimal stock of health capital at any age, i.

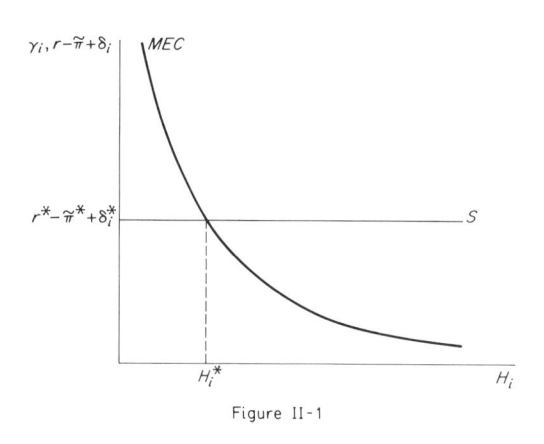

$\gamma_i, r - \tilde{\pi} + \delta_i$ | MEC

$r^* - \tilde{\pi}^* + \delta_i^*$ .... S

H_i^* H_i

Figure II-1

The demand curve, MEC, shows the relationship between the stock of health (H_i) and the rate of return on an investment in health or the marginal efficiency of health capital (γ_i). The marginal efficiency of capital is defined as WG/π, where W is the wage rate, G is the marginal product of health capital—the increase in healthy time caused by a one-unit increase in the stock of health—and π is the marginal cost of gross investment. Since the output produced by health capital has a finite upper limit of 365 healthy days, diminishing marginal productivity is assumed. Therefore, the MEC schedule slopes downward. The supply curve, S, shows the relationship between the stock of health and the cost of capital. The latter variable equals the sum of the real-own rate of interest ($r - \tilde{\pi}$) and the rate of depreciation (δ_i). Since the cost of capital is independent of the stock of health, the supply curve is infinitely elastic. The equilibrium stock is given by H_i^*, where the demand and supply curves intersect.[1]

Two novel features of the model are the roles it assigns to age and education. The interpretation of the effects of these two variables on the demand for health and medical care follows.

1. An increase in the rate of depreciation with age would increase the cost of capital and reduce the demand for health over the life cycle. At the same time, if the elasticity of the demand curve in Figure II-1 were less than unity, medical expenditures would tend to rise with age. Put differently, with a relatively inelastic demand curve for health, older persons would have an incentive to offset *part* of the reduction in health caused by an increase in the rate of depreciation by increasing their medical outlays.

2. It is well-documented that more-educated persons are more efficient producers of money earnings than their less-educated colleagues. Since education improves market productivity, it may be expected to improve nonmarket productivity as well. This implies a positive correlation between education and the efficiency of the gross investment production process. In other words, an increase in education would increase the amount of health capital obtained from given amounts of medical care and other inputs, lower the marginal cost of gross investment, and shift the MEC schedule to the right. With the wage rate and the cost of capital held constant, the more-educated would demand a larger optimal stock of health. If the demand curve were relatively inelastic, however, the correlation between expenditures on medical

---

[1] The above presentation assumes that the marginal disutility of sick time equals zero. This analysis is modified in the study to take account of the consumption aspects of the demand for health.

care and education would be negative.

The empirical sections of the study estimate demand curves for health and medical care and gross investment production functions. The demand curves are fitted by ordinary least squares, and the production functions by two-stage least squares. The principal data source is the 1963 health interview survey conducted by the National Opinion Research Center and the Center for Health Administration Studies of the University of Chicago. Healthy time, the output produced by health capital, is measured either by the complement of the number of restricted-activity days due to illness and injury or by the complement of the number of work-loss days.

The most important regression results follow.

1. Education has a positive and statistically significant coefficient in the health demand curve. The marginal cost of producing gross additions to health capital is roughly 7.1 per cent lower for consumers with, say, eleven years of formal schooling than for those with ten years.

2. An increase in age simultaneously reduces health and increases medical expenditures. Computations based on the age coefficients reveal that the continuously compounded rate of growth of the depreciation rate is 2.1 per cent per year over the life cycle.

3. The best estimate of the elasticity of the demand curve in Figure II-1 is 0.5.

4. Estimates of the elasticity of health with respect to medical care range from 0.1 to 0.3.

The empirical analysis also explores the effects of changes in wage rates and property income on the demand for health and medical care. In addition, the impact of disability insurance—insurance that finances earnings lost due to illness—on work-loss is assessed. Moreover, to check the results obtained when ill-health is measured by sick time, variations in death rates across states of the United States are studied. This analysis reveals a remarkable qualitative and quantitative agreement between the mortality and sick time regression coefficients.

Michael Grossman

An Economic Analysis of Accidents

Accidents impose significant losses on property and persons—for example, accidents are exceeded only by heart disease and cancer as a cause of death in the United States. So far, there has been little systematic economic analysis of accidents, yet, they can be viewed as an economic problem in the sense that inputs of scarce resources can reduce both the probabilities of and the losses from accidents. In this study a model is first developed which identifies those factors that determine the level of one's resource inputs to reduce expected accident losses. These factors include (1) the initial probability and loss from an accident, (2) the individual's wealth, (3) the productivity and cost of safety devices, (4) the availability of insurance, (5) attitudes toward risk, and (6) legal liability rules.

The second part of the study will be an empirical analysis of accidents. Data are available by states on deaths in 1960 from all accidents by color and by sex. Cross-section regressions will be estimated with independent variables, such as income, years of schooling, medical service inputs, population density, and industrial and occupational characteristics. A cross-section analysis of deaths from specific types of accidents—for example, automobile accidents—will also be undertaken.

A striking feature of the accident data being

TABLE II-3

Deaths from Accidents per 100,000 Persons, U.S., 1959-61

Age Group	Whites Males	Whites Females	Nonwhites Males	Nonwhites Females
All Ages (age-adjusted)	70.2	25.1	98.6	34.9
15-24	92.4	19.3	95.8	19.9
25-34	67.4	14.0	103.8	24.3
35-44	60.3	15.5	110.3	29.1
45-54	71.4	21.5	122.7	32.9
55-64	83.8	29.2	130.8	45.8

Source: Iskrant and Joliet, *Accidents and Homicides*.

studied is the higher rates for nonwhites than for whites in the United States. In Table II-3, nonwhite accident deaths are more than 30 per cent greater than for whites, and similar differences exist in every region of the country. It is interesting to note further the pattern of accident deaths by age for whites and nonwhites. For white males accidents peak at ages 15-24 and decline continuously down to the 45-54 age group, while for nonwhites accident rates rise continuously as age increases. An attempt will be made to explain not only the difference in over-all rates between whites and nonwhites but also the widening differential with age.

William M. Landes

Expenditures for Physicians' Services

This study, which is being undertaken at the request of the National Center for Health Services Research and Development (Department of H.E.W.), is concerned with expenditures for physicians' services in the United States in the post-World War II period. These expenditures rose from $2.6 billion in 1948 to $11.6 billion in 1968. The rate of increase was substantially more rapid than that recorded for the gross national product, personal consumption expenditures, or expenditures on other services. Moreover, the gap has been widening in recent years.

The purpose of our study is twofold: first, we will identify the "sources" of growth in expenditures for the entire period and significant subperiods. These sources include changes in population (size and composition), price (several variants will be considered), number of visits, quantity of service per visit (tests, X-rays, etc.), and quality of service (specialization, length of training).

The second part of the study will be an analysis of the behavior of physicians and patients. Supply and demand elasticities will be estimated from time series and cross-section data. We hope to shed some light on the growth of specialization, the simultaneous existence of excess demand (in general practice) and excess supply (in surgery), and the growth of insurance and prepayment.

Victor R. Fuchs
Marcia J. Kramer

Socioeconomic Determinants of Hospital Use

In rewriting a portion of my manuscript, I became aware of the need to formulate explicit models. New models have been constructed and, to test them, it has become necessary to run a few more regressions. I plan to rewrite my paper as soon as I get the results. In the meantime, I am working on a short paper with Richard Auster entitled "Income and the Consumption of Hospital Services."

K. K. Ro

The Ownership Income of Management

I have revised my study and it has been sent to the Board for review under the title, "The Ownership Income of Management." The Table of Contents is as follows:
1. Introduction
2. Methodology and the Data
3. Executive Compensation Patterns
4. Study: Stock Ownership and Income: Large Manufacturers
5. Study: Stock Ownership and Income: Retail Trade
6. Study: Stock Ownership and Income: Small Manufacturers
7. Summary and Evaluation
   Appendixes
A. Numerical Example of Compensation Calculation

B. Corporations in the Three Samples
C. Sample Sizes by Year and Executive Rank
D. Ownership Income and Compensation Within the Large Manufacturing Sample: Adjusted for Extreme Values
E. Ownership Income and Compensation Within the Retail Trade Sample: Adjusted for Extreme Values
F. Ownership Income and Compensation Within the Small Manufacturing Sample: Adjusted for Extreme Values

Wilbur G. Lewellen

Diversification in American Industry

Our work has been focused until recently on developing the necessary basic data for analysis. Future work will proceed in two directions.

First, we have completed the compilation of data on the diffusion of thirteen product innovations as measured by the number of firms producing the products at successive points in time in the 1920-68 period. These products are spread over a broad spectrum of industries. We are now examining the identity of early and later entrants into production in terms of their asset size. The next step will be an attempt to "explain" the rate of diffusion or entry by the rate of change in sales, price movements, and major technical modifications in these products subsequent to their introduction. Thus far, it appears there is at least one fairly consistent pattern: the number of producers does not remain at a plateau after reaching its maximum but rather the rise is followed by a marked decline. The interval from innovation to peak in number of producers varies considerably. One of our objectives is to explain this variation.

The second direction taken by our work involves the analysis of product diversification patterns for a large number of individual firms. We now have a reliable record for 1968 of the activities of roughly 350 manufacturing and 140 nonmanufacturing firms. This record, based on Dun and Bradstreet data, shows for each firm the breakdown of employment by 4-digit industry classified on the basis of the primary activity of each plant. For each firm, the entire "compustat" record of financial data, covering a considerable span of years, is also available. The sample was selected after tests were carried out to ensure that both the "compustat" and the Dun and Bradstreet data referred to the same configurations of parent and subsidiary companies. We now intend to examine two interrelated questions with the help of these data:

1. What is the nature of the linkages between the primary and the secondary activities of companies? For example, do these linkages appear to be in the production or in the marketing characteristics of the activities? To what extent can the spectrum of activities be explained by vertical integration?

2. What is the relative importance of individual company versus industry characteristics in explaining diversification? Among individual company characteristics, one would include past profitability, growth rates, and expenditures on research and development and on advertising. Among the industry characteristics, one would include capital intensiveness, marketing costs, the composition of labor and other attributes of the production processes of the primary industries by which the companies are classified, as well as the growth and profitability of these industries.

In addition to the problems discussed above, our manuscript will also contain some description and analysis of trends in diversification since 1954, based on aggregative census data.

I expect to complete a manuscript for this study by early fall of 1970. Robert McGuckin, a graduate student at the State University of New York at Buffalo, is collaborating with me in the project. The study is financed by the National Bureau of Economic Research with some supplemental financing by the General Electric Foundation.

Michael Gort

8. INTERNATIONAL STUDIES

Introduction

Several projects in the international area have matured during the past year. The largest in terms of the amount of new information collected and analyzed is the study of "Price Competitiveness in World Trade," by Irving B. Kravis and Robert E. Lipsey, which will soon go to press. This study serves a dual purpose, providing both a contribution toward improved methods of international price collection and comparison and an analysis of relative price levels and trends in the international trade of the United States and its leading competitors. Further work that makes use of the data collected and other price series is reported on below by Kravis and Lipsey under the heading "The Role of Prices in International Trade."

Another study now in press is Michael Michaely's "The Responsiveness of Demand Policies to the Balance of Payments: Postwar Patterns." Michaely's objective is to examine the behavior of monetary and fiscal policy variables in the United States and other leading countries and to try to determine, by systematic statistical investigation, to what extent the direction of movement in these variables has been consistent with changes in the international payments positions of these countries. The analysis is pursued both on a comparative basis and in detail for each of nine countries.

A monograph on "Measuring International Capital Movements," by Walther P. Michael, undertaken much earlier as part of a project on the structure of world trade and payments,[1] has been sent to the Board. It is a unique attempt to construct detailed matrices of different types of capital movements by drawing on data from both capital-exporting and capital-importing countries.

Among the work completed, mention should also be made of the conference volume on *The Technology Factor in International Trade,* edited by Raymond Vernon, which was recently published. The proceedings of the Conference on the International Mobility and Movement of Capital, held in January 1970 under the chairmanship of Fritz Machlup, are being edited for publication.

The major new research endeavor recently undertaken as part of the international studies program concerns exchange controls and liberalization in developing countries. This project, for which financing is being provided by the Agency for International Development, is under the joint direction of Jagdish Bhagwati and Anne Krueger, and will entail the participation of a number of other leading scholars having first-hand knowledge of the problems to be studied. Plans for the study are given below in the report by Bhagwati and Krueger. Further support to another major project has been received from the National Science Foundation in the form of a second grant for the Robert Lipsey and Merle Yahr Weiss study of the relation between U.S. manufacturing abroad and U.S. exports. This is one of several international projects originally undertaken with the support of a grant by the Ford Foundation. Others in this group are the Michaely study and the conference on technology and trade, mentioned above, the Furth-Mikesell study reported on below, and my own volume published in 1968 on *Imports of Manufactures from Less Developed Countries.* Research in this last area is being carried on by Seiji Naya, who is continuing his work on the striking growth in the foreign trade of Korea.

The project on determinants of rates of intracountry diffusion of new technological processes, in which the National Bureau is cooperating with several European research institutes, is now well under way and beginning to yield questionnaire returns with the data needed for analysis. Alfred H. Conrad gives a detailed report below on the statistical design for the study of the basic oxygen process, for which the National Bureau has particular re-

---
[1] See Herbert B. Woolley, *Measuring Transactions Between World Areas,* New York, NBER, 1966.

sponsibility as its part in this cooperative research venture.

Among the international studies on which separate reports follow is that by George Garvy on money and banking systems in the Soviet Union and Eastern Europe.

Hal B. Lary

The Relation of U.S. Manufacturing Abroad to U.S. Exports

This study of interrelationships between manufacturing abroad by affiliates of U.S. companies and the export trade of the United States has been devoted mainly to data collection during the past year. The Office of Business Economics has completed its re-editing of data from several years of voluntary returns relating to trade between U.S. companies and their foreign affiliates. The only government data we are still waiting for are those of the Office of Foreign Direct Investments, covering the location and size of all foreign affiliates of U.S. companies and the exports of a large sample of U.S. parent companies. Both of these sets of data, after they are combined with information supplied by the National Bureau, are to be processed by the Bureau of the Census in such a way as to insure the confidentiality of the government records.

Of the data to be provided by the National Bureau, those on exports of the United States and its main competitors, by detailed commodity class and destination, have now been collected and processed. For many of the main countries in which U.S. direct investment is located, the affiliates of U.S. firms have been classified by industry and main product group. We expect to complete this aspect of the work soon. Data have also been collected on the sales, assets, and other characteristics of the parent companies. Of particular interest for this study is the information on the distribution, by SIC group, of parent companies' employment in the United States. The company identifications have been matched with those used by government agencies in order to permit the assembly of a single unified file.

A description of the plans for the study, the data to be used, and the relationships to be measured was read at the 1969 Annual Meeting of the American Statistical Association. The paper, entitled "The Relation of U.S. Manufacturing Abroad to U.S. Exports: A Framework for Analysis," was published in the *1969 Proceedings of the Business and Economics Section,* American Statistical Association.

The study has been financed by grants from the Ford Foundation and the National Science Foundation. Marianne Lloris and Susan Tebbetts have been the research assistants responsible for most of the data collection and computer processing.

Robert E. Lipsey
Merle Yahr Weiss

The Role of Prices in International Trade

The new indexes of international price competitiveness compiled in our study, "Price Competitiveness in World Trade," that is now being readied for publication, offer opportunities to test the role of price levels and price changes in determining the level and direction of trade. Chapter 6 of that study includes some experiments along that line, but these did not take into account any of the factors other than prices that we might expect to influence trade flows. The present study is an attempt to exploit the data and the methods developed in the earlier study.

The first aspect of this work is an examination of the asymmetry between increases and decreases in U.S. price competitiveness during the period covered by the indexes, 1953 to 1964, for which we found that decreases in U.S. price competitiveness produced much stronger effects on trade than increases. One hypothesis we are testing is that the elasticity of substitution is sensitive to the initial share of each exporter in the market for a product. Preliminary results suggest that this is indeed the case.

A second question we are investigating is whether the price level difference between two countries influences subsequent shifts in trade. If it does, the implication would be that the response to price changes is slow, and that this year's changes in trade shares may be a response to price changes in past periods. If the price level difference is not a significant factor, the implication would be that the adjustment is fairly rapid and that the trade pattern of each period already reflects recent price levels.

A further step in the analysis, for which the data collection is now complete, will involve a disaggregation of the trade data by major markets. In this way we will eliminate the influence of each country's domestic market on the results and take account of the possibility that substitution elasticities differ significantly among markets.

In addition to these analyses, which will be conducted using price data from the price competitiveness study, we plan to construct wholesale price indexes for the main trading countries on the same principles used for the international price indexes; that is, with a common weighting system based on international trade weights. These indexes will then be used to interpolate and extend our international price indexes and also, by themselves, to study changes in trade. We will make use of these wholesale price data despite their serious deficiencies, which we discussed in the Price Competitiveness volume, because our own international price indexes are not available beyond 1964 and there is no immediate prospect of any official program to bring them up to date. For the near future, therefore, current analyses will have to rely on wholesale prices and other less suitable series.

We have now collected all the basic price data needed for the calculation of these indexes, to cover the period 1953 through 1968 for the United States, the United Kingdom, Germany, and Japan. We have also assembled trade data for the period since 1964 in addition to that collected earlier. Christine Mortensen and Eva Wyler have been assisting us with the price collection and data processing.

The first results of this project, based entirely on the international price indexes, were presented in a paper at the Conference on Research in Income and Wealth in May 1970.

Irving B. Kravis
Robert E. Lipsey

The Diffusion of New Technologies

During the second full year of the New Technology Project, the European group drafted and distributed questionnaires on special presses in paper-making (Industriens Utredningsinstitut, Stockholm), shuttleless looms in textiles (National Institute for Economic and Social Research, London), numerically controlled machine tools (Institut für Wirtschaftsforschung, Munich), and continuous- or strand-casting in steel manufacture (Osterreichisches Institut für Wirtschaftsforschung, Vienna). At the National Bureau, in addition to the reworking of some of the questionnaire materials to fit American practices more closely, and their subsequent distribution among American firms, a second, company-level questionnaire was prepared for the basic oxygen process in steel. Secondly, in the face of the reluctance of many European firms to reveal capacity figures and the refusal of American manufacturers to report capacities after 1960, Wharton School capacity series were prepared here from steel output data for each of the participating countries. In addition, financial data were gathered by us at the European Economic Community and the High Authority of the European Iron and Steel Community to supplement the limited availability of balance sheets and income statements by European steelmakers. Finally, work has gone forward on the two-stage statistical design for the steel study, based upon a partial-adjustment investment function of the Koyck-Nerlove type (and similar to John Lintner's dividend model).

The second-stage questionnaire in steel asks for information on (1) the technological environment at the plant level, (2) managerial patterns, or style, and (3) research and development activity by the companies. Following the emphasis in the NBER design upon the technological background to the cost advantages of the innovation, the new inquiry concentrates on scrap balance, hot metal capacity, and operating improvements in existing furnaces. Management style is approached in terms of educational backgrounds, patterns of executive compensation, and turnover rates in the executive group. The research and development questions include specific chronologies as well as information on expenditures and personnel.

The Wharton capacity-utilization indexes were prepared from national data on steel production and investment. In addition to the obvious test of comparison with the period for which independent series are available for the United States from the American Iron and Steel Institute, the European series were sent to the participating institutes to be checked against unpublished indicators (or even more informally within the industry); the results have been generally reassuring on the usefulness of this crucial set of estimates for the "acceleration-principle" part of the diffusion model.

The empirical model starts from a comparison between the desired or optimal level of diffusion at time t, and the actual level. Let Y_t stand for the actual level of diffusion at time t, measured as the relative share of the new-technique capacity in the total capacity of the industry. Y_t^*, similarly, is the desired or optimal level of diffusion at time t. We can then write

(1) $\quad Y_t - Y_{t-1} = \alpha(Y_t^* - Y_{t-1})$

where α is the partial adjustment coefficient, measuring the degree to which the actual rate of diffusion, $Y_t - Y_{t-1}$, approaches the desired (or "desirable") rate of diffusion.[1] The desired

rate is defined by

(2) $\quad Y_t^* = a + b_1 X_{1t-1} + b_2 X_{2t-1} + \ldots + b_k X_{kt-1}$

where X_1, X_2, etc., are the profitability, output growth, capacity utilization, and other (national level, i.e., average or aggregate) market and technical variables mentioned earlier.

Combining (1) and (2), we have

(3) $\quad Y_t = \alpha a + \alpha b_1 X_{1t-1} + \alpha b_2 X_{2t-1} + \ldots + \alpha b_k X_{kt-1} + (1-\alpha) Y_{t-1}$

which relates the actual level of diffusion to the postulated economic determinants. The stochastic form of equation 3 (equation 3.1) includes the addition of a random disturbance term, u_t. By applying ordinary least squares to (3.1) we can, in theory, get direct estimates of the parameters, α, a, b_1, b_2, etc. Returning to equation 2, the estimated $\hat{a}$ and $\hat{b}_i$ should enable us to define the optimal diffusion level $\hat{Y}_t^*$. (The limits of inference, in addition to the problem of the adequacy of the sample, require that the equation be fitted to the full set of international observations. An alternative procedure is to derive the parameters, b_i, extraneously from engineering estimates.)

We now have two ways of specifying the dependent variable in the second stage. If the managerial variables can be operationally defined over time, then the expression $\hat{Y}_t^* - Y_t = (Y_t - Y_{t-1}) - (\hat{Y}_t^* - Y_{t-1})$ may be regressed upon time series of the management-style variables. But management style as we have discussed it is likely to be a long-run stable characteristic of firms within a country, perhaps even without regard to industry or sector, so that $\hat{\alpha}$, the adjustment or response *coefficient*, would itself provide a more plausible second-stage dependent *variable*. The analysis of covariance analogue to the pooled regression procedure suggested for (3.1) will deliver a set of $\hat{\alpha}$'s as country constants, but a simpler, though crude, procedure is also available. Given the estimates $\hat{b}_i$, we can use the raw data on Y_t and X_{it} in equation 3, country by coun-

---

[1] In this *deterministic* form, the adjustment function does not include a random disturbance term, u_t, say. In the stochastic estimating form of the equation, such a term should of course be included.

101

try, to estimate the individual national $\hat{\alpha}$'s.

Up to this point, we have dealt with the profit-maximizing aspect of the decision to adopt a new technique. By introducing the adjustment factor, which is obviously intended here to be something more than a random error term, we are able to go beyond the maximizing decision to consider questions of innovating style. The technique suggested earlier was to relate the optimal-actual difference, or the adjustment coefficient itself, to a set of variables specified to approximate both financial behavior and the availability of funds, as well as management style and attitudes toward innovative behavior.

The explanation of observed diffusion patterns, then, is broken into two parts. The first part is derived from an orthodox profit-maximization model, applied to a specific kind of investment decision: the adoption of a new process. The second part of the theory is an attempt to relate the observed rates of response to the technological opportunity, on the one hand, with variations in management motivation and style, on the other. Because the innovating spirit is a value-loaded concept, we are attempting to go beyond stated attitudes, which may express desirable images as much as actual behavior, and consider such evidence of motivation as can be found in varying policies toward liquidity, research budget practice, and the executive structure of the firm.

In view of the severity of our specification and data problems, how are we proceeding to implement the empirical model of diffusion?

First, in order to generate a series of Y^* for each country for the given industry, it is necessary to have estimates of the $\hat{b}_i$ for those variables which enter the cost-saving relationship. Cost differences between the new processes and existing techniques will be a function of the scale of operations, the relative prices of primary inputs, and the other technical economic variables observed in the first-stage questionnaires. The problem is how we can most effectively incorporate the cost-advantage variable into the diffusion model.

Two approaches have been considered. The first would be to derive a measure of cost-advantage directly, which (let us call it the γ variable) then becomes one of the arguments on the right-hand side of equation 2, which, in turn, determines the desired rate of diffusion. But, in order to predict the γ values—since that is how the cost advantage enters the investment decision—we must have estimates of the elasticities of total cost with respect to the technical conditions mentioned in the paragraph above. As was suggested earlier, it may be most convenient to estimate these elasticities directly from best-practice engineering data. We have engineering cost comparisons under varying conditions for steelmaking. Again, recall that the purpose of these elasticities is to make possible a set of γ estimates which are indicative of the technical conditions *specific to each country*. Ideally, and where there are sufficient time series, we should generate a series of such observations on γ. I have discussed previously the simultaneity problem involved at this stage of the analysis, where the conditions themselves may change in anticipation of or in response to the adoption of the new technique. The problem is equally grave at the next step, the estimation of the $\hat{b}$ coefficients in equation 3.1 for subsequent use in (2).

The second approach would be to enter the cost-advantage variables directly into equation 2. However, while it is possible to estimate the cost-saving elasticities extraneously in order to use the cost-advantage in (2), it is not obvious how we could identify any direct relationships between the cost-determining variables and the desired diffusion rate. In general, the estimation of the $\hat{b}$ coefficients, either directly or in terms of the γ variables, depends upon the significance we are able to attach to the α estimates in equation 3.1.

In addition to the cost-advantage variables, the first-stage analysis must take account of product specifications (the proportion of special steels, essentially) which directly condition the appropriateness of the new technique. Another conditioning variable is the presence of a sufficient supply of hot metal for the basic oxygen converter. Preliminary investigation suggests that the necessity to construct new blast furnace capacity, which would in any event not be required in order to introduce an electric steelmaking furnace, would be an almost entirely dominant negative influence in the decision with respect to the basic oxygen process.

The final group of first-stage variables in the model is drawn from the theory underlying the acceleration principle, rather than from marginal theories of the capital decision. If the productive capacity is increasing in an industry, the possibility of increasing the share of a new technology in the total is obviously greater than when adoption of the new technique involves a decision to retire (replace) existing active capacity. Similarly, if the stock of capital is of relatively early vintage—in calendar terms, not simply technologically—so that a large proportion of the stock is approaching the age of physical retirement and has been written off, then the new capital decision is a choice between techniques, essentially, and not a decision to replace active capacity. The variables measuring the rate of growth of output in the given industry within each country and, where it is available, a measure of the vintage of the capital stock, are entered directly into equation 3. In addition, the capacity-utilization series mentioned earlier are part of the set of acceleration variables.

These variables seem to me to be sufficient to generate the "desired" diffusion rates, Y^*. In those cases especially where a complete time series is not possible because of gaps in the basic data, we will try to redesign the first stage to provide an optimal "prediction" of new technique proportions at a pair of dates, *e.g.*, two and seven years from the data of first commercial application.

Since the optimal rate is a manufactured measure, rather than an observed datum, it can in no way be tested for statistical significance. (I omit discussion of the obvious Bayesian argument with regard to the decision-making significance of the Y^* measure, beyond observing that the Bayesian approach may be more relevant than classical significance for a theory derived from the investment decision.) There is still the possibility of testing a single-stage model in the general form of equation 3. In that event, of course, the managerial variables must be added to equation 3.1, in which case we shall quickly run into problems of statistical degrees of freedom and the more serious interdependence difficulties already discussed with respect to the $\hat{b}$ estimates. It may be possible to avoid this by careful grouping and the use of binary dummy variables or other nonparametric techniques; but in the grouping case, I would be anxious about heteroscedasticity, and in the use of dummies, I would regret the inevitable loss of richness.

The first-stage national data series are in hand now. The second-stage company-level responses are beginning to come in. The group's timetable is now aimed toward a final editorial meeting in June 1971.

During the past year, the project staff at the National Bureau has included, for varying lengths of time, Guy Herregat, concentrating on the steel questionnaires; Mansing Lee and Neville Beharie on the textile, paper, and machine-tool questionnaires; Pamela Mash on the capacity utilization series and textile trade statistics; and Jae Won Lee on statistical problems.

Alfred H. Conrad

Exchange Control, Liberalization, and Economic Development

This study is concerned with the exchange control systems applied in most of the developing countries, the effects of these controls upon economic growth, and ways in which liberalization of restrictionist regimes can be accomplished. Quantitative controls in the developing countries affect virtually every aspect of economic activity: production levels are frequently determined by the availability of imports; the implicit protection afforded to import-competing producers leads to high-cost import substitution and, frequently, to domestic monopoly positions; and export growth is inhibited by overvaluation of the exchange rate. Liberalization is not easily achieved, however, and little is known about how it can be successfully carried out.

In the course of the project, the experience of a number of developing countries with exchange control and liberalization efforts will be carefully and systematically examined. Each of the country studies will be undertaken by an economist already familiar with that country, and coordination of the individual research projects will be sought through a basic "analytic framework" prepared by us in consultation with the other participants and through periodic meetings of the group. On the basis of the individual studies, which will be carried on over the next year and a half, the project directors will prepare an over-all synthesis with the aim of providing better answers than are now available concerning the effects of controls and the most promising means of liberalization. It is anticipated that the systematic and parallel investigation of a number of cases will provide, among other things, new insights into the costs of exchange control systems, in terms of the effects on the growth rates of developing countries and the viability of their economic development.

Countries whose experience will be subjected to detailed examination will probably include Brazil, Chile, Colombia, Egypt, Ghana, India, Israel, Pakistan, Philippine Islands, South Korea, Turkey, and several others yet to be determined. The initial meeting of economists participating in the project was held at the National Bureau on May 28 and 29.

Jagdish N. Bhagwati
Anne O. Krueger

The Pattern of Exports and Import-Substitution in an Outward-Looking Economy: Korea

In continuation of a study of Korea's trade pattern, my research during the past year has been primarily concerned with the extent to which the country's tariff structure affords protection to value added by production, as distinguished from the gross value of production, of its industries. In measuring this "effective rate of protection," 158 manufacturing sectors have been selected from 299 interindustry sectors for the year 1966. Nominal tariffs and special customs duties are combined as tariff measures (with both import-weighted and output-weighted tariffs employed for different computations).

One result of the various computations made is that the pattern of effective rates across industries, measured under the assumption of fixed input coefficients, closely reflects that obtained when substitution between inputs is allowed. In testing for possible distortion of effective rates when measured with fixed input coefficients, I have computed proportionate changes in the price of value-added inputs based on the CES production function and an assumed value of 0.5 for the elasticity of substitution between value-added and intermediate inputs. Under the fixed coefficients assumption, both the average rate and the coefficient of variation are found to be more than 50 per cent larger than under the substitution assumption. Yet the pattern given by these two sets of estimates is virtually identical (the correlation between them being .9919).

Since the above finding is based on assumptions with respect to the production function and the elasticity of substitution, two more sets of effective rates have been computed as an additional test. These are based on 1963 and 1966 input coefficients but use the same 1965 tariffs. A close similarity in the pattern of effective rates is again disclosed, despite the use of different input coefficients.

My work on the export performance and trade structure of Korea is now being extended to other Asian countries. This work, which employs Lary's value-added-per-employee as a proxy for capital intensity, is being financed by a grant from the Southeast Asia Development Advisory Group.

Seiji Naya

Foreign Holdings of Liquid Dollar Assets

The purpose of the study is to analyze the behavior of foreign holdings of liquid dollar assets over the period 1957-69 in order to improve our understanding of the international functions of the dollar and of the position of the United States as an international financial center.

The study focuses on the different types of liquid dollar holders, i.e., foreign official agencies, foreign commercial banks, foreign branches of U.S. banks, and other foreigners. The published breakdown by types of holders of direct foreign dollar claims on the United States ("American dollars") is unsatisfactory for the purpose of the study because the data do not reflect the impact of the Eurodollar market on both the size and the distribution of total liquid dollar assets held by foreigners. Similarly, the published Eurodollar statistics of the Bank for International Settlements need to be modified for the purpose of the study in order to eliminate double counting. The integration of American dollar and Eurodollar statistics presents many conceptual and statistical difficulties but is essential for estimating and analyzing the behavior of foreign holdings of liquid dollar assets.

On the basis of our estimates, the changes in foreign-held dollar assets will be compared with the corresponding changes in foreign-owed dollar liabilities, again including liabilities both to U.S. residents and to other foreigners, so as to arrive at estimates of foreign "net" dollar holdings by type of holder. We also plan to analyze the foreign demand for liquid dollar assets by category of holder, in terms of the major determinants of foreign demand which have been dealt with in the literature on international short-term capital movements. These determinants include: (a) interest rates or interest rate differentials; (b) trade flows or total transactions involving dollars; (c) exchange rate expectations; (d) various measures of foreign confidence in U.S. dollars; (e) portfolio balance prescripts; and (f) institutional factors.

We believe the previous analyses of these determinants of foreign dollar balances have been inadequate because of their failure to disaggregate balances by type and by category of holder.

A complete analysis of the foreign demand for liquid dollar assets would require the formulation and testing of a comprehensive econometric model, which would include among the variables all liquid assets that serve as a substitute for liquid dollar assets and those transactions governing the supply of liquid dollar assets. Our purpose is the more modest one of providing the conceptual and statistical basis for such an analysis. However, we do plan to undertake a preliminary study of variations in categories of foreign liquid dollar assets in relation to the determinants noted above. This study will provide the basis for a critical review of several models that have been formulated (and tested) in the literature relating foreign dollar balances to central bank asset preferences, the transactions demand for dollar balances, and balanced portfolio hypotheses.

Our initial work has consisted of bringing up to date the data contained in an earlier draft of this study prepared by Herbert Furth, and subjecting the data to some tentative statistical tests. Readjustment of the "net" value of the Eurodollar market has resulted in a figure considerably lower than that used by the Bank for International Settlements but still large enough to influence decisively the aggregate amount of foreign dollar holdings. The data confirm our suspicion that, on balance, only foreign official agencies are holders of sizable net liquid dollar assets, while foreign commercial banks tend to maintain a zero net position, and other foreigners are on balance substantial net dollar debtors. The data also show how closely the rise in foreign net dollar holdings is associated with the increase in the net value of the Eurodollar market, and how the participation of foreign official agencies in that market has caused, on occasion, the paradox of a U.S. payments surplus on "official reserve transactions" account at a time of record deficits on the "liquidity" account. Similarly, disaggregation between dollar assets held by foreign banks and by foreign branches of U.S. banks, together with further disaggregation by regions, brings to light the differences in the behavior of foreign banks in Western Europe (where banks have been substituting Eurodollars for American dollar holdings) and in the rest of the world (where banks have continued to expand working balances in American dollars in line with the growth in international commerce).

J. Herbert Furth
Raymond F. Mikesell

Credit, Banking, and Financial Flows in Eastern Europe

The main objective of my project is to analyze the functioning of the banking and credit systems in the socialist countries of Eastern Europe and their relation to central planning. Because money and credit are largely implementary rather than dynamic elements of the socialist economies, and fiscal rather than monetary policy is relied upon to achieve macroeconomic equilibrium, a full evaluation of the contribution of monetary policy to economic stability and growth will not be attempted.

The monograph will cover all the socialist countries of Europe with the exception of Albania. The Soviet system was introduced in the other countries of Eastern Europe about thirty years after the Bolshevik Revolution, in the course of which the old Russian monetary and banking system had been liquidated and, after a series of experiments, replaced by the present system. The smaller countries of Eastern Europe did not start *de novo,* they merely copied an existing system. Thus, the main part of the project will deal with what I have called the "standard system" developed in the Soviet Union after the credit reform of 1930-32. In carrying out this project the role of money and credit in a centrally directed economy will be explored, as well as the structure and functioning of the banking system, which I have called the "monobank."

Part I of the monograph will provide a general historical introduction. It will first trace some elements of the standard system to the deep involvement of the Czarist State Bank in creating the Russian banking system and in using it to achieve specific goals of government policy. A second chapter will show that some of the ideas embodied in the standard system were, in fact, developed by several academic and financial economists of prerevolutionary Russia. In another chapter the sources of Lenin's views that the banking system should be used as a means for the socialist transformation of the Russian economy will be traced. As it happened, partly because of the Civil War, the money and banking system collapsed, and the blueprint proved inapplicable. The nationalization and liquidation of the prerevolutionary banking system will be the subject of the final chapter of the historical part.

The "standard system" emerged in the Soviet Union in the early 1930's, and has undergone little change since then. Since all the elements of the socialist monetary and credit system adopted by the countries of Eastern Europe in the late 1940's derive from the Soviet prototype, the latter will be examined in some detail in Part II. Successive chapters will describe the monetary system structured to serve a centrally directed economy, the role of credit in such an economy, the structure and functioning of the banking system, the various instruments and processes of "socialist credit," and finally, the nature of financial flows and the financial planning designed to project and to control these flows.

The proposed plan for Part II will permit an analytical treatment of the "standard case," while the institutional and policy differences which emerged in the other countries will be reserved for Part III. In the smaller countries, the Soviet credit system was introduced against the background of a financial structure which, in most cases, was much more developed than in Russia at the time of the Revolution, and more of the traditional elements of their respective banking structures were carried into the standard system. Other differences in the smaller countries compared with the Soviet system relate to the greater relative importance of the financing of foreign trade and the provision of credit to households and to the nonsocialized sector of the economy. Soon after its adoption, the Russian system began to be modified to fit the particular needs of each of the smaller countries embarked upon a program of economic reforms. Credit became one of the main instruments for channeling funds into investment and for achieving a more decentralized and flexible system of production and distribution responding to demands by ultimate consumers. Part III, then, will be a comparative study of the credit systems of the smaller socialist countries. It will show significant differences in policies and techniques among these countries, as well as the way in which the standard system had been adapted and in some cases developed beyond the Soviet example. A separate chapter will deal with foreign monetary relations and operations, including the role of the International Bank for Economic Cooperation and the "transferable ruble."

Yugoslavia, which originally had also slavishly copied the Russian system, has gradually evolved a system which is geared to a competitive socialist market economy. It pioneered some of the ideas embodied in the economic reforms now being undertaken by its neighbors. Because banking and credit in Yugoslavia can no longer be adequately described as just a variant of the Soviet prototype, a separate chapter on Yugoslavia will conclude Part III.

Part IV will discuss the role of credit in the economic reforms in Eastern Europe. A significant part of these reforms concerns the use of financial incentives and the rechanneling of financial flows through the use of credit in preference to the financing of investment by nonreturnable grants. Developments up to the end of 1969 will be covered.

George Garvy

9. ECONOMETRICS AND MEASUREMENT METHODS

Analysis of Long-Run Dependence in Time Series: The R/S Technique

This study is concerned with testing out and improving R/S analysis,[1] a new and extremely promising statistical technique that can be used either to test for the presence of very long-run nonperiodic statistical dependence, or to define and estimate the intensity of such dependence. Very long-run nonperiodic dependence manifests itself by the presence of "cycles," clear cut but of variable periodicity, superimposed upon a variety of "variable trends," "slow cycles," and "long swings"; where the slowest swing period is roughly of the order of magnitude of the total available record. Such behavior is well-known to be characteristic of many economic records.

Since the sources of the R/S analysis are not readily accessible,[2] the basic definitions must be repeated. Let $X(t)$ be a stationary random function with $\sum_{\hat{u}=1}^{t} X(u)$ denoted by $X^*(t)$. For every value of d (called the lag) one defines

$$R(t,d) = \max_{0 \le u \le d} \{X^*(t+u) - X^*(t) - (u/d)[X^*(t+d) - X^*(t)]\} - \min_{0 \le u \le d} \{X^*(t+u) - X^*(t) - (u/d)[X^*(t+d) - X^*(t)]\}$$

and

---

[1] R/S symbolizes cumulative range divided by the standard deviation.

[2] Two articles by myself and J. R. Wallis: "Robustness of the Rescaled Range R/S in the Measurement of Noncyclic Long-Run Statistical Dependence," *Water Resources Research*, October 1969, pp. 967-988; and "Computer Experiments with Fractional Gaussian Noises," *Water Resources Research*, February 1969, pp. 228-267.

$$S^2(t, d) = d^{-1} \sum_{u=1}^{d} X^2(t+u) - d^{-2} [\sum_{u=1}^{d} X(t+u)]^2$$

and one forms the expression

$$\text{Ros}(d) = E[R(t, d)/S(t, d)].$$

R/S is a very useful statistic because the dependence of the function Ros(d) on the lag happens to separate the effects due to the marginal distribution of $X(t)$ and the effects due to the presence or the absence of long-run statistical dependence.

When the variables $X(t)$ are statistically independent, one has Ros(d) ~ Cd^H, with $H = 0.5$ and C a constant; ~ designates a relation valid asymptotically. When $X(t)$ is a Markov process or a more general finite autoregressive process, the relation Ros(d) ~ $Cd^{0.5}$ still holds asymptotically, but the value of C is different and the asymptotic behavior is more slowly attained than in the case of independence. Independent, Markov, and finite autoregressive processes are all such that their values at instants sufficiently apart in time are near independent. For all those processes one has: Ros(d) ~ $Cd^{0.5}$, where C is affected by the precise rule of interdependences, but the exponent is $H = 0.5$ irrespective of the marginal distribution of $X(t)$. H is the same whether $X(t)$ is Gaussian or long tailed, including the cases where $X(t)$ has infinite variance.[3]

But the law Ros(d) ~ $Cd^{0.5}$ fails for random processes that generate sample functions characterized by slow swings, because for such processes the interdependence of values very far apart cannot be neglected. In the simplest cases, one has Ros(d) ~ Cd^H, where H lies between 0.5 and 1. In such cases, the value of H can be used to measure the intensity of long-run dependence, namely, the degree of "tendency to slow swinging."

[3] B. Mandelbrot, "The Variation of Certain Speculative Prices," *Journal of Business*, October 1963, pp. 394-419.

When $X(t)$ is an empirical time series of length T, the definitions of $R(t, d)$ and $S(t, d)$ remain meaningful and the expression Ros $(d) =$

$$(T\text{-}s) \sum_{t=1}^{T\text{-}s} R(t, d)/S(t, d) \text{ can be considered an}$$

estimate of Ros(d). R/S testing consists in testing whether or not the departure of Ros(d) from Ros^ (d) ~ $Cd^{0.5}$ is statistically significant. R/S estimation consists in estimating from Ros (d) the value of the exponent H that best represents Ros^ (d) in the form Cd^H.

One of the main weaknesses of conventional econometrics has been that its tools lose part or all of their validity when applied to time series whose variance is very large or infinite. The robustness of the statistic Ros(d) with respect to the marginal distribution is therefore extremely valuable. The main thrust of this study is to perfect R/S analysis for small samples and to apply it to an increasing variety of time series.

Benoit B. Mandelbrot

Analysis of Time Series

During the first few months of my tenure as a postdoctoral Research Fellow at the Bureau, I have completed two papers dealing with the analysis of economic time series. The first is "Spectral Analysis and the Detection of Lead-Lag Relations." This paper is concerned with invalid attempts by some economists to infer timing relationships between pairs of economic series directly from phase statistics calculated from the cross spectrum of the series. The paper points out fundamental differences between the engineering and economic definitions of lead and lag that have caused some confusion in the economist's interpretation of phase statistics. Assumptions about the model linking the time series play an essential role in the correct interpretation of phase statistics. This conclusion is illustrated with several explicit models. The stringent conditions required for the existence of a simple relationship between phase statistics and the economist's concept of lead and lag are briefly discussed.

The second paper is "Dynamic Equivalents of Distributed Lags." Much econometric work using distributed lags starts with loose qualitative notions that, in some manner, the effect of one variable on another is spread over time. Without further development, this approach sometimes leads economists to estimate lagged structures without much attention to dynamic considerations that make theoretical sense. This paper argues that qualitative characteristics of distributed lags can often be represented by functions that are mathematically equivalent to simple dynamic mechanisms (such as linear differential equations). These may be more fruitful for further theoretical and empirical work than the initial distributed lag formulation. Hence a careful analysis of distributed lags and equivalent dynamic systems may be a useful approach to developing better dynamic models in economics. After an introductory section, the paper discusses the formal relationship between distributed lags and other linear dynamic systems. A third section makes use of a simple example to illustrate theoretical advantages that may arise from analyzing a distributed lag system by some dynamically equivalent system. In the final section, several examples are further developed to indicate the usefulness of this approach. If distributed lags are constructed from exponentials (possibly complex) and polynomials of time, the equivalent dynamic forms reduce to differential equations (difference equations in discrete time) that may have relatively simple theoretical interpretations. Lags generated by so-called "rational polynomial generating functions" are equivalent to this class. Hence this analysis has some important implications for interpreting distributed lag coefficients of dynamic structures estimated from completely ad hoc rational polynomial generating functions.

John C. Hause

Papers on Statistical and Economic Methodology

Provisional plans have been made to publish as NBER Technical Papers two collections of papers which I wrote while a Research Fellow at the Bureau. The first collection will be on multicollinearity and measurement errors and will include the following papers (two of which have been previously published as journal articles):

1. "Multicollinearity in Regression Analysis: An Experimental Evaluation of Alternative Procedures," read at the Joint Statistical Meetings of the American Statistical Association (Section on Physical and Engineering Sciences) and the Biometric Society in August 1969

2. "On Multicollinearity in Regression Analysis: A Comment," published in *Review of Economics and Statistics,* September 1969

3. "On the Correlations Between Estimated Parameters in Linear Regression"

4. "A Note on Regression on Principal Components," published in *The American Statistician,* October 1966

5. "A Note on Regression on Principal Components and Constrained Least Squares"

6. "On Errors of Measurements in Regression Analysis"

The second Technical Paper will be devoted to missing observations in regression analysis and will include: (1) a modified and expanded version of my paper in the *Journal of the Royal Statistical Society,* No. 1, 1968, (2) "Estimation of Regression Equations when a Block of Observations is Missing," *1968 Proceedings of the Business and Economic Statistics Section* of the American Statistical Association; and a third paper entitled "On the Use of Auxiliary Information for Estimating Missing Observations in Regression," prepared jointly with Neil Wallace. Most of the theory in the last paper has been developed, but modifications are necessary in light of some results obtained by a Monte Carlo study designed to evaluate the small-sample properties of our suggested estimators.

Another research project under way is a study of the comparative properties of forecasting and estimation of time series models with the first difference transformation vs. "zero difference transformation." This is being carried on jointly with Professor P. J. Verdoorn of the Netherlands Central Planning Bureau and Rotterdam University. We plan to have it ready for publication by the end of the academic year.

Finally, a computer program for Monte Carlo studies entitled "REGEN-Computer Program to Generate Multivariate Observations for Linear Regression Equations," prepared jointly with Sidney Jacobs of the Data Processing Unit, has been reviewed by a staff reading committee. After revision, it will be submitted for publication as a Technical Paper.

Yoel Haitovsky

Experimentation with Nonlinear Regression Programs

Available programs to estimate a nonlinear equation of the form

$$Y = \alpha M^{\eta_1}(1 + r_1)^t X_1 + \beta M^{\eta_2}(1 + r_2)^t X_2$$

have proven unsatisfactory in two respects: they use too much machine time, and some of the estimated coefficient values are unrealistic. We have found it preferable to program our own method for estimating this equation. Our program computes the two modified Cobb-Douglas terms at points in a grid of parameter values for the parameters η_1, r_1, η_2, and r_2. At each grid point selected, the two nonlinear terms enter into a linear regression in which α and β are estimated; this determines what area of the grid is to be searched more closely. The search procedure converges to a best grid point. Substantial computer time is saved by tailoring the program to the specific equation at hand.

In principle, the method could be generalized to handle any nonlinear equation, but this would reduce the saving of machine time. A more promising approach to a general nonlinear regression program proceeds by making a first-order approximation of the regression, using the first partials of the equation with respect to the parameters to be estimated. A linear regression in these partials is run, obtaining a correction to the initial guess of the parameters. By successive approximations, convergence to parameter estimates is achieved.[1] If any of the estimated values lie outside of their expected range, one should repeat the regression with boundary constraints on the parameters. Even if the results fall within the expected range, it may be worthwhile to experiment with alternative boundry constraints.

While this method is used in some existing nonlinear regression programs, we are incorporating several innovations:

1. The nonlinear regression equation will usually be analytic in the parameters. Hence the variance-covariance matrix of partials can be computed by first-order approximation formulas applied to the variance-covariance matrix of the original variables.[2] The original matrix is computed just once, at the beginning of the program; thereafter the program need no longer refer to the individual observations. When the number of observations is large, this procedure will result in substantial savings of computer time. It may be desirable, however, to recompute the exact matrix from the original observations periodically, after a specified number of iterations, to prevent the procedure from going astray.

2. The program operates in a thoroughly conversational manner, via keyboard terminal. It requests data as needed, offers alternative modes of operation, and asks what to do next—all in plain English. Thus the program explains itself to the user as it runs, and requires no previous study of instruction manuals. In the con-

---

[1] E. J. Williams, *Regression Analysis,* 1967, pp. 60-62.

[2] M. G. Kendall and A. Stuart, *The Advanced Theory of Statistics,* Vol. 1, 1963, pp. 231-232.

versational mode, the user sees his answers almost immediately and can decide on the spot what further equations he may want to run on the same or other data.

3. The program language used is APL, which is particularly suited to the conversational mode and which offers a highly condensed notation for mathematical operations. A typical sixty-line page of FORTRAN statements can usually be expressed in two or three lines of APL statements.

Parts of the above innovations have been successfully tested in a prototype APL regression program written for the IBM-1130.

Sidney Jacobs

A Study of the Properties of the Minimum-Sum-of-Absolute-Errors Estimator

In this study, an attempt is being made to determine the sampling distribution of the minimum-sum-of-absolute-errors (MSAE) estimator of the parameters of a linear regression. The estimator is known to out-perform the least-squares estimator in applications where disturbances are characterized by very dense extreme tails, as, for example, where the disturbances follow the symmetric stable distributions with characteristic parameter α very much less than two. Mandelbrot has argued persuasively that such fat-tailed distributions are the appropriate model for many economic processes, which suggests that MSAE may be a good estimator for economists to employ.

Developing a sampling theory for MSAE is made difficult by the fact that there exists no analytic expression for the MSAE estimator. Instead, it is calculated via a linear-programming algorithm. However, by utilizing some results on the distributions of order statistics, it should be possible to characterize the asymptotic distribution of the MSAE estimator. Monte Carlo experiments can then be used to supplement the asymptotic results and enable us to assess how seriously the small-sample distributions seem to depart from the asymptotic distributions.

Reports on some preliminary work on this topic are contained in last year's *Annual Report*, as well as in a forthcoming volume of *Econometrica*. The study is being conducted jointly with Robert Blattberg of the University of Chicago.

Thomas J. Sargent

10. ELECTRONIC COMPUTER SERVICES IN SUPPORT OF ECONOMIC RESEARCH

Introduction

The Bureau's electronic data processing operations encompass a large variety of activities, such as programming, consulting, and other services connected with individual research projects; improvement of data storage and retrieval; and development of programmed approaches to statistical problems. While major services are provided in response to internal demands, we are increasingly attempting to make our resources available to outsiders.

In the supporting operations there are three developments worth pointing out: (1) with the increasing size and complexity of data sets received from government agencies and other sources, data retrieval has become more important and more difficult; (2) the fact that programming is taught in schools and universities has led to an increase in the importance of our consulting functions as compared with our programming activities; (3) easier access to various computer systems, via remote terminals and time-sharing, has increased the necessity for system selection, job channeling, and similar operations. These changes are described below in the report on the activities of the E.D.P. unit.

The availability of ever-increasing quantities of statistical data requires the development of efficient methods for data retrieval and manipulation, as well as of the documentation describing the meaning, the coverage, and other characteristics of the data. New methods of storage, retrieval, presentation, and documentation are described by Richard and Nancy Ruggles in their report on project RIPP. Our effort to facilitate the accessibility and manipulation of the Bureau's time series collection is described in my report on the National Bureau's data bank. A third approach to developing more efficient methods is that pursued in the newly organized Universities-National Bureau Conference on the Application of the Computer to Economic Research, reported on in Part III of this report.

Several new programs and improvements of old programs were developed during the report period, particularly in reference to business cycle analysis. A description of our efforts in this area is found below.

Another effort is aimed at the improvement of nonlinear regression programs. A major shortcoming of existing programs is that the accommodation of nonlinear relationships involves large expenditure of effort and machine time. Our attempts to remedy this condition are described by Sidney Jacobs in Section 9 of this report.

Charlotte Boschan

Operations of the Data Processing Unit

The use of electronic computers in the Bureau's research operations continues to increase. Our small IBM-1130 computer is being used for at least two shifts. In addition, we are using computing facilities of Yale, Columbia, various other universities, and some commercial service bureaus. The most important of these operations, those at Yale, are described below by Sanford Berg. Access to some of these facilities is via remote terminal. In view of the increasing importance of time-sharing arrangements, particularly in connection with data bank operations, we are always experimenting with new systems in order to establish their relative efficiency and cost. These experiments are helping us to select the systems most appropriate for our operations.

A significant change in the operations of the E.D.P. unit has been brought about by the trend towards large data sets. Much of the work done in the Bureau's research projects requires retrieval of data from magnetic tapes and involves various storing and merging operations. These tapes are originally generated by a large number of different systems with different characteristics; the lack of standardization, or even compatibility, makes merging information from two different sources a somewhat complicated undertaking, particularly if neither source is compatible with our own computer system. These conditions emphasize the need for standardization and documentation, planned for the future by Richard and Nancy Ruggles. At present, however, a large part of our time is spent in writing tape utility programs for various machines and in helping researchers to handle heterogeneous data sets.

Because many research projects now have their own programmers, whose skills range from simple coding to sophisticated programming, our central programming staff, instead of writing ad hoc programs for one-time use, spends considerable time in teaching, advising, and assisting. Among our supporting operations is electronic charting on a Calcomp Plotter attached to the IBM-1130. This operation is increasingly replacing hand charting, both for analysis and for publications.

In principle, all members of the data processing unit are taking part in all its operations. To the extent that there is specialization, Lora Weinstein and Susan Crayne do counseling; mathematical and complicated statistical matters are handled by Sidney Jacobs; Antonette Delak takes care of charting operations including some programming; and Irene Abramson helps with operations, programming, and maintenance of the 1130. Assistance and advice concerning the operation of the IBM-1130 is given by Martha Jones, who also handles the unit-record equipment, and Dora Thompson takes care of card and paper-tape punching.

Charlotte Boschan

NBER Computer Operations at New Haven

The NBER computer operations at New Haven consist of three parts: (1) development of administrative information processing, ADMIN (2) development of research information processing, RIPP, and (3) support of current research activities.

In the ADMIN project, we are exploring ways to computerize administrative tasks and information dissemination processes. At the present stage of development, computer programs exist to create labels for mass mailings to specified classes of NBER subscribers and to facilitate budgeting operations. A description of the RIPP project is contained in the report by Richard and Nancy Ruggles.

The use of Yale computer facilities by NBER research projects has increased. Daily United Parcel delivery service is connecting New York and New Haven operations. While we have not the staff to handle substantial debugging of programs, all output is examined so that minor changes might be made if it appears that this will result in a successful run. A series of seminars has been initiated in order to introduce NBER staff members in New York to Yale's IBM-360/50. Warren Sanderson presented the first seminar on the general principles of this system. Later seminars will examine programming techniques and research strategy within the framework of an interactive computer system.

Sanford Berg

Progress Report on Project RIPP

The Research Information Processing Project (RIPP) has been set up by the National Bureau to develop computer techniques for large scale storing and retrieving of information useful in economic research. The function of the project is to provide for the long-run development of computer capabilities rather than to assist in the day-to-day problems encountered by specific research programs.

A major portion of the project is focused on the development and utilization of machine readable documentation systems. These documentation systems are concerned with handling three kinds of information. First, the time series which the National Bureau has on hand are being documented in such a manner that they can be processed and retrieved by standard programs and used in conjunction with existing statistical packages designed for analyzing time series. Second, methods of generating worksheets and tables in machine readable form are being developed so that the research analyst can call on such information and produce tabulations suitable for further research or publication. Finally, work is under way on the development of machine readable documentation describing the organization and content of magnetic tape and disk files so that they can be accessed and operated upon by standard programs.

The project is considered to be part of the development work underlying the National Bureau's effort to create a machine readable data library for research purposes. Although the problems involved are basic to any computer configuration and to the statistical processing of any body of research data, the work is geared to random access third generation computers, in particular the IBM-360/50 at Yale University.

Richard Ruggles
Nancy D. Ruggles

The National Bureau Data Bank

The National Bureau makes a part of its collection of time series available in the form of a machine readable data bank. Users may be outsiders as well as members of the Bureau's staff. At present this data bank contains about 1,000 monthly and quarterly time series. We plan to increase the collection to about 1,500 series by the end of 1970. Series are updated and revised as soon as the data become available. A list of the available series can be provided.

Typically, the outside user belongs to a group centered around a computer system; access to the data base is obtained via remote terminals or other means. This arrangement is advantageous for the outside user as well as for the Bureau. For the user it permits the sharing of transmission cost, storage cost, software development, and so forth; for the Bureau it reduces the effort involved in the mechanical transmission of updating. At present, only one user organization (Project Economics, on the Rapidata System) uses the NBER data bank; the Information Service Department of General Electric has about completed arrangements for a similar relationship on their own computer system, and other user groups have approached the Bureau. Some outsiders use the data bank as individual subscribers, e.g., the Department of Economic Research of IBM.

The National Bureau is compensated for its services through a fee paid by the individual user; each user must agree to a set of specified terms of cooperation. Academic users pay a nominal fee for once-a-month tape service. These fees do not include any costs incurred by users in connection with the services of their computer system.

Day-to-day operations of the data bank are supervised by Peggy Cahn. Hanna Stern is working on source material and data documentation. Others involved in the project are Constance Lim, Young Lee and Wan-Lee Hsu (updating and revisions), Dorothy O'Brien (seasonal adjustments, checking for comparability), and Lora Weinstein (computer operations).

Charlotte Boschan

Programmed Determination of Cyclical Turning Point and Timing Measures

Determination of turning points. The program for the determination of specific cyclical turns in individual time series, developed by Gerhard Bry and myself, has been used in various Bureau projects and stands up rather well.[1] There are, however, a few shortcomings which should be known to prospective users, although they show up infrequently.

The program may designate shallow fluctuations as cyclical, even in series that typically exhibit steep cycles. On occasion, this might be undesirable. However, we hesitate to modify the program, since shallow fluctuations might well have become a characteristic of present-day economic developments.

Another problem arises in connection with the use of the program for the analysis of current business conditions; the program reflects considerable caution in recognizing turns close to the end of a series. In order to avoid recognizing temporary reversals as cyclical, the program requires at least six months of reversed direction. This conflicts with the need for early recognition of cyclical changes in individual series and in the economy as a whole. Rather than change criteria, we shall provide options to the user for varying the duration of reversals required for recognizing turns.

Finally, in excluding turns associated with "short" phases (less than five months), the alternative peak selected by the program may be lower than the eliminated one, or the alternative trough may be higher. This result is justified if the eliminated turn is randomly extreme but not if it reflects a cyclical reversal. Further experience with this problem may lead to program modification.

Timing relationships. Timing comparisons describe the relationship among cyclical turning points in different economic time series.

---

[1] The program is described in the forthcoming book by Gerhard Bry and Charlotte Boschan on "Cyclical Analysis of Time Series: Selected Procedures and Computer Programs."

These comparisons are carried out by determining leads, lags, and coincidences of cyclical turns in specific time series relative to reference turning points (which may be turns in business conditions at large or turns in a designated reference activity).

It might appear that the determination of timing measures is simple, once the specific and reference turns are established. This is indeed the case, if the series is identified as positively or inversely conforming, if every specific turn can be matched with a reference turn, and vice versa, and if no opposite turns occur between matching peaks and between matching troughs. However, a number of difficulties occur when these conditions are not met; these, in fact, led to the prediction that timing comparisons would prove intractable to a programmed approach. The primary problem is to determine which specific turn should be related to which reference turn. This decision may involve many considerations, such as proximity, typical timing behavior at other turns, and amplitudes. In the present program, which is still in the early stages of development, we restricted the decision rules to proximity and typical timing, but we shall consider other criteria if this proves necessary. We are fairly confident that timing comparisons can be successfully programmed.

Charlotte Boschan

III

Conferences on Research

Conference on Research in Income and Wealth

The conference volume, *Education, Income, and Human Capital,* W. Lee Hansen, editor, is to be published in the fall of 1970. Papers prepared for the Conference on Econometric Models of Cyclical Behavior, held at Harvard University in November 1969, have been revised and will soon undergo preparation for press. A small "follow-up" conference was held on February 27, 1970, to discuss the completed results of the Zarnowitz/Boschan/Moore paper on "Business Cycle Analysis of Econometric Model Simulations." Future research growing out of the Econometric Models Conference was also discussed.

On May 21-22, 1970, the Conference on International Comparisons of Prices and Real Incomes, under the chairmanship of D. J. Daly, was held at the Keele Street Campus of York University. The program consisted of:

The Theory of International Comparisons of Prices and Real Output
    Sidney Afriat, University of North Carolina

The Comparative National Income of the U.S.S.R. and the U.S.A.
    A. Bergson, Harvard University

The Role of Prices in Trade
    I. B. Kravis and R. E. Lipsey, NBER

International Price Comparison of Selected Capital Goods Industries
    Barend A. deVries, International Bank for Reconstruction and Development

Price Differences and Economic Integration in Latin America
    J. Grunwald and J. Salazar, Brookings Institution

Relative Prices in Planning for Economic Development
    Gustav Ranis, Yale University

A Conference on Measurement of Economic and Social Performance has been authorized by the Executive Committee, tentatively for the fall of 1971. The Program Committee consists of Milton Moss (Chairman), F. Thomas Juster, and Dale W. Jorgenson.

Members of the Executive Committee are: Harold W. Watts (Chairman), Edward C. Budd, Jean B. Crockett, W. Lee Hansen, Dale W. Jorgenson, F. Thomas Juster, Maurice Liebenberg, Herman P. Miller, Stephen P. Taylor, Malcolm C. Urquhart, and Mildred E. Courtney (Secretary).

Universities-National Bureau Committee for Economic Research

The Conference on International Mobility and Movement of Capital was held January 30-February 1, 1970, at the Brookings Institution, Washington, D.C. Fritz Machlup was chairman of the Conference planning committee whose members were Richard N. Cooper, Ilse Mintz, Walter S. Salant, David W. Slater, and Edward S. Shaw. The Conference proceedings are being prepared for publication.

The Conference volume, *The Role of Agriculture in Economic Development,* Erik Thorbecke, editor, was published in February 1970. Proceedings of the two later conferences are expected to be published later this year under the titles, *The Technology Factor in International Trade,* Raymond Vernon, editor, and *The Analysis of Public Output,* Julius Margolis, editor.

The annual meeting of the Universities-National Bureau Committee for Economic Research was held on January 30, 1970, in conjunction with the Conference on International Mobility and Movement of Capital. A Conference on Education as an Industry, Joseph Froomkin, chairman, was tentatively scheduled to be held in the spring of 1971. A Conference on Secular Inflation was authorized at the meeting and tentatively scheduled to be held during the fall of 1971. Jürg Niehans is chairman of the planning committee.

In addition, conditional authorization for a Conference on Poverty and Welfare Systems was approved at the annual meeting, with the Executive Committee of the Universities-National Bureau Committee delegated the power to approve it after a revised exploratory committee report has been presented.

The Universities-National Bureau Committee expressed its interest in two other exploratory committee proposals and voted to return them to the committees for further elaboration. The proposals dealt with potential conferences on Security Prices, Henry Latané, chairman, and on Medical Care, Herbert E. Klarman, chairman. Further, the Committee authorized the creation of an exploratory committee to investigate a potential future conference on the Economics of Environmental Quality, Edwin S. Mills, chairman. Reports recommending or rejecting conferences on these subjects will be presented to the next annual meeting of the Universities-National Bureau Committee for Economic Research, tentatively scheduled for the spring of 1971.

Thirty-seven universities offering graduate work in economics and emphasizing research, together with the National Bureau, are represented on the Committee. The Conference program is assisted by a grant from the National Science Foundation. The participating universities and their present representatives are:

Buffalo	Daniel Hamberg
California, Berkeley	John M. Letiche
California, Los Angeles	J. C. La Force
Carnegie-Mellon	Norman Miller
Chicago	H. Gregg Lewis
Columbia	Phillip Cagan
Cornell	George J. Staller
Duke	John O. Blackburn
Harvard	James S. Duesenberry
Illinois	Marvin Frankel
Indiana	Robert W. Campbell
Iowa State	Dudley G. Luckett
Johns Hopkins	Carl F. Christ
Massachusetts Institute of Technology	Richard S. Eckaus
McGill	A. Deutsch
Michigan State	Carl E. Liedholm
Michigan	Harvey E. Brazer
Minnesota	James M. Henderson
New School for Social Research	Thomas Vietorisz
New York	Bruno Stein
North Carolina	Henry A. Latané
Northwestern	Richard B. Heflebower
Ohio State	Jon Cunnyngham
Pennsylvania	Almarin Phillips
Pittsburgh	Jacob Cohen
Princeton	Albert Rees
Queen's	David C. Smith
Rochester	Richard N. Rosett
Stanford	Moses Abramovitz
Texas	Wendell C. Gordon
Toronto	D. C. MacGregor
Vanderbilt	Rendigs Fels
Virginia	Richard T. Selden
Washington (Seattle)	Yoram Barzel
Washington (St. Louis)	Werner Hochwald
Wisconsin	Leonard W. Weiss
Yale	Richard Ruggles

Other members of the Committee elected as members at large for a four-year term, July 1, 1970 to June 30, 1974, are: Daniel Creamer, Simon Goldberg, George Jaszi, Rudolf R. Rhomberg, Walter S. Salant, Julius Shiskin, and George J. Stigler. Robert E. Lipsey is the representative from the National Bureau of Economic Research.

The members of the Executive Committee are Carl F. Christ (Chairman), Walter S. Salant (Vice Chairman), Moses Abramovitz, Rendigs Fels, James M. Henderson, Robert E. Lipsey, and Almarin Phillips. Robert P. Shay is Secretary.

Universities interested in membership on the Universities-National Bureau Committee for Economic Research should get in touch with the Chairman of the Universities-National Bureau Committee, indicating by letter the extent to which they meet the criteria for membership. These criteria are: (a) The extent to which graduate training in economics is given as indicated by the awarding of the Ph.D. degree in economics; (b) The extent to which economic research is emphasized, supported, and carried on at the institution.

If accepted for membership the University will be invited, by letter addressed to the appropriate university officer, usually the chairman of the Department of Economics, to designate a member of its faculty to serve on the Committee. It is understood that the University will provide for its representative's expenses when attending the annual meeting of the Committee.

Universities-National Bureau Conference on the Application of the Computer to Economic Research

The first meeting of the Universities-National Bureau Conference on the Application of the Computer to Economic Research was held on February 26, 1970, at the National Bureau. The topic of the meeting was the exchange of information about various economic data banks and their methods of retrieval. The following data banks were represented: The Brookings Institution, Bureau of Labor Statistics, Data Resources Inc., Dominion Bureau of Statistics, I.B.M. Corporation, National Bureau of Economic Research, University of California (Berkeley), University of Michigan, and the University of Wisconsin. The central issues considered were to define areas of duplication among the data banks and to set up some ad hoc committees to follow up specific suggestions, such as the standardization of procedures for transferring data among the various research institutions. The description of the data banks and their methods of retrieval were presented and discussed during the meeting, and the proceedings of the conference will be made available to the interested research institutions. The next conference will be held in October of 1970, and it will focus on the problems in the usage of microdata in economic analysis.

IV

Report on New Publications

Introduction

Since June 1969 thirteen reports on research conducted by the staff and three conference volumes have been published. Four research reports and two conference volumes are in press.

Two issues of the *National Bureau Report,* each accompanied by a research supplement, have been issued in the past year. The supplements included the following:

The Evaluation and Planning of Social Programs—John R. Meyer (Supplement to *Report No. 5)*

NBER 50th Anniversary Dinner Proceedings, February 27, 1970 (Supplement to *Report No. 6)*

Publications issued since June 1969 and those forthcoming by mid-1971 are listed below.

Joan R. Tron

Reports Published Since June 1969

Essays on Interest Rates, Volume 1, Jack M. Guttentag and Phillip Cagan, editors (General Series 88, 1969, xxvi + 282 pp., $10.00).

Each of the six essays in this volume is concerned with a different aspect of interest rates; together they form a comprehensive study of the field as a whole. The two essays on the mortgage market—one by Jack Guttentag on residential mortgages, one by Royal Shipp on nonresidential mortgages—are drawn from larger studies that will be forthcoming. Phillip Cagan's three essays are products of his study of the cyclical behavior of interest rates. The Joseph Conard-Mark Frankena essay examines the *prima facie* puzzling fact that new corporate bond issues carry a higher yield than similar outstanding issues. The essays, although different in approach and method, have the common objective of illuminating some aspect of the effect of financial variables on economic activity, and the efficiency of financial markets.

The Design of Economic Accounts, by Nancy and Richard Ruggles (General Series 89, 1970, xvi + 184 pp., $8.00).

In response to society's need for measures of economic progress and guidelines for future policy, elaborate systems of economic accounting have evolved over the past decades. In this survey of present United States and United Nations accounts, Nancy and Richard Ruggles make specific recommendations for the design of future national economic accounting systems. More than just a general framework into which different kinds of data can be fitted, the proposed system is built around specific economic constants and, in considering economic activity in terms of the interrelations between enterprises, government, and households, it provides a means for interrelating economic accounts not only in these areas but with many other kinds of information, both economic and social.

The Behavior of Industrial Prices, by George J. Stigler and James K. Kindahl (General Series 90, 1970, xvi + 202 pp., $7.50).

This comparison of the behavior of industrial price indexes involved the creation of a new index, using somewhat different procedures and sources of data than those used by the Bureau of Labor Statistics, and comparing the results with the BLS index. Whereas the BLS obtains from the sellers of the products a few well-defined "typical" prices and transactions, the prices for the new index are obtained from the buyers. Since it is seldom that any two buyers will purchase the identical physical product, to say nothing of the other terms of the transaction, this study combines the diverse prices into one index. In short, the BLS lets the well-defined product represent the class of product, while the NBER index combines the prices paid by buyers for similar products within the class. The resulting indexes were compared over the ten-year period 1957-66 for cyclical responsiveness, trend, and short-run fluctuation.

Home Mortgage Delinquency and Foreclosures, by John P. Herzog and James S. Earley (General Series 91, 1970, xx + 170 pp., $7.50).

This National Bureau study evaluates the significance of various loan and borrower characteristics culled from the data of some 13,000 conventional FHA and VA mortgage loans made throughout the United States since 1946, in an effort to determine their individual relationship to the risk of delinquency and foreclosure. Among the variables examined are: loan purpose, the presence or absence of junior financing, loan-to-value ratio, loan type, initial maturity of loan, and borrower age and occupation.

The Business Cycle in a Changing World, by Arthur F. Burns (Studies in Business Cycles 18, 1969, xvi + 352 pp., $8.50).

"Economic change is a law of life," says Arthur Burns in the opening essay of this memorial volume. The essays in the book draw upon the research and thinking of an economist who has devoted the major portion of his professional life to study of the nature and causes of prosperity and depression. The writing provides a scholarly and scientific review of the factors that have long needed to be considered in shaping policy toward the goal of a rapid economic growth and a high level of employment without inflation. Collectively, the essays may be viewed as diagnoses of economic problems, though they do not represent policy recommendations. The first article summarizes Burns' views of the business cycle as well as those held by other economists today. The twelve following reports illuminate that review by illustrating more specifically many of its propositions and findings. The National Bureau of Economic Research, celebrating its Fiftieth Anniversary in 1970, presents this compilation of Dr. Burns' writings in honor of his dedicated service to the research and administration of the Bureau during most of its history.

Economic Forecasts and Expectations: Analyses of Forecasting Behavior and Performance, Jacob Mincer, editor (Studies in Business Cycles 19, 1969, xix + 251 pp., $10.00).

What will happen to GNP, prices, interest rates, and unemployment rates over the near term is a matter of deep concern and interest to the business community, the government, and the public. Certainly the forecasts of these economic factors have a powerful influence on the behavior of those who make use of them. There has, however, been very little systematic analysis of the forecasts themselves. We do not know, for example, how accurate they have actually been, which types of forecasts tend to be more reliable, and how the forecasts themselves are generated. What can we tell from forecasts about the expectations held by business and consumers? Are the expectations and plans of economic units a reliable basis for predicting future behavior? These are only some of the questions explored in this collection of essays, the fourth in a series of National Bureau studies on short-term economic forecasting. Taken together, the studies focus on methods of determining forecast accuracy, analysis of the errors most commonly met and the reasons for them, and attempts to determine the factors that influence forecasters in the creation of their projections. Contributors to the volume include F. Thomas Juster, Victor Zarnowitz, Jacob Mincer, Rosanne Cole, and Stanley Diller.

Monetary Statistics of the United States: Estimates, Sources, Methods, by Milton Friedman and Anna J. Schwartz (Studies in Business Cycles 20, 1970, xxii + 629 pp., $15.00).

Together with the authors' earlier *A Monetary History of the United States, 1867-1960,* the present volume forms part of what will eventually be a series of five volumes devoted to the study of the quantity of money in the United States. While the previous volume analyzed the role of changes in the money stock in the nation's history, this book provides a compendium of estimates of the quantity of money in the United States, together with a thorough treatment of the historical background, the sources of data, and the techniques for the construction of estimates of the quantity of money at any given time.

Errors in Provisional Estimates of Gross National Product, by Rosanne Cole (Studies in Business Cycles 21, 1970, xiv + 109 pp., $6.00).

Economists concerned with the dependability of gross national product information will observe with interest this study of some of the sources of measurement error connected with present forecasting methods; as well as its examination of the potential of later revisions of provisional estimates in reducing such errors. Among the errors to which particular attention is given are those connected with the measurement of the major components of GNP, the gathering of quarterly data, and the estimation of cyclical changes and long-term rates of growth. The author also examines the degree to which preliminary estimates have improved in accuracy during the postwar period. Miss Cole's book, the latest in a series of NBER publications on short-term forecasting, also presents an error model which illustrates the types of error GNP estimates may contain, as well as some of the properties of those errors.

Dating Postwar Business Cycles: Methods and Their Application to Western Germany, 1950-67, by Ilse Mintz (Occasional Paper 107, 1970, xiv + 111 pp., $3.75).

This new study of the German economy reveals clearly that cycles, although milder ones, continue to manifest themselves, despite the absence of absolute declines in activity. The author shows that the German economy, despite a strong upward trend, experienced three and one-half well-marked cycles in the period from 1950 to 1967. Observers of the German economy have characterized certain periods as times of relatively rapid change. The concepts and methods used in this study pinpoint these periods more precisely. Mintz is able to identify, in each instance, a particular date at which the German economy turned from relatively rapid to relatively slow growth, or vice versa. Reference dates of this sort facilitate the analysis of cyclical changes in the German economy as they have done in the past for the United States economy.

The Seasonal Variation of Interest Rates, by Stanley Diller (Occasional Paper 108, 1970, xv + 112 pp., $4.50).

In this examination of variations in interest rates, Stanley Diller finds considerable evidence of seasonal movements in both long- and short-term rates during the period 1955-60. While the indicators of seasonality are less distinct before 1955 and after 1960, the author finds reasonable grounds for concluding that seasonal variations (with a much smaller amplitude) existed in the two or three years on either side of this period. Further, recent evidence suggests a recurrence of seasonal variation in interest rates within the last few years. An interesting aspect of this study is the author's demonstration of the ways in which the incidence and extent of the seasonal in Treasury bill rates is related to the seasonal amplitude of money supply and total bills outstanding, indicating that variations in the seasonal patterns of both money supply and government borrowing contribute to the sharp rise and subsequent decline in the size of the seasonal swing in interest rates.

The Value of Time in Passenger Transportation: The Demand for Air Travel, by Reuben Gronau (Occasional Paper 109, 1970, xiv + 74 pp., $4.00).

This report, essentially an outgrowth of investigations concerning the effect of time limitations on economic behavior, is related to previous NBER work done in connection with the service industries, where the value of time plays an important role. Gronau limits his investigation to the issue of passenger demand for air transportation. One of the results of his research concerns the way the price of time affects the choice between air transportation and other modes of travel, as well as the related question of the various ways in which differing groups estimate the value of their time. In conclusion, it considers the application of the price of time to several problems currently facing policy makers in transportation, most importantly the impact of the new supersonic plane and the increases in train speed.

The Changing Position of Philanthropy in the American Economy, by Frank G. Dickinson (Occasional Paper 110, 1970, xii + 214 pp., $8.00).

In this volume, which presents the follow-up study to his earlier *Philanthropy and the Public Policy* (1962), the late Frank G. Dickinson continues his investigation into philanthropy in the American economy, this time during the period 1929-59. An extensive introduction by Solomon Fabricant examines the basic premises on which Dickinson conducted his study, with particular attention to the items comprised in Dickinson's definition of philanthropy, the validity of his estimates, and the soundness of the conclusions based upon them. Fabricant also enlarges on the motivational aspects and provides an explanation for the significant increase of nearly 300 per cent in dollars of constant purchasing power which Dickinson traced during the period.

Economic Factors in the Growth of Corporation Giving, by Ralph L. Nelson (Occasional Paper 111, 1970, xvii + 113 pp., $6.50*).

Changes in corporate attitudes toward giving reflect changes in the role of the business corporation not only as an economic unit but also as a social institution shaped by noneconomic forces. This study examines the growth of corporate giving from the period 1936 through 1964 and measures the separate effects of changes in corporate attitudes and giving behavior; as well as developments of a more strictly economic character. The author pays particular attention to the complex noneconomic role that the corporation—particularly the large corporation—plays in society. The corporation is viewed as a citizen responsible to its several constituencies of employees, shareholders, customers, suppliers, government, and general society.

Education, Income, and Human Capital, by W. Lee Hansen, editor (Income and Wealth Conference 35, 1970, x + 320 pp., $10.00).

The objective of these conference papers is to take stock of our knowledge of a subject of rapidly growing interest—the relationship between education and income and the role of the human-capital approach in illuminating these relationships. This volume attempts to pull together what has been learned and to plot some of the directions that future research on this subject should take. The work itself spills over into a wide range of fields, among them economic theory, production economics, public finance, labor economics, and development. Through much of this work there are two underlying themes: (1) there are important links between education and productivity – and therefore income; and (2) the role of education can be fruitfully explored when viewed as an income-generating form of human capital. Contributors to the volume include Samuel Bowles, Zvi Griliches, Yoram Ben-Porath, Barry R. Chiswick, Peter B. Kenen, Anthony Scott, Theodore W. Schultz, and W. Lee Hansen.

The Role of Agriculture in Economic Development, Erik Thorbecke, editor (Universities-NBER Conference 21, 1970, x + 480 pp., $12.50).

In 1967, a Universities-NBER conference was held for the purpose of examining the relationship between agriculture and foreign trade at regional, national, and global levels. Three main subject areas were emphasized and also eventually became the basis for the

---

* Published jointly with the Russell Sage Foundation.

reports published in this volume: agriculture in the world economy, the relationship between agriculture and other sectors, and national studies analyzing the transformation of traditional agriculture. Contributors to the volume include Louis M. Goreux, J. A. C. Brown, Karl A. Fox, John C. H. Fei, Gustav Ranis, Alfred J. Field, Jan Sandee, Jerzy F. Karcz, Kazushi Ohkawa, Bruce F. Johnston, John Cownie, William H. Nicholls, and Hylke Van de Wetering.

The Technology Factor in International Trade, Raymond Vernon, editor (Universities-NBER Conference 22, 1970, x + 535 pp., $15.00).

For the last two decades, the evolution of international trade theory has been marked by the increasingly important role of technology. Although the importance of this factor has long been recognized, it was not until the advent of large-scale data processing that real progress could be made towards accommodating it. At about the same time, the introduction of the Leontief Paradox gave additional stimulus to empirical testing. These two developments brought about a torrent of new research. To meet this challenge, the Universities-National Bureau Committee prepared the conference, held in October 1968, of which this book is the result. The value of this volume to those concerned with international trade theory lies in its recapitulation of what has been accomplished to date, and in its crystallization of the key problems for further research.

Publications Forthcoming

New Series on Home Mortgage Yields Since 1951, by Jack M. Guttentag and Morris Beck.

Demand-Policy Responsiveness to the Balance of Payments: The Postwar Pattern, by Michael Michaely.

Analysis of Public Output (Universities-NBER Conference), Julius Margolis, editor.

Cyclical Analysis of Time Series, by Gerhard Bry and Charlotte Boschan.

Price Competitiveness in World Trade, by Irving B. Kravis and Robert E. Lipsey.

Fluctuations in Job Vacancies: An Analysis of Available Measures, by Charlotte Boschan.

Measures of Credit Risk and Experience, by Edgar R. Fiedler

The Postwar Quality of State and Local Debt, by George H. Hempel.

Econometric Models of Cyclical Behavior (Income and Wealth Conference), Bert Hickman, editor.

International Mobility and Movement of Capital (Universities-NBER Conference), Fritz Machlup, Walter S. Salant, and Lorie Tarshis, editors.

V

Organization

Directors and Officers

The annual meeting of the Board of Directors, held on September 19 and 20, 1969, was coordinated with a staff conference at which seventy members of the research staff participated in a comprehensive review of work in process and in prospect. Developments in the research program were further considered by the Board at their special meeting on April 27, 1970. Three meetings of the Executive Committee were held during the year to take actions within the general policies approved by the Board.

At the annual meeting, three new directors at large were elected: David L. Grove, Chief Economist, International Business Machines Corporation; James J. O'Leary, Executive Vice President and Economist, United States Trust Company of New York, and Lazare Teper, Director, Research Department of the International Ladies' Garment Workers' Union. Arthur F. Burns, who had resigned from Columbia University and as that University's representative director, was also elected a director at large.

With the annual meeting, Albert J. Hettinger, Jr. became a director emeritus. He was honored by his colleagues for his continuous service since 1953 as a member of the Board, the Executive Committee, and the Finance Committee. He had also served as Vice President and Chairman of the Board. Mr. Hettinger continues to serve as a member of the Finance Committee and Chairman of the Fiftieth Anniversary Committee.

Upon nomination by Columbia University, Gary S. Becker was elected to complete the term of representative director from which Arthur F. Burns had resigned. Thomas A. Wilson was elected as the University of Toronto's representative director to replace Douglas G. Hartle who had resigned from that University.

The Board amended the section of the by-laws relating to the election of directors who are nominated by universities. In the past, directors by university appointment have been nominated by specific universities which had been designated by resolutions of the Board, and fifteen universities had been so designated. It was not deemed advisable to increase the number of directors by university appointment above fifteen, but it was decided to broaden the group of institutions from which these directors could be selected. Accordingly the by-laws were changed to provide that directors by university appointment shall be nominated by any university which is represented on the Universities-National Bureau Committee for Economic Research and which is invited to submit a nomination by the National Bureau's nominating committee.

Willard L. Thorp was re-elected director by appointment of the American Economic Association. The Board also added the Canadian Economics Association to the organizations that are designated to nominate directors. Douglas G. Hartle was subsequently nominated by the Canadian Economics Association, and he was elected as their representative director by the Bureau's Executive Committee on November 24, 1969.

Officers elected at the annual meeting were: Arthur F. Burns, Honorary Chairman, Theodore O. Yntema, Chairman, Walter W. Heller, Vice Chairman, John R. Meyer, President, Donald B. Woodward, Treasurer, Victor R. Fuchs and F. Thomas Juster, Vice Presidents-Research, Douglas H. Eldridge, Vice President-Executive Secretary, Hal B. Lary, Director of International Studies, and Donald S.

Shoup, Director of Research Services and Planning.

In January 1970, Donald Shoup resigned from the National Bureau to assume a position with the Social Science Research Council.

By action of the Executive Committee on February 16, 1970, Edward K. Smith, of Colorado State University and formerly Deputy Assistant Secretary for Economic Policy, U.S. Department of Commerce, was elected Vice President. Hal B. Lary and Robert E. Lipsey were elected to additional positions of Vice Presidents-Research. Joan R. Tron was elected Director of Publications.

At the time of the April meeting of the Board, Donald B. Woodward resigned as Treasurer. Thomas D. Flynn was elected as his successor. A new position of Assistant Treasurer was established and Douglas H. Eldridge was elected to assume these duties.

Soma Golden, formerly assistant economics editor of *Business Week,* joined the Bureau's administrative staff in May as Assistant to the President.

The directors and the staff were saddened by the deaths during the year of three of the Bureau's distinguished directors emeriti. Harry Scherman, a director at large from 1942 to 1967, died on November 12, 1969. Harold M. Groves, who served as a director by appointment of the University of Wisconsin from 1939 to 1968, died on December 2, 1969. George Soule, a director at large from 1922 to 1967, died on April 14, 1970.

Douglas H. Eldridge

Research Fellowships

Each year the National Bureau appoints several Research Fellows who spend approximately a year at the Bureau. These fellowships are intended to provide further educational opportunities to scholars of outstanding promise, generally, but not always, at an early post-doctoral stage of their careers.

The Research Fellows for 1969-70 are:

Name	University	Area of Interest
V. K. Chetty	Columbia University	Economics of education
H. Laurence Miller, Jr.	Carleton College	Economics of information and transaction costs
Lewis Solmon	Purdue University	Economics of education
Finis Welch	Southern Methodist University	Economics of education

The following Research Fellows have been appointed for 1970-71 (or calendar year 1970 in the case of Professor Hause):

John C. Hause	University of Minnesota	Economics of education
Christopher Sims	Harvard University	Econometric studies of production functions and the construction industry
Robert Willis	Wesleyan University	Economics of population

Victor R. Fuchs

Staff Seminars

In 1968 the National Bureau inaugurated a program of weekly seminars. These meetings encourage a vigorous exchange of ideas on a wide spectrum of economic research interests. The program is designed principally as a forum for members of the staff, and also benefits from guest lectures by scholars from various universities and research institutions in the United States and abroad. A list of speakers and of the topics discussed at these seminars in the past year is given below.

M. Ishaq Nadiri	Consumption, Human Capital, and Labor Supply	July 13, 1969
Paul Taubman & Terence Wales	Ability and Education Since 1905— A Cohort Analysis	July 16, 1969
Bruce Petersen	The Balance of Trade Effects of a Value-Added Tax/Corporate Profits Tax Substitution	July 23, 1969
V. Karuppan Chetty	An International Comparison of Production Functions in Manufacturing	July 30, 1969
Neil Wallace	An Approach to the Study of Barter and Market Structures	August 6, 1969
Thomas Sargent & Neil Wallace	Market Transaction Costs, Asset Demand Functions, and the Potency of Monetary and Fiscal Policy	August 13, 1969
Paul Wachtel	Models of Durable Goods Demand	August 20, 1969
Finis Welch	The Distributional Incidence of Changes in Aggregate Employment	Sept. 3, 1969
V. Karuppan Chetty	Estimation of Distributed Lag Models	Sept. 10, 1969
Lewis Solmon	Human Capital and Aggregate Savings Behavior	Sept. 26, 1969
Roger Alcaly	Food Prices in Relation to Income in New York City	Oct. 17, 1969
Warren Sanderson	Toward an Econometric Model of the American Birth Rate: 1920-65	Oct. 24, 1969
Stephen Dresch	Intra- and Interstate Analyses of Grants-in-Aid	Oct. 31, 1969
G. S. Maddala	Some Neglected Aspects of Large Econometric Models	Nov. 7, 1969
William Landes	The Economics of the Courts: A Theoretical and Empirical Analysis	Nov. 14, 1969
Hrishikesh Vinod	Integer Programming and the Theory of Grouping	Nov. 21, 1969
Sherwin Rosen	Some Aspects of the Supply of Human Capital	Dec. 5, 1969
Lawrence Miller	Some Economics of Information	Dec. 12, 1969
Robert J. Willis	Income and Substitution Effects as Determinants of Household Fertility	Dec. 19, 1969

V. Karuppan Chetty	On the Relation Between Short-Run and Long-Run Elasticities	Jan. 9, 1970
Finis Welch	Risk, Uncertainty, and Profit	Jan. 16, 1970
Joseph Persky	Migration and Employment in Southern Metropolitan Areas	Jan. 23, 1970
Donald Straszheim	The Income and Occupational Structure of College Graduates by Academic Discipline	Jan. 30, 1970
Gregory Chow	Optimal Stochastic Control of Linear Economic Systems	Feb. 6, 1970
Hiroki Tsurumi	Effects of Wage-Parity Between Canada and the United States on the Canadian Economic Growth: Simulation Experiments With a Macro-Model	Feb. 13, 1970
Peter Temin	The Beginnings of the Depression in Germany	Feb. 20, 1970
Seiji Naya	The Economic Impact of the Vietnam Conflict on Asian Countries	March 6, 1970
Giora Hanoch	Generation of New Production Functions Through Duality	March 13, 1970
Masanori Hashimoto	State Differences in the Incidence of Cyclical and Secular Unemployment	April 3, 1970
John Hause	The Measurement of Welfare Changes or Variations on a Major Theme by Dupuit	April 10, 1970
Michael Tannen	Economic Growth and the Distribution of Labor Income: A Human Capital Approach	April 17, 1970
Thomas Wilson	Diversification Mergers and the Growth of Large Companies, 1954-58	April 28, 1970
Robert Eisner	Non-Income Income—Directions and Progress	May 8, 1970
David Gordon	The Economics of "The Promised Land": Glimpses of the Ghetto Labor Market	May 22, 1970
Zvi Griliches	Education and All That	June 2, 1970
Victor Fuchs	Male-Female Differentials in Hourly Earnings	June 5, 1970
Robert Eisner	Non-Income Income—Directions and Progress	June 10, 1970
Roger Findlay	Comparative Advantage, Effective Protection, and the Domestic Resource Cost of Foreign Exchange	June 17, 1970
Peter Workman	Biological Perspectives on Economic Problems	June 24, 1970

W. M. Landes

The National Bureau's Fiftieth Anniversary Program

Celebration of the Bureau's Fiftieth Anniversary began with a reception and dinner at the Waldorf-Astoria Hotel on Friday, February 27, 1970. Theodore O. Yntema, Chairman of the Bureau's Board of Directors, welcomed the five hundred guests and thanked them for their continued participation in and support of the National Bureau's program. He then read messages from President Nixon and former Vice President Humphrey, both of whom congratulated the Bureau on its fifty years of accomplishment. In addition, Dr. Yntema read excerpts of a letter from Dr. Harry W. Laidler, reminiscing about the Bureau's past. Dr. Laidler, former Executive Director of the League for Industrial Democracy and for fifty years editor of the "Intercollegiate Socialist," was the only surviving member of the Bureau's original Board of Directors and served as director emeritus until his death on July 14, 1970.

In recognition of his many years of outstanding service to the Bureau, Arthur F. Burns, Chairman of the Federal Reserve Board and Honorary Chairman of the Bureau's Board of Directors, attended the dinner as guest of honor. George P. Shultz, Secretary of Labor, and Wassily W. Leontief, Henry Lee Professor of Economics at Harvard University, and President of the American Economic Association, were the featured speakers of the evening. Walter W. Heller, Vice Chairman of the Bureau's Board of Directors, presided over the evening's program, which also included remarks by John R. Meyer, President of the Bureau.

In addition to Dr. Burns, two other former Directors of Research were honored for their substantial contributions to the first half-century of the Bureau's successful operation: Solomon Fabricant, who joined the Bureau in 1930 and who is now a member of the senior research staff and a professor of economics at New York University, and Geoffrey H. Moore, who has been affiliated with the Bureau since 1936 and who is currently on leave to fill the post of Commissioner of Labor Statistics.

As a continuation of the Anniversary program, six colloquia will be held during the fall of 1970, each devoted to an appraisal of research efforts in areas in which the Bureau has been involved in the past and expects to be involved in the future: business cycles, public expenditures and taxation, finance and money markets, industrial organization, human capital, and economic growth. Each colloquium is designed to bring selected business and governmental leaders together with economists for the purpose of examining past research findings and relating these findings to current and future policy issues. It is expected that new research needs within each area will become apparent as the discussions progress.

The first of the colloquia will be concerned with business cycle analysis, and it will be held at the Hotel Pierre in New York City on Thursday, September 24, 1970. The morning session will be devoted to an analysis of NBER methods of analyzing cyclical episodes. Two papers will be presented: Ilse Mintz will analyze the effect of using rates-of-change to define the business cycle and will compare the results so obtained with the more conventional absolute change definitions; Geoffrey Moore will focus on the cyclical behavior of prices. During the afternoon session, Victor Zarnowitz, Yoel Haitovsky, and Neil Wallace will present papers concerning the performance, forecasting reliability, and policy sensitivity of various econometric models. A major portion of each session will be devoted to a discussion of future research priorities. To stimulate such discussion, which will invite audience participation, Otto Eckstein, Harvard University, Henry Wallich, Yale University, and Arthur Okun of The Brookings Institution will comment on the presentations. Paul A. Samuelson of the Massachusetts Institute of Technology will serve as moderator of the proceedings. In addition, Herbert Stein, a member of the President's Council of Economic Advisers, will address the luncheon session of the business cycle colloquium.

On Friday, October 9, 1970, a colloquium on public expenditures and taxation will be held at the Wisconsin Center of the University of Wisconsin in Madison. Carl Shoup, Columbia University, will open the colloquium session with a presentation surveying the research done in this area to date, with particular reference to those research activities which relate to current policy issues. His survey paper and presentation will serve as a basis for audience and panel discussion of future research directions necessitated by current and future policy issues. Walter W. Heller will moderate and participate in the panel discussion, which will also include remarks by Richard Musgrave of Harvard University, and James Buchanan of Virginia Polytechnic Institute. Senator William Proxmire[1] will address the luncheon which will be held in conjunction with the public expenditures and taxation colloquium.

A third colloquium, on finance and money markets, will be held at Delmonico's Hotel in New York City on Thursday, October 22. John Lintner of Harvard University and the Harvard Business School will make the basic presentation. The current and future research and policy ramifications of his presentation will be explored by a panel chaired by Robert V. Roosa of Brown Brothers Harriman, and consisting of James J. O'Leary, executive vice president of the United States Trust Company of New York, and William Baumol, Princeton University. The Hon. Richard Smith, member of the U.S. Securities and Exchange Commission, will speak at the dinner session of this colloquium.

On Thursday, November 5, on the campus of the University of Chicago, the Bureau will hold a roundtable on policy issues and research opportunities in industrial organization. The discussion, which will invite audience comment, will be chaired by Victor R. Fuchs, professor of economics at City University of New York and a member of the Bureau's staff. It will include presentations and comments by Ronald H. Coase, University of Chicago, James W. McKie, Vanderbilt University, Richard R. Nelson, Yale University, and Oliver E. Williamson, University of Pennsylvania.

The campus of Clark University in Atlanta will be the site of a colloquium on human capital, which will be held on Wednesday, November 11, 1970. Theodore W. Schultz of the University of Chicago is preparing the survey paper for this area. Alice Rivlin of The Brookings Institution and Gerald G. Somers of the University of Wisconsin will participate in the discussion of future research objectives, which will be moderated by Gary Becker, professor of economics at the University of Chicago and a Bureau staff member.

Economic growth is the subject of the final colloquium in the series, which will be held in the A. P. Giannini Auditorium of the new Bank of America Building in San Francisco on Thursday, December 10. James Tobin and William Nordhaus of Yale University are collaborating on the survey paper for this area. The discussion of future research needs will be chaired by R. A. Gordon of the University of California, and will include Moses Abramovitz, Stanford University, and R. C. O. Matthews of All Souls College, Oxford, England, as discussants. Representative Henry S. Reuss has accepted the Bureau's invitation to address the dinner that will be held in conjunction with this session.

---

[1] Senator Proxmire's participation will be dependent upon the Senate calendar.

The Anniversary program will conclude on Friday, April 23, 1971, at the American Academy of Arts and Sciences in Boston, with a conference entitled, "The Future of Economic Research." Simon Kuznets, the principal speaker, will focus on the future directions of empirical and quantitative research. It is expected that his remarks will, in some measure, summarize and evaluate the views developed within the various colloquia discussions.

The papers to be developed for the Fiftieth Anniversary series of colloquia and Dr. Kuznets' presentation will be published as part of the Bureau's Anniversary series.

The Fiftieth Anniversary program was created and guided by the Fiftieth Anniversary Committee of the Bureau's Board of Directors. This Committee was chaired by Albert J. Hettinger, Jr., and included the participation of Emilio G. Collado, Solomon Fabricant, Eugene P. Foley, Eli Goldston, Harry W. Laidler, J. Irwin Miller, Geoffrey H. Moore, J. Wilson Newman, George B. Roberts, Robert V. Roosa, Boris Shishkin, and Joseph H. Willits. Walter W. Heller, John R. Meyer, Donald B. Woodward, and Theodore O. Yntema assisted the committee in an ex-officio capacity.

Nancy Steinthal

VI

Roster of
National Bureau Staff

The following is a list of staff members as of about mid-1970, excluding temporary employees and others whose connection with the National Bureau was then drawing to a close. The list includes part-time as well as full-time members and also newly appointed members not yet on duty. More details on new members and Research Fellows are given in Part V.

SENIOR ADMINISTRATIVE PERSONNEL
John R. Meyer, President
Douglas H. Eldridge, Vice President-Executive Secretary
Victor R. Fuchs, Vice President—Research
F. Thomas Juster, Vice President—Research
Hal B. Lary, Vice President—Research
Robert E. Lipsey, Vice President—Research
Edward K. Smith, Vice President
Joan R. Tron, Director of Publications
Charlotte Boschan, Chief of Data Processing
Soma Golden, Assistant to the President
Ruth LaPan, Coordinator of Support Services
Nancy Steinthal, Administrative Assistant
Sapfo Chacona, Chief Accountant

SENIOR RESEARCH STAFF

Gary S. Becker	Irving B. Kravis
Charlotte Boschan	Hal B. Lary
Phillip Cagan	Robert E. Lipsey
Alfred H. Conrad	John R. Meyer
James S. Earley	Jacob Mincer
Solomon Fabricant	Ilse Mintz
Milton Friedman	Geoffrey H. Moore*
Victor R. Fuchs	M. I. Nadiri
Raymond W. Goldsmith	Nancy Ruggles
Jack M. Guttentag	Richard Ruggles
Daniel M. Holland	Anna J. Schwartz
F. Thomas Juster	Robert P. Shay
C. Harry Kahn	Carl S. Shoup**
John F. Kain	George J. Stigler
John W. Kendrick	Victor Zarnowitz

RESEARCH ASSOCIATES AND FELLOWS

Roger E. Alcaly	J. Royce Ginn	Benoit B. Mandelbrot	Christopher Sims
Albert E. Beaton	Robert J. Gordon	Robert T. Michael	Paul F. Smith
Sanford Berg	Michael Gort	Michael Michaely	Lewis C. Solmon
Jagdish N. Bhagwati	Manuel Gottlieb	Raymond F. Mikesell	David K. Stout
John D. Bossons	Michael Grossman	Seiji Naya	Mahlon R. Straszheim
H. James Brown	Yoel Haitovsky	Ralph L. Nelson	Raymond J. Struyk
V. K. Chetty	John C. Hause	Kong Kyun Ro	Paul J. Taubman
Barry R. Chiswick	Edward F. X. Hughes	T. Russell Robinson	George I. Treyz
Stephen P. Dresch	Donald P. Jacobs	Sherwin Rosen	Terence J. Wales
Isaac Ehrlich	Philip A. Klein	Warren Sanderson	Neil Wallace
Robert Eisner	David T. Kresge	Thomas J. Sargent	Merle Y. Weiss
Franklin M. Fisher	Anne O. Krueger	Richard T. Selden	Finis R. Welch
J. Herbert Furth	William M. Landes	Irving R. Silver	Robert J. Willis
George Garvy	Michael Landsberger	Morris Silver	Peter Workman

*On leave.
**Special consultant.

RESEARCH ANALYSTS AND ASSISTANTS

Neville Beharie	Masanori Hashimoto	An Loh Lin	Jorge A. Sanguinetty
Veena H. Bhatia	Guy Herregat	Marianne Lloris	Johanna Stern
Nadeschda Bohsack	Colin J. Hindle	Stephen Mayo	Richard P. Strauss
Carol Breckner	James L. Hosek	Christine Mortensen	Josephine Su
Peggy Cahn	Wan-Lee Hsu	Dorothy M. O'Brien	Vincent Su
Mervin Daub	Gregory K. Ingram	Sara Paroush	Murad Taqqu
Chantal Dubrin	Franklin J. James, Jr.	Joseph J. Persky	Susan Tebbetts
Ann B. Dukes	Jane Kenworthy	Bruce L. Petersen	Paul Wachtel
Avrohn Eisenstein	Marcia J. Kramer	Elizabeth Pinkston	Elizabeth Simpson Wehle
Barry J. Geller	Young Lee	Doris Preston	Robert L. Welch
Gilbert Ghez	Dianne R. Levine	John M. Quigley	Eva Wyler
David M. Gordon	Eugene Lewit	Teresita Rodriguez	
Morris Harf	Constance Lim	Jennifer Rowley	

PROGRAMMING AND DATA PROCESSING

Irene Abramson
Susan Crayne
Antonette Delak
Robert D. Goldberg
Orin C. Hansen
Sidney Jacobs
Martha Jones
Dora Thompson
Lora Weinstein

PUBLICATIONS

H. Irving Forman
Gnomi Gouldin
Richard Koo
Virginia Meltzer
Ester Moskowitz
Ruth Ridler
Elizabeth M. Ruth
Monika Shoffman

ADMINISTRATIVE AND SECRETARIAL STAFF

William Alladice	Rose Ferro	Simone Leeser
Vivian Batts	Georgette Gelormini	Charles E. Mitchell
Hermeta Benjamin	Margaret Gibbons	Muriel Moeller
Theresa Brilliante	Beatrice Grabiner	Beatrice Nielsen
Ruth Brody	Catherine S. Grant	Elisabeth Parshley
Helen Cheperak	James H. Hayes	Catherine Pavone
Dorothy Chesterton	Carolyn Hughes	Guido Pittaccio
Mildred E. Courtney	Ulla C. Jeremitsky	Nancy Scotton
Margaret W. Cozens	Rose D. Kalnin	Carolyn Terry
Virginia K. Crowley	Doris Kayne	
Maria D'Ambrosia	William Kennedy	

VII

Publications
1920-1970

Contributions and Subscriptions

Contributors or subscribers of $75 or more a year receive a complimentary copy of each new NBER publication—books, Occasional Papers, Technical Papers, newsletter, and annual report—in advance of release to the public. In addition, the subscriber is entitled to a 33⅓ per cent discount on any publication purchased from the National Bureau.

A special subscription rate of $35, providing the same privileges as above, is open to government employees and to employees of research/educational institutions, and faculty members.

A student subscription rate of $10, renewable for a total of three years, provides students with copies of all NBER publications issued during the subscription year. The 33⅓ per cent discount privilege is not applicable by students to newly published books but may be used on purchases of titles that have appeared in previous years.

For persons wishing to subscribe only to Occasional and Technical Papers, the subscription rate is $10 for five issues, along with 33⅓ per cent discount book purchase privileges for the duration of the subscription.

Address contributions, subscriptions, and inquiries to the attention of Douglas H. Eldridge, Vice President-Administration.

Contributions to the National Bureau are deductible in calculating income taxes.

How to Order Publications

Noncontributors and nonsubscribers: Order directly from the distributor of the publication, as indicated in the list of abbreviations or in the footnotes. Columbia University Press is distributor of publications too recent to be listed.

Contributors and Subscribers: Order all publications marked NBER, CUP, or PUP from National Bureau of Economic Research, Inc., 261 Madison Avenue, New York, New York 10016. Order all others from the distributor as indicated in the footnotes.

Please be sure to include state and local sales taxes.

Abbreviations

- **CUP—** Available from Columbia University Press, 136 South Broadway, Irvington-on-Hudson, N. Y. 10533.

- **PUP—** Available from Princeton University Press, Princeton, New Jersey 08540.

- **UM—** Available from University Microfilms Library Services, Xerox Corporation, 300 North Zeeb Road, Ann Arbor, Mich. 48106. Books marked UM are no longer in print at the National Bureau. These are available from University Microfilms on microfilm, xerox, or offset copy.

- **NBER—** Available from the National Bureau of Economic Research, Inc., 261 Madison Avenue, New York, N. Y. 10016.

BOOKS
GENERAL SERIES

1. *Income in the United States: Its Amount and Distribution, 1909-1919. I, Summary*
Wesley C. Mitchell, Willford I. King, Frederick R. Macaulay, and Oswald W. Knauth
UM, 1921, 168 pp.

2. *Income in the United States: Its Amount and Distribution, 1909-1919. II, Detailed Report*
Wesley C. Mitchell (ed.), Willford I. King, Frederick R. Macaulay, and Oswald W. Knauth
UM, 1922, 454 pp.

3. *Distribution of Income by States in 1919*
Oswald W. Knauth
UM, 1922, 35 pp.

4. *Business Cycles and Unemployment*
Committee of the President's Conference on Unemployment, and a special staff of the National Bureau
UM, 1923, 445 pp.

5. *Employment Hours and Earnings in Prosperity and Depression, United States, 1920-1922*
Willford Isbell King
UM, 1923, 2nd ed., 151 pp.

6. *The Growth of American Trade Unions, 1880-1923*
Leo Wolman
UM, 1924, 170 pp.

7. *Income in the Various States: Its Sources and Distribution, 1919, 1920, and 1921*
Maurice Leven
UM, 1925, 306 pp.

8. *Business Annals*
Willard Long Thorp
UM, 1926, 380 pp.

9. *Migration and Business Cycles*
Harry Jerome
UM, 1926, 256 pp.

10. *Business Cycles: The Problem and Its Setting*
Wesley C. Mitchell
NBER, 1927, 511 pp., $5.00

11. *The Behavior of Prices*
Frederick C. Mills
UM, 1927, 598 pp.

12. *Trends in Philanthropy: A Study in a Typical American City*
Willford Isbell King assisted by Kate E. Huntley
UM, 1928, 78 pp.

13. *Recent Economic Changes in the United States*
Committee on Recent Economic Changes of the President's Conference on Unemployment, and a special staff of the National Bureau
UM, 1929, 2 vols., 986 pp.

14. *International Migrations, I, Statistics*
Imre Ferenczi, edited by Walter F. Willcox
UM, 1929, 1112 pp.

15. *The National Income and Its Purchasing Power*
Willford Isbell King assisted by Lillian Epstein
UM, 1930, 394 pp.

16. *Corporation Contributions to Organized Community Welfare Services*
Pierce Williams and Frederick E. Croxton
UM, 1930, 347 pp.

17. *Planning and Control of Public Works*
Leo Wolman
UM, 1930, 291 pp.

18. *International Migrations, II, Interpretations*
Walter F. Willcox (ed.)
UM, 1931, 715 pp.

19. *The Smoothing of Times Series*
Frederick R. Macaulay
UM, 1931, 172 pp.

20. *The Purchase of Medical Care through Fixed Periodic Payment*
Pierce Williams assisted by Isabel C. Chamberlain
UM, 1932, 324 pp.

21. *Economic Tendencies in the United States: Aspects of Pre-War and Post-War Changes*
Frederick C. Mills
UM, 1932, 659 pp.

22. *Seasonal Variations in Industry and Trade*
Simon Kuznets
UM, 1933, 479 pp.

*23. *Production Trends in the United States since 1870*
Arthur F. Burns
1934, 395 pp.

*24. *Strategic Factors in Business Cycles*
John Maurice Clark
1934, 253 pp.

25. *German Business Cycles, 1924-1933*
Carl T. Schmidt
UM, 1934, 302 pp.

26. *Industrial Profits in the United States*
Ralph C. Epstein assisted by Florence M. Clark
UM, 1934, 689 pp.

27. *Mechanization in Industry*
Harry Jerome
UM, 1934, 515 pp.

28. *Corporate Profits as Shown by Audit Reports*
W. A. Paton
UM, 1935, 162 pp.

29. *Public Works in Prosperity and Depression*
Arthur D. Gayer
UM, 1935, 480 pp.

30. *Ebb and Flow in Trade Unionism*
Leo Wolman
UM, 1936, 268 pp.

31. *Prices in Recession and Recovery: A Survey of Recent Changes*
Frederick C. Mills
UM, 1936, 596 pp.

32. *National Income and Capital Formation, 1919-1935*
Simon Kuznets
UM, 1937, 96 pp.

33. *Some Theoretical Problems Suggested by the Movements of Interest Rates, Bond Yields and Stock Prices in the United States since 1856*
Frederick R. Macaulay
CUP, 1938, 604 pp., $7.50
The Social Sciences and the Unknown Future
Introductory chapter from the above.
NBER, 25¢

34. *Commodity Flow and Capital Formation, Volume I*
Simon Kuznets
UM, 1938, 514 pp.

35. *Capital Consumption and Adjustment*
Solomon Fabricant
UM, 1938, 291 pp.

---
* Available from Augustus M. Kelley, Bookseller, 24 East 22nd Street, New York, N. Y. 10010.

36 *The Structure of Manufacturing Production: A Cross-Section View*
Charles A. Bliss UM, 1939, 248 pp.

†37 *The International Gold Standard Reinterpreted, 1914-1934*
William Adams Brown, Jr. 2 vols., 1420 pp.

38 *Residential Real Estate: Its Economic Position as Shown by Values, Rents, Family Incomes, Financing, and Construction, Together with Estimates for All Real Estate*
David L. Wickens UM, 1941, 327 pp.

39 *The Output of Manufacturing Industries, 1899-1937*
Solomon Fabricant assisted by Julius Shiskin UM, 1940, 708 pp.

40 *National Income and Its Composition, 1919-1938*
Simon Kuznets assisted by Lillian Epstein and Elizabeth Jenks CUP, 1941, 1,009 pp., $12.50

41 *Employment in Manufacturing, 1899-1939: An Analysis of Its Relation to the Volume of Production*
Solomon Fabricant UM, 1942, 381 pp.

42 *American Agriculture, 1899-1939: A Study of Output, Employment and Productivity*
Harold Barger and Hans H. Landsberg UM, 1942, 462 pp.

43 *The Mining Industries, 1899-1939: A Study of Output, Employment and Productivity*
Harold Barger and Sam H. Schurr UM, 1944, 474 pp.

44 *National Product in Wartime*
Simon Kuznets UM, 1945, 166 pp.

45 *Income from Independent Professional Practice*
Milton Friedman and Simon Kuznets CUP, 1945, 632 pp., $5.50

46 *National Product since 1869*
Simon Kuznets assisted by Lillian Epstein and Elizabeth Jenks UM, 1946, 256 pp.

47 *Output and Productivity in the Electric and Gas Utilities, 1899-1942*
Jacob Martin Gould CUP, 1946, 207 pp., $3.00

48 *Value of Commodity Output since 1869*
William Howard Shaw UM, 1947, 320 pp.

49 *Business Incorporations in the United States, 1800-1943*
George Heberton Evans, Jr. CUP, 1948, 192 pp., $6.00

50 *The Statistical Agencies of the Federal Government: A Report to the Commission on Organization of the Executive Branch of the Government*
Frederick C. Mills and Clarence D. Long UM, 1949, 215 pp.

51 *The Transportation Industries, 1889-1946: A Study of Output, Employment, and Productivity*
Harold Barger CUP, 1951, 304 pp., $4.00

52 *Deterioration in the Quality of Foreign Bonds Issued in the United States, 1920-1930*
Ilse Mintz CUP, 1951, 111 pp., $2.00

53 *Wesley Clair Mitchell: The Economic Scientist*
Arthur F. Burns (ed.) CUP, 1952, 396 pp., $4.00

54 *A Study of Moneyflows in the United States*
Morris A. Copeland UM, 1952, 611 pp.

55 *Shares of Upper Income Groups in Income and Savings*
Simon Kuznets assisted by Elizabeth Jenks CUP, 1953, 766 pp., $9.00

56 *The Trend of Government Activity in the United States since 1900*
Solomon Fabricant assisted by Robert E. Lipsey UM, 1952, 286 pp.

*57 *The Frontiers of Economic Knowledge*
Arthur F. Burns UM, 1954, 378 pp.

58 *Distribution's Place in the American Economy since 1869*
Harold Barger UM, 1955, 240 pp.

59 *Trends in Employment in the Service Industries*
George J. Stigler PUP, 1956, 183 pp., $3.75

60 *The Growth of Public Employment in Great Britain*
Moses Abramovitz and Vera F. Eliasberg UM, 1957, 164 pp.

61 *Concentration in Canadian Manufacturing Industries*
Gideon Rosenbluth UM, 1957, 167 pp.

62 *The Demand and Supply of Scientific Personnel*
David M. Blank and George J. Stigler UM, 1957, 219 pp.

63 *A Theory of the Consumption Function*
Milton Friedman PUP, 1957, 259 pp., $6.50

64 *The National Economic Accounts of the United States: Review, Appraisal, and Recommendations*
National Accounts Review Committee
Report made at the request of the Bureau of the Budget and submitted in hearings before the Subcommittee on Economic Statistics of the Joint Economic Committee in October 1957; reprinted from the published *Hearings*
UM, 1958, 204 pp.

65 *The Labor Force under Changing Income and Employment*
Clarence D. Long UM, 1958, 464 pp.
Supplement *Appendixes G, H, and I*
NBER, $1.00 net

---

† Available from A.M.S. Press, 56 East 13th Street, New York, N. Y. 10003.

* Paperback edition available from John Wiley & Sons, Inc., 605 3rd Avenue, New York, N. Y. 10016.

66 *Merger Movements in American Industry, 1895-1956*
Ralph L. Nelson   UM, 1959, 198 pp.

67 *Wages and Earnings in the United States, 1860-1890*
Clarence D. Long   UM, 1960, 186 pp.

68 *Wages in Germany, 1871-1945*
Gerhard Bry assisted by Charlotte Boschan
                       UM, 1960, 513 pp.

69 *Soviet Statistics of Physical Output of Industrial Commodities: Their Compilation and Quality*
Gregory Grossman   UM, 1960, 167 pp.

70 *Real Wages in Manufacturing, 1890-1914*
Albert Rees   UM, 1961, 179 pp.

71 *Productivity Trends in the United States*
John W. Kendrick assisted by Maude R. Pech
                       UM, 1961, 682 pp.

72 *The Growth of Public Expenditure in the United Kingdom*
Alan T. Peacock and Jack Wiseman
                       UM, 1961, 244 pp.

73 *The Price Statistics of the Federal Government*
Report of the Price Statistics Review Committee
Report made at the request of the Bureau of the Budget and submitted in hearings before the Subcommittee on Economic Statistics of the Joint Economic Committee; reprinted from the *Hearings*   CUP, 1961, 518 pp., $1.50

74 *The Share of Top Wealth-Holders in National Wealth, 1922-56*
Robert J. Lampman   UM, 1962, 313 pp.

75 *Growth of Industrial Production in the Soviet Union*
G. Warren Nutter assisted by Israel Borenstein and Adam Kaufman   UM, 1962, 733 pp.
Supplement, *Statistical Abstract of Industrial Output in the Soviet Union, 1913-1955*
                       NBER, $10.00 net

76 *Freight Transportation in the Soviet Union, including Comparisons with the United States*
Ernest W. Williams, Jr.
                       PUP, 1962, 242 pp., $4.50

77 *Diversification and Integration in American Industry*
Michael Gort   UM, 1962, 259 pp.

78 *Capital and Rates of Return in Manufacturing Industries*
George J. Stigler   UM, 1963, 242 pp.

79 *Anticipations and Purchases: An Analysis of Consumer Behavior*
F. Thomas Juster   PUP, 1964, 321 pp., $6.50

80 *Human Capital: A Theoretical and Empirical Analysis, with Special Reference to Education*
Gary S. Becker   CUP, 1964, 203 pp., $6.50

81 *The Behavior of Interest Rates: A Progress Report*
Joseph W. Conard   CUP, 1966, 159 pp., $5.00

82 *Source Book of Statistics Relating to Construction*
Robert E. Lipsey and Doris Preston
                       CUP, 1966, 317 pp., $12.50

83 *Household Capital Formation and Financing, 1897-1962*
F. Thomas Juster   CUP, 1966, 160 pp., $6.00

84 *Yields on Corporate Debt Directly Placed*
Avery B. Cohan   CUP, 1967, 202 pp., $7.50

85 *Economic Aspects of Pensions: A Summary Report*
Roger F. Murray   CUP, 1968, 148 pp., $4.50

86 *Population, Labor Force, and Long Swings in Economic Growth: The American Experience*
Richard A. Easterlin
                       CUP, 1968, 318 pp., $10.00

Also available from Recording for the Blind, Inc., 215 East 58th Street, New York, N. Y. 10022.

87 *The Service Economy*
Victor Fuchs assisted by Irving F. Leveson
                       CUP, 1968, 308 pp., $10.00
Paperback available from CUP, $3.75

88 *Essays on Interest Rates, Vol. I*
Jack M. Guttentag and Phillip Cagan (eds.)
                       CUP, 1969, 308 pp., $10.00

89 *The Design of Economic Accounts*
Nancy Ruggles and Richard Ruggles
                       CUP, 1970, 196 pp., $8.00

90 *The Behavior of Industrial Prices*
George J. Stigler and James K. Kindahl
                       CUP, 1970, 100 pp., $7.50

91 *Home Mortgage Delinquency and Foreclosure*
John P. Herzog and James S. Earley
                       CUP, 1970, 128 pp., $7.50

STUDIES IN BUSINESS CYCLES

1 *Business Cycles: The Problem and Its Setting*
Wesley C. Mitchell
                       NBER, 1927, 511 pp., $5.00

2 *Measuring Business Cycles*
Arthur F. Burns and Wesley C. Mitchell
                       CUP, 1946, 587 pp., $5.00
Also available from Recording for the Blind, Inc., 215 East 58th Street, New York, N. Y. 10022

3 *American Transportation in Prosperity and Depression*
Thor Hultgren   UM, 1948, 431 pp.

4 *Inventories and Business Cycles, with Special Reference to Manufacturers' Inventories*
Moses Abramovitz   UM, 1950, 668 pp.

5 *What Happens during Business Cycles: A Progress Report*
Wesley C. Mitchell   CUP, 1951, 417 pp., $7.50

6 *Personal Income during Business Cycles*
Daniel Creamer assisted by Martin Bernstein
PUP, 1956, 208 pp., $4.00

7 *Consumption and Business Fluctuations: A Case Study of the Shoe, Leather, Hide Sequence*
Ruth P. Mack   UM, 1956, 310 pp.

8 *International Financial Transactions and Business Cycles*
Oskar Morgenstern   UM, 1959, 624 pp.

9 *Federal Receipts and Expenditures During Business Cycles, 1879-1958*
John M. Firestone   PUP, 1960, 192 pp., $4.00

10 *Business Cycle Indicators*
Geoffrey H. Moore (ed.)   PUP, 1961
Vol. I, 792 pp., $12.50
Vol. II, 196 pp., $ 4.50
Both vols., $15.00

11 *Postwar Cycles in Manufacturers' Inventories*
Thomas M. Stanback, Jr.   UM, 1962, 160 pp.

12 *A Monetary History of the United States, 1867-1960*
Milton Friedman and Anna Jacobson Schwartz
PUP, 1963, 884 pp., $15.00
The Great Contraction, 1929-33, Chapter 7 from the above   PUP, 1965, 162 pp., $1.95

13 *Determinants and Effects of Changes in the Stock of Money, 1875-1960*
Phillip Cagan   CUP, 1965, 408 pp., $10.00

14 *Cost, Prices, and Profits: Their Cyclical Relations*
Thor Hultgren assisted by Maude R. Pech
CUP, 1965, 255 pp., $6.00

15 *Cyclical Fluctuations in the Exports of the United States since 1879*
Ilse Mintz   CUP, 1967, 352 pp., $10.00

16 *Information, Expectations, and Inventory Fluctuation: A Study of Materials Stock on Hand and on Order*
Ruth P. Mack   CUP, 1967, 318 pp., $10.00

17 *Forecasting and Recognizing Business Cycle Turning Points*
Rendigs Fels and C. Elton Hinshaw
CUP, 1968, 148 pp., $4.50

18 *The Business Cycle in a Changing World*
Arthur F. Burns   CUP, 1969, 366 pp., $8.50

19 *Economic Forecasts and Expectations: Analysis of Forecasting Behavior and Performance*
Jacob Mincer (ed.)   CUP, 1969, 269 pp., $10.00

20 *Monetary Statistics of the United States: Estimates, Sources, Methods*
Milton Friedman and Anna Jacobson Schwartz
CUP, 1970, 517 pp., $15.00

21 *Errors in Provisional Estimates of Gross National Product*
Rosanne Cole   CUP, 1970, 106 pp., $6.00

STUDIES IN CAPITAL FORMATION AND FINANCING

1 *Capital Formation in Residential Real Estate: Trends and Prospects*
Leo Grebler, David M. Blank, and Louis Winnick   PUP, 1956, 549 pp., $10.00

2 *Capital in Agriculture: Its Formation and Financing since 1870*
Alvin S. Tostlebe   UM, 1957, 258 pp.

*3 *Financial Intermediaries in the American Economy since 1900*
Raymond W. Goldsmith
PUP, 1958, 450 pp., $10.00

4 *Capital in Transportation, Communications, and Public Utilities: Its Formation and Financing*
Melville J. Ulmer NBER, 1960, 577 pp., $12.00

5 *Postwar Market for State and Local Government Securities*
Roland I. Robinson   PUP, 1960, 251 pp., $5.00

6 *Capital in Manufacturing and Mining: Its Formation and Financing*
Daniel Creamer, Sergei Dobrovolsky, and Israel Borenstein, assisted by Martin Bernstein
UM, 1960, 398 pp.

7 *Trends in Government Financing*
Morris A. Copeland   UM, 1961, 236 pp.

8 *The Postwar Residential Mortgage Market*
Saul B. Klaman   UM, 1961, 332 pp.

9 *Capital in the American Economy: Its Formation and Financing*
Simon Kuznets assisted by Elizabeth Jenks
PUP, 1961, 693 pp., $12.00

10 *The National Wealth of the United States in the Postwar Period*
Raymond W. Goldsmith
PUP, 1962, 463 pp., $12.50

11 *Studies in the National Balance Sheet of the United States*   PUP, 1963
Vol. I, Raymond W. Goldsmith and Robert E. Lipsey   458 pp., $8.50
Vol. II, Raymond W. Goldsmith, Robert E. Lipsey, and Morris Mendelson 551 pp., $7.50
Both vols., $15.00

12 *The Flow of Capital Funds in the Postwar Economy*
Raymond W. Goldsmith
CUP, 1965, 338 pp., $7.50

TWENTY-FIFTH ANNIVERSARY SERIES

1 *National Income: A Summary of Findings*
Simon Kuznets   UM, 1946, 154 pp.

2 *Price-Quantity Interactions in Business Cycles*
Frederick C. Mills   UM, 1946, 152 pp.

---

* Appendixes out of print.

3 *Economic Research and the Development of Economic Science and Public Policy*
UM, 1946, 208 pp.

4 *Trends in Output and Employment*
George J. Stigler UM, 1947, 76 pp.

FISCAL STUDIES

1 *Fiscal Planning for Total War*
William Leonard Crum, John F. Fennelly, and Lawrence Howard Seltzer UM, 1942, 383 pp.

2 *Taxable and Business Income*
Dan Throop Smith and J. Keith Butters
UM, 1949, 367 pp.

3 *The Nature and Tax Treatment of Capital Gains and Losses*
Lawrence H. Seltzer assisted by Selma F. Goldsmith and M. Slade Kendrick
UM, 1951, 576 pp.

4 *Federal Grants and the Business Cycle*
James A. Maxwell UM, 1952, 134 pp.

5 *The Income-Tax Burden on Stockholders*
Daniel M. Holland PUP, 1958, 266 pp., $5.00

6 *Personal Deductions in the Federal Income Tax*
C. Harry Kahn PUP, 1960, 266 pp., $5.00

7 *Dividends Under the Income Tax*
Daniel M. Holland UM, 1962, 206 pp.

8 *Business and Professional Income Under the Personal Income Tax*
C. Harry Kahn PUP, 1964, 208 pp., $4.00

9 *Accelerated Depreciation in the United States, 1954-60*
Norman B. Ture CUP, 1967, 257 pp., $7.50

10 *Employee Compensation Under the Income Tax*
C. Harry Kahn CUP, 1968, 153 pp., $5.00

11 *Executive Compensation in Large Industrial Corporations*
Wilbur G. Lewellen
CUP, 1968, 396 pp., $13.50

12 *The Personal Exemptions in the Income Tax*
Lawrence H. Seltzer CUP, 1968, 233 pp., $8.50

13 *Tax Changes and Modernization in the Textile Industry*
Thomas M. Stanback, Jr.
CUP, 1969, 134 pp., $6.75

FINANCIAL RESEARCH PROGRAM

I A Program of Financial Research

A Program of Financial Research
Vol. One: *Report of the Exploratory Committee on Financial Research*
Exploratory Committee on Financial Research
NBER, 1937, 91 pp., $1.00

Vol. Two: *Inventory of Current Research on Financial Problems*
Exploratory Committee on Financial Research
CUP, 1937, 261 pp., $1.50

II Studies in Consumer Instalment Financing

1 *Personal Finance Companies and Their Credit Practices*
Ralph A. Young and associates
UM, 1940, 192 pp.

2 *Sales Finance Companies and Their Credit Practices*
Wilbur C. Plummer and Ralph A. Young
UM, 1940, 321 pp.

3 *Commercial Banks and Consumer Instalment Credit*
John M. Chapman and associates
UM, 1940, 342 pp.

4 *Industrial Banking Companies and Their Credit Practices*
Raymond J. Saulnier UM, 1940, 213 pp.

5 *Government Agencies of Consumer Instalment Credit*
Joseph D. Coppock UM, 1940, 238 pp.

6 *The Pattern of Consumer Debt, 1935-36: A Statistical Analysis*
Blanche Bernstein UM, 1940, 255 pp.

7 *The Volume of Consumer Instalment Credit, 1929-1938*
Duncan McC. Holthausen in collaboration with Malcolm L. Merriam and Rolf Nugent
UM, 1940, 156 pp.

8 *Risk Elements in Consumer Instalment Financing*
David Durand UM, 1941, General Ed., 121 pp.
Technical Ed., 186 pp.

9 *Consumer Instalment Credit and Economic Fluctuations*
Gottfried Haberler UM, 1942, 258 pp.

10 *Comparative Operating Experience of Consumer Instalment Financing Agencies and Commercial Banks, 1929-41*
Ernst A. Dauer NBER, 1944, 239 pp., $3.00

11 *Consumer Credit Costs, 1949-1959*
Paul F. Smith PUP, 1964, 179 pp., $4.50

12 *Consumer Credit Finance Charges: Rate Information and Quotation*
Wallace P. Mors CUP, 1965, 150 pp., $5.00

13 *The Quality of Consumer Instalment Credit*
Geoffrey H. Moore and Philip A. Klein
CUP, 1967, 282 pp., $8.50

III Studies in Business Financing

1 *Term Lending to Business*
Neil H. Jacoby and Raymond J. Saulnier
UM, 1942, 180 pp.

2 *Financing Small Corporations in Five Manufacturing Industries, 1926-36*
Charles L. Merwin   UM, 1942, 189 pp.

3 *Accounts Receivable Financing*
Raymond J. Saulnier and Neil H. Jacoby
    UM, 1943, 172 pp.

4 *The Financing of Large Corporations, 1920-39*
Albert Ralph Koch   UM, 1943, 156 pp.

5 *Financing Equipment for Commercial and Industrial Enterprise*
Raymond J. Saulnier and Neil H. Jacoby
    UM, 1944, 110 pp.

6 *Financing Inventory on Field Warehouse Receipts*
Neil H. Jacoby and Raymond J. Saulnier
    CUP, 1944, 104 pp., $1.50

7 *The Pattern of Corporate Financial Structure: A Cross-Section View of Manufacturing, Mining, Trade and Construction, 1937*
Walter A. Chudson   UM, 1945, 162 pp.

8 *Corporate Cash Balances, 1914-43: Manufacturing and Trade*
Friedrich A. Lutz   UM, 1945, 146 pp.

9 *Business Finance and Banking*
Neil H. Jacoby and Raymond J. Saulnier
    UM, 1947, 259 pp.

10 *Corporate Income Retention, 1915-43*
Sergei P. Dobrovolsky   UM, 1951, 140 pp.

IV Studies in Urban Mortgage Financing

1 *Urban Mortgage Lending by Life Insurance Companies*
Raymond J. Saulnier CUP, 1950, 201 pp., $2.50

2 *The Impact of Government on Real Estate Finance in the United States*
Miles L. Colean   UM, 1950, 189 pp.

3 *Urban Real Estate Markets: Characteristics and Financing*
Ernest M. Fisher   CUP, 1951, 207 pp., $3.00

4 *History and Policies of the Home Owners' Loan Corporation*
C. Lowell Harriss   CUP, 1951, 223 pp., $3.00

5 *Commercial Bank Activities in Urban Mortgage Financing*
Carl F. Behrens   CUP, 1952, 150 pp., $2.50

6 *Urban Mortgage Lending: Comparative Markets and Experience*
J. E. Morton   NBER, 1956, 207 pp., $4.00

V Studies in Corporate Bond Financing

1 *The Volume of Corporate Bond Financing since 1900*
W. Braddock Hickman
    NBER, 1953, 460 pp., $7.50

2 *Corporate Bond Quality and Investor Experience*
W. Braddock Hickman
    PUP, 1958, 565 pp., $10.00

3 *Statistical Measures of Corporate Bond Financing since 1900*
W. Braddock Hickman assisted by Elizabeth T. Simpson   PUP, 1960, 612 pp., $9.00

4 *Trends in Corporate Bond Quality*
Thomas R. Atkinson assisted by Elizabeth T. Simpson   CUP, 1967, 122 pp., $5.00

VI Studies in Agricultural Financing

1 *Mortgage Lending Experience in Agriculture*
Lawrence A. Jones and David Durand
    PUP, 1954, 255 pp., $5.00

2 *Patterns of Farm Financial Structure: A Cross-Section View of Economic and Physical Determinants*
Donald C. Horton   PUP, 1957, 205 pp., $4.50

VII Other Studies

1 *The Pattern of Financial Asset Ownership: Wisconsin Individuals, 1949*
Thomas R. Atkinson
    PUP, 1956, 194 pp., $3.75

2 *Federal Lending and Loan Insurance*
Raymond J. Saulnier, Harold G. Halcrow, and Neil H. Jacoby   PUP, 1958, 596 pp., $12.00

STUDIES IN INTERNATIONAL ECONOMIC RELATIONS

1 *Problems of the United States as World Trader and Banker*
Hal B. Lary   CUP, 1963, 191 pp., $6.00

2 *Price and Quantity Trends in the Foreign Trade of the United States*
Robert E. Lipsey   PUP, 1963, 505 pp., $10.00

3 *Measuring Transactions Between World Areas*
Herbert B. Woolley CUP, 1966, 175 pp., $7.50

4 *Imports of Manufactures from Less Developed Countries*
Hal B. Lary   CUP, 1968, 303 pp., $8.50

STUDIES IN INCOME AND WEALTH

Conference on Research in Income and Wealth

1 Eight papers on concepts and measurement of national income   UM, 1937, 366 pp.

2 Six papers on wealth measurement, price changes, savings, capital gains, and government product   UM, 1938, 354 pp.

3 Seven papers on income size distribution, savings, national product, and distribution of income by states UM, 1939, 502 pp.

4 *Outlay and Income in the United States, 1921-1938*
Harold Barger UM, 1942, 418 pp.

5 *Income Size Distributions in the United States, Part I* UM, 1943, 157 pp.

6 Seven papers on income measurement, government product, parity, international transactions, forecasting national income, income differences among communities, and net capital formation UM, 1943, 301 pp.

7 *Changes in Income Distribution during the Great Depression*
Horst Mendershausen UM, 1946, 191 pp.

8 Eleven papers on estimating national income for use in dealing with war problems and postwar adjustments UM, 1946, 311 pp.

9 *Analysis of Wisconsin Income*
Frank A. Hanna, Joseph A. Pechman, and Sidney M. Lerner CUP, 1948, 279 pp., $3.50

10 Eight papers on standardizing basic concepts of national bookkeeping by American, British, and Canadian statisticians; problems of international comparisons of income and wealth; the nation's economic budget and forecasting gross national product and employment; savings and income distribution; and resource distribution patterns UM, 1947, 351 pp.

11 Six papers on the industrial distribution of manpower, real incomes in dissimilar geographic areas, national income forecasting, and the savings-income ratio UM, 1949, 462 pp.

12 Thirteen papers on national wealth UM, 1950, 599 pp.

13 Ten papers on size distribution of income UM, 1951, 601 pp.

14 Seven papers on wealth, the value of reproducible tangible assets, the concentration of wealth, the Estates Survey, real property assets, and the relation of asset holdings to economic behavior and motivation UM, 1951, 286 pp.

15 Eight papers on size distribution of income UM, 1952, 240 pp.

16 *Long-Range Economic Projection* PUP, 1954, 486 pp., $10.00

17 *Short-Term Economic Forecasting* UM, 1955, 517 pp.

18 *Input-Output Analysis: An Appraisal* PUP, 1955, 381 pp., $9.00
Technical supplement, *Input-Output Analysis* NBER, $4.00 net

19 *Problems of Capital Formation: Concepts, Measurement, and Controlling Factors* UM, 1957, 623 pp.

20 *Problems in the International Comparison of Economic Accounts* UM, 1957, 414 pp.

21 *Regional Income* UM, 1957, 418 pp.

22 *A Critique of the United States Income and Product Accounts* UM, 1958, 599 pp.

23 *An Appraisal of the 1950 Census Income Data* PUP, 1958, 460 pp., $10.00

24 *Trends in the American Economy in the Nineteenth Century* UM, 1960, 791 pp.

25 *Output, Input, and Productivity Measurement* (contains author and title indexes for Studies in Income and Wealth, Volumes 1-25) PUP, 1961, 516 pp., $12.50

26 *The Flow-of-Funds Approach to Social Accounting* UM, 1962, 497 pp.

27 *The Behavior of Income Shares: Selected Theoretical and Empirical Issues* PUP, 1964, 404 pp., $8.00

28 *Models of Income Determination* PUP, 1964, 436 pp., $10.00

29 *Measuring the Nation's Wealth* UM, 1964, 866 pp.

30 *Output, Employment, and Productivity in the United States After 1800*
Dorothy S. Brady (ed.) CUP, 1966, 674 pp., $12.50

31 *The Theory and Empirical Analysis of Production*
Murray Brown (ed.) CUP, 1967, 525 pp., $12.50

32 *The Industrial Composition of Income and Product*
John W. Kendrick (ed.) CUP, 1968, 508 pp., $14.00

33 *Six Papers on the Size Distribution of Wealth and Income*
Lee Soltow (ed.) CUP, 1969, 281 pp., $10.00

34 *Production and Productivity in the Service Industries*
Victor R. Fuchs (ed.) CUP, 1969, 404 pp., $12.50

CONFERENCE ON PRICE RESEARCH

1 *Report of the Committee on Prices in the Bituminous Coal Industry* UM, 1938, 164 pp.

2 *Textile Markets: Their Structure in Relation to Price Research* UM, 1939, 286 pp.

3 *Price Research in the Steel and Petroleum Industries* UM, 1939, 183 pp.

4 *Cost Behavior and Price Policy*
Committee on Price Determination
UM, 1943, 375 pp.

5 *Minimum Price Fixing in the Bituminous Coal Industry*
Waldo E. Fisher and Charles M. James
PUP, 1955, 554 pp., $10.00

UNIVERSITIES–NATIONAL BUREAU CONFERENCE SERIES

1 *Problems in the Study of Economic Growth*
UM, 1949, 254 pp.

2 *Conference on Business Cycles*
UM, 1951, 445 pp.

3 *Conference on Research in Business Finance*
UM, 1952, 358 pp.

4 *Regularization of Business Investment*
PUP, 1954, 539 pp., $8.00

5 *Business Concentration and Price Policy*
PUP, 1955, 524 pp., $12.50

6 *Capital Formation and Economic Growth*
UM, 1955, 690 pp.

7 *Policies to Combat Depression*
UM, 1956, 427 pp.

8 *The Measurement and Behavior of Unemployment*
PUP, 1957, 615 pp., $7.50

*9 *Problems in International Economics*
1958, 142 pp.

10 *The Quality and Economic Significance of Anticipations Data*
UM, 1960, 477 pp.

11 *Demographic and Economic Change in Developed Countries*
CUP, 1960, 547 pp., $12.00

12 *Public Finances: Needs, Sources, and Utilization*
PUP, 1961, 526 pp., $12.50

13 *The Rate and Direction of Inventive Activity: Economic and Social Factors*
PUP, 1962, 646 pp., $12.50

14 *Aspects of Labor Economics*
UM, 1962, 361 pp.

†15 *Investment in Human Beings*
1962, 157 pp.

16 *The State of Monetary Economics*
CUP, 1963, 155 pp., $3.00

17 *Transportation Economics*
CUP, 1965, 482 pp., $10.00

---

* Out of print at the National Bureau. Available from Kraus Reprint Corp., 16 East 46th Street, New York, N. Y. 10017.

† Out of print at the National Bureau. Available from University of Chicago Press, 5750 Ellis Avenue, Chicago, Ill. 60637, $3.50.

18 *Determinants of Investment Behavior*
Robert Ferber (ed.) CUP, 1967, 622 pp., $15.00

19 *National Economic Planning*
Max F. Millikan (ed.)
CUP, 1967, 423 pp., $10.00

20 *Issues in Defense Economics*
Roland N. McKean (ed.)
CUP, 1967, 297 pp., $7.50

21 *The Role of Agriculture in Economic Development*
Erik Thorbecke (ed.)
CUP, 1970, 490 pp., $12.50

22 *The Technology Factor in International Trade*
Raymond Vernon (ed.)
CUP, 1970, 535 pp., $15.00

OTHER CONFERENCES

1 *Consumer Instalment Credit: Conference on Regulation*
Order from Superintendent of Documents, Washington, D. C. 20025
1957, Vol. 1, 579 pp., $1.75
1957, Vol. 2, 171 pp., 60¢

2 *Philanthropy and Public Policy*
Frank G. Dickinson (ed.)
CUP, 1962, 155 pp., $3.50

3 *The Role of Direct and Indirect Taxes in the Federal Revenue System*
A Conference Report of the National Bureau of Economic Research and the Brookings Institution
PUP, 1964, 333 pp., $7.50
PUP, paperbound, $2.95

4 *Foreign Tax Policies and Economic Growth*
A Conference Report of the National Bureau of Economic Research and the Brookings Institution
CUP, 1966, 503 pp., $10.00
CUP, paperbound, $3.50

5 *The Measurement and Interpretation of Job Vacancies*
CUP, 1966, 602 pp., $12.50

EXPLORATORY REPORTS

1 *Research in Securities Markets*
Exploratory Committee on Research in Securities Markets
CUP, 1946, 38 pp., 50¢

2 *Research in the Capital and Securities Markets*
Exploratory Committee on Research in the Capital and Securities Markets
NBER, 1954, 88 pp., $1.00

3 *Suggestions for Research in the Economics of Pensions*
NBER, 1957, 64 pp., $1.00

4 *The Comparative Study of Economic Growth and Structure: Suggestions on Research Objectives and Organization*
CUP, 1959, 201 pp., $3.00

5 *Research in the Capital Markets*
CUP, 1964, 48 pp., $1.00

OCCASIONAL PAPERS

1 *Manufacturing Output, 1929-1937*
Solomon Fabricant   UM, 1940, 28 pp.

2 *National Income, 1919-1938*
Simon Kuznets   UM, 1941, 32 pp.

3 *Finished Commodities since 1879: Output and Its Composition*
William H. Shaw   UM, 1941, 49 pp.

4 *The Relation between Factory Employment and Output since 1899*
Solomon Fabricant   UM, 1941, 39 pp.

5 *Railway Freight Traffic in Prosperity and Depression*
Thor Hultgren   UM, 1942, 51 pp.

6 *Uses of National Income in Peace and War*
Simon Kuznets   UM, 1942, 42 pp.

7 *Productivity of Labor in Peace and War*
Solomon Fabricant   UM, 1942, 28 pp.

8 *The Banking System and War Finance*
Charles R. Whittlesey   UM, 1943, 53 pp.

9 *Wartime 'Prosperity' and the Future*
Wesley C. Mitchell   UM, 1943, 40 pp.

10 *The Effect of War on Business Financing: Manufacturing and Trade, World War I*
Charles H. Schmidt and Ralph A. Young
UM, 1943, 95 pp.

11 *The Effect of War on Currency and Deposits*
Charles R. Whittlesey   UM, 1943, 50 pp.

12 *Prices in a War Economy: Some Aspects of the Present Price Structure of the United States*
Frederick C. Mills   UM, 1943, 102 pp.

13 *Railroad Travel and the State of Business*
Thor Hultgren   UM, 1943, 35 pp.

14 *The Labor Force in Wartime America*
Clarence D. Long   UM, 1944, 73 pp.

15 *Railway Traffic Expansion and Use of Resources in World War II*
Thor Hultgren   UM, 1944, 31 pp.

16 *British and American Plans for International Currency Stabilization*
J. H. Riddle   UM, 1943, 42 pp.

17 *National Product, War and Prewar*
Simon Kuznets   UM, 1944, 54 pp.

18 *Production of Industrial Materials in World Wars I and II*
Geoffrey H. Moore   UM, 1944, 81 pp.

19 *Canada's Financial System in War*
Benjamin H. Higgins   NBER, 1944, 82 pp., 50¢

20 *Nazi War Finance and Banking*
Otto Nathan   UM, 1944, 100 pp.

21 *The Federal Reserve System in Wartime*
Anna Youngman   UM, 1945, 67 pp.

22 *Bank Liquidity and the War*
Charles R. Whittlesey   UM, 1945, 86 pp.

23 *Labor Savings in American Industry, 1899-1939*
Solomon Fabricant   UM, 1945, 56 pp.

24 *Domestic Servants in the United States, 1900-1940*
George J. Stigler   NBER, 1946, 44 pp., 50¢

25 *Recent Developments in Dominion-Provincial Fiscal Relations in Canada*
J. A. Maxwell   UM, 1948, 62 pp.

26 *The Role of Inventories in Business Cycles*
Moses Abramovitz   UM, 1948, 26 pp.

27 *The Structure of Postwar Prices*
Frederick C. Mills   UM, 1948, 66 pp.

28 *Lombard Street in War and Reconstruction*
Benjamin H. Higgins   UM, 1949, 115 pp.

29 *The Rising Trend of Government Employment*
Solomon Fabricant   UM, 1949, 30 pp.

30 *Costs and Returns on Farm Mortgage Lending by Life Insurance Companies, 1945-1947*
R. J. Saulnier   UM, 1949, 55 pp.

31 *Statistical Indicators of Cyclical Revivals and Recessions*
Geoffrey H. Moore   UM, 1950, 96 pp.

32 *Cyclical Diversities in the Fortunes of Industrial Corporations*
Thor Hultgren   UM, 1950, 34 pp.

33 *Employment and Compensation in Education*
George J. Stigler   UM, 1950, 77 pp.

34 *Behavior of Wage Rates during Business Cycles*
Daniel Creamer assisted by Martin Bernstein
UM, 1950, 66 pp.

35 *Shares of Upper Income Groups in Income and Savings*
Simon Kuznets   NBER, 1950, 68 pp., $1.00

36 *The Labor Force in War and Transition: Four Countries*
Clarence D. Long   CUP, 1952, 61 pp., $1.00

37 *Trends and Cycles in Corporate Bond Financing*
W. Braddock Hickman   UM, 1952, 37 pp.

38 *Productivity and Economic Progress*
Frederick C. Mills   UM, 1952, 36 pp.

39 *The Role of Federal Credit Aids in Residential Construction*
Leo Grebler   UM, 1953, 76 pp.

40 *Transport and the State of Trade in Britain*
Thor Hultgren assisted by William I. Greenwald
UM, 1953, 126 pp.

41 *Capital and Output Trends in Manufacturing Industries, 1880-1948*
Daniel Creamer assisted by Martin Bernstein
UM, 1954, 104 pp.

42 *The Share of Financial Intermediaries in National Wealth and National Assets, 1900-1949*
Raymond W. Goldsmith   UM, 1954, 120 pp.

43 *Trends and Cycles in Capital Formation by United States Railroads, 1870-1950*
Melville J. Ulmer   UM, 1954, 70 pp.

44 *The Growth of Physical Capital in Agriculture, 1870-1950*
Alvin S. Tostlebe   UM, 1954, 104 pp.

45 *Capital and Output Trends in Mining Industries, 1870-1948*
Israel Borenstein   UM, 1954, 81 pp.

46 *Immigration and the Foreign Born*
Simon Kuznets and Ernest Rubin
UM, 1954, 119 pp.

47 *The Ownership of Tax-Exempt Securities, 1913-1953*
George E. Lent   UM, 1955, 150 pp.

48 *A Century and a Half of Federal Expenditures*
M. Slade Kendrick assisted by Mark Wehle
UM, 1955, 112 pp.

49 *The Korean War and United States Economic Activity, 1950-1952*
Bert G. Hickman   UM, 1955, 72 pp.

50 *Agricultural Equipment Financing*
Howard G. Diesslin
NBER, 1955, 111 pp., $1.25

51 *Interest as a Source of Personal Income and Tax Revenue*
Lawrence H. Seltzer   CUP, 1955, 82 pp., $1.25

52 *Resource and Output Trends in the United States since 1870*
Moses Abramovitz   UM, 1956, 23 pp.

53 *Productivity Trends: Capital and Labor*
John W. Kendrick   UM, 1956, 23 pp.

54 *Bank Stock Prices and the Bank Capital Problem*
David Durand   UM, 1957, 86 pp.

55 *Some Observations on Soviet Industrial Growth*
G. Warren Nutter   NBER, 1957, 12 pp., 50¢

56 *Distribution of Union Membership among the States, 1939 and 1953*
Leo Troy   UM, 1957, 40 pp.

57 *Electronic Computers and Business Indicators*
Julius Shiskin   CUP, 1957, 52 pp., $1.50

58 *Federal Lending: Its Growth and Impact*
A summary, prepared by the National Bureau's editorial staff, of *Federal Lending and Loan Insurance*, by R. J. Saulnier, Harold G. Halcrow, and Neil H. Jacoby   UM, 1957, 56 pp.

59 *Corporate Bonds: Quality and Investment Performance*
W. Braddock Hickman   UM, 1957, 43 pp.

60 *The Postwar Rise of Mortgage Companies*
Saul B. Klaman   UM, 1959, 117 pp.

61 *Measuring Recessions*
Geoffrey H. Moore   UM, 1958, 57 pp.

62 *The Demand for Currency Relative to Total Money Supply*
Phillip Cagan   UM, 1958, 37 pp.

63 *Basic Facts on Productivity Change*
Solomon Fabricant   CUP, 1959, 57 pp., $1.00

64 *The Role of Middleman Transactions in World Trade*
Robert M. Lichtenberg
CUP, 1959, 102 pp., $1.50

65 *Freight Transportation in the Soviet Union: A Comparison with the United States*
Ernest W. Williams, Jr.
NBER, 1959, 47 pp., 75¢

66 *City Expenditures in the United States*
Harvey E. Brazer   UM, 1959, 93 pp.
Supplement, *Appendix E*   NBER, 50¢

67 *Trade Balances during Business Cycles: U.S. and Britain since 1880*
Ilse Mintz   UM, 1959, 109 pp.

68 *The Demand for Money: Some Theoretical and Empirical Results*
Milton Friedman   CUP, 1959, 25 pp., $1.50

69 *The Average Workweek as an Economic Indicator*
Gerhard Bry   UM, 1959, 122 pp.

70 *Consumer Expectations, Plans, and Purchases: A Progress Report*
F. Thomas Juster   UM, 1959, 192 pp.

71 *Changes in the Share of Wealth Held by Top Wealth-Holders, 1922-1956*
Robert J. Lampman   UM, 1960, 32 pp.

72 *Housing Issues in Economic Stabilization Policy*
Leo Grebler   CUP, 1960, 140 pp., $2.75

73 *Regional Cycles of Manufacturing Employment in the United States, 1914-1953*
George H. Borts   NBER, 1960, 60 pp., 75¢

74 *Changes in Labor Cost During Cycles in Production and Business*
Thor Hultgren   UM, 1960, 102 pp.

75 *New Measures of Wage-Earner Compensation in Manufacturing, 1914-57*
Albert Rees   UM, 1960, 35 pp.

76 *American Exports During Business Cycles, 1879-1958*
Ilse Mintz   UM, 1961, 104 pp.

77 *Signals of Recession and Recovery: An Experiment with Monthly Reporting*
Julius Shiskin   CUP, 1961, 203 pp., $3.00

78 *The Postwar Rise in the Velocity of Money: A Sectoral Analysis*
Richard T. Selden   UM, 1962, 72 pp.

*79 *The American Baby Boom in Historical Perspective*
Richard A. Easterlin   1962, 64 pp.

80 *Small-Scale Industry in the Soviet Union*
Adam Kaufman   UM, 1962, 111 pp.

81 *The United States Savings Bond Program in the Postwar Period*
George Hanc   CUP, 1962, 122 pp., $1.50

82 *The Quality of Bank Loans: A Study of Bank Examination Records*
Albert M. Wojnilower   CUP, 1962, 88 pp., $1.50

83 *Cost of Providing Consumer Credit: A Study of Four Major Types of Financial Institutions*
Paul F. Smith   CUP, 1962, 27 pp., 50¢

84 *Unfilled Orders, Price Changes, and Business Fluctuations*
Victor Zarnowitz   CUP, 1962, 32 pp., 75¢

85 *Trends and Cycles in the Commercial Paper Market*
Richard T. Selden   UM, 1963, 133 pp.

86 *New-Automobile Finance Rates, 1924-62*
Robert P. Shay   CUP, 1963, 37 pp., 75¢

87 *The Quality of Trade Credit*
Martin H. Seiden   CUP, 1964, 149 pp., $3.00

88 *Consumer Sensitivity to Finance Rates: An Empirical and Analytical Investigation*
F. Thomas Juster and Robert P. Shay   CUP, 1964, 116 pp., $2.50

89 *Productivity Trends in the Goods and Service Sectors, 1929-61: A Preliminary Survey*
Victor R. Fuchs   CUP, 1964, 57 pp., $1.75

90 *Evidences of Long Swings in Aggregate Construction Since the Civil War*
Moses Abramovitz   CUP, 1964, 252 pp., $4.00

91 *The Cyclical Behavior of the Term Structure of Interest Rates*
Reuben A. Kessel   CUP, 1965, 125 pp., $3.00

92 *Trade Union Membership, 1897-1962*
Leo Troy   CUP, 1965, 90 pp., $2.00

93 *Financial Adjustments to Unemployment*
Philip A. Klein   CUP, 1965, 88 pp., $2.50

94 *Measuring International Price Competitiveness: A Preliminary Report*
Irving B. Kravis, Robert E. Lipsey, and Philip J. Bourque   CUP, 1965, 48 pp., $1.75

95 *The Effect of Pension Plans on Aggregate Saving: Evidence from a Sample Survey*
Phillip Cagan   CUP, 1965, 117 pp., $3.00

96 *The Growing Importance of the Service Industries*
Victor R. Fuchs   CUP, 1965, 38 pp., $1.00

97 *Private Pension Funds: Projected Growth*
Daniel M. Holland   CUP, 1966, 166 pp., $4.00

98 *Comparative Prices of Nonferrous Metals in International Trade, 1953-64*
Irving B. Kravis and Robert E. Lipsey   CUP, 1966, 64 pp., $2.00

99 *Consumer Buying Intentions and Purchase Probability: An Experiment in Survey Design*
F. Thomas Juster   CUP, 1966, 60 pp., $2.00

100 *Changes in the Cyclical Behavior of Interest Rates*
Phillip Cagan   CUP, 1966, 32 pp., $1.00

101 *Differentials in Hourly Earnings by Region and City Size, 1959*
Victor R. Fuchs   CUP, 1967, 60 pp., $1.00

102 *Productivity Differences Within the Service Sector*
Victor R. Fuchs and Jean Alexander Wilburn   CUP, 1967, 122 pp., $3.00

103 *Indicators of Business Expansions and Contractions*
Geoffrey H. Moore and Julius Shiskin   CUP, 1967, 140 pp., $6.00

104 *An Appraisal of Short-Term Economic Forecasts*
Victor Zarnowitz   CUP, 1967, 156 pp., $5.00

105 *Pension Funds of Multiemployer Industrial Groups, Unions, and Nonprofit Organizations*
H. Robert Bartell and Elizabeth T. Simpson   CUP, 1968, 64 pp., $2.25

106 *Balance-of-Payments Adjustment Policies: Japan, Germany, and the Netherlands*
Michael Michaely   CUP, 1968, 122 pp., $2.75

107 *Dating Postwar Business Cycles: Methods and Their Application to Western Germany, 1950-67*
Ilse Mintz   CUP, 1970, 110 pp., $3.75

108 *The Seasonal Variation of Interest Rates*
Stanley Diller   CUP, 1970, 128 pp., $4.50

109 *The Value of Time in Passenger Transportation: The Demand for Air Travel*
Reuben Gronau   CUP, 1970, 92 pp., $4.00

110 *The Changing Position of Philanthropy in the American Economy*
Frank G. Dickinson   CUP, 1970, 214 pp., $8.00

---

* Out of print at the National Bureau. Reprinted in the Bobbs-Merrill Reprint Series in the Social Sciences, S-381 (Bobbs-Merrill, Inc., 4300 West 62 Street, Indianapolis, Ind. 46206).

TECHNICAL PAPERS

1. *A Significance Test for Time Series and Other Ordered Observations*
   W. Allen Wallis and Geoffrey H. Moore
   UM, 1941, 59 pp.

2. *The Relation of Cost to Output for a Leather Belt Shop*
   Joel Dean   UM, 1941, 72 pp.

3. *Basic Yields of Corporate Bonds, 1900-1942*
   David Durand   UM, 1942, 34 pp.

4. *Currency Held by the Public, the Banks, and the Treasury, Monthly, December 1917-December 1944*
   Anna Jacobson Schwartz and Elma Oliver
   UM, 1947, 65 pp.

5. *Concerning a New Federal Financial Statement*
   Morris A. Copeland   UM, 1947, 63 pp.

6. *Basic Yields of Bonds, 1926-1947: Their Measurement and Pattern*
   David Durand and Willis J. Winn
   UM, 1947, 40 pp.

7. *Factors Affecting the Demand for Consumer Instalment Sales Credit*
   Avram Kisselgoff   UM, 1952, 70 pp.

8. *A Study of Aggregate Consumption Functions*
   Robert Ferber   UM, 1953, 72 pp.

9. *The Volume of Residential Construction, 1889-1950*
   David M. Blank   UM, 1954, 111 pp.

10. *Factors Influencing Consumption: An Experimental Analysis of Shoe Buying*
    Ruth P. Mack   UM, 1954, 124 pp.

11. *Fiscal-Year Reporting for Corporate Income Tax*
    W. L. Crum   UM, 1956, 65 pp.

12. *Seasonal Adjustments by Electronic Computer Methods*
    Julius Shiskin and Harry Eisenpress
    UM, 1958, 34 pp.

13. *The Volume of Mortgage Debt in the Postwar Decade*
    Saul B. Klaman   UM, 1958, 158 pp.

14. *Industrial Demands upon the Money Market, 1919-57: A Study in Fund-Flow Analysis*
    Wilson F. Payne   UM, 1961, 158 pp.

15. *Methods for Improving World Transportation Accounts, Applied to 1950-1953*
    Herman F. Karreman
    CUP, 1961, 138 pp., $1.50

16. *The Interpolation of Time Series by Related Series*
    Milton Friedman   UM, 1962, 33 pp.

17. *Estimates of Residential Building, United States, 1840-1939*
    Manuel Gottlieb   UM, 1964, 115 pp.

18. *The Measurement of Corporate Sources and Uses of Funds*
    David Meiselman and Eli Shapiro
    CUP, 1964, 297 pp., $4.50

19. *Some Measures of the Quality of Agricultural Credit*
    George K. Brinegar and Lyle P. Fettig
    CUP, 1968, 63 pp., $2.25

ANNUAL REPORTS

(Those available from NBER will be sent gratis on request)

25th *The National Bureau's First Quarter-Century*
     UM, May 1945

27th *Stepping Stones Towards the Future*
     UM, March 1947

29th *Wesley Mitchell and the National Bureau*
     UM, May 1949

30th *New Facts on Business Cycles* UM, May 1950

33rd *Business Cycle Research and the Needs of Our Times*   UM, May 1953

34th *Economic Progress and Economic Change*
     UM, May 1954

46th *Anticipating the Nation's Needs for Economic Knowledge*   NBER, June 1966

47th *Contributions to Economic Knowledge Through Research*   NBER, June 1967

48th *Toward Improved Social and Economic Measurement*   NBER, June 1968

49th *New Challenges for Economic Research*
     NBER, October 1969

VIII

Finances
and Sources
of Support

Finances and Sources of Support

During the fiscal year ending June 30, 1970, expenditures for the National Bureau's program of research, publication, and related activities were $2,606,808. Current income was $2,162,224. Unrestricted sustaining funds of the National Bureau were drawn on to finance the $444,584 deficit.

Current financial support was received from philanthropic foundations, government agencies, business associations, companies, labor unions, and individuals.

About two-fifths of current income was obtained from restricted fund grants or contracts for the support of specific research projects. These sources of support for particular studies included: Agency for International Development—exchange control, liberalization, and economic development; American Bankers Association—banking structure and performance; Carnegie Commission on the Future of Higher Education—benefits of higher education; Carnegie Corporation of New York—economics of education; Commonwealth Fund—economics of health; Ford Foundation—international economic relations, technological diffusion; International Business Machines Corporation—inter-university computer workshop; National Science Foundation—household capital formation and savings, relation of U.S. manufacturing abroad and U.S. exports, and the conference series; Rockefeller Foundation—a program in international economics; Scherman Foundation—eastern European credit institutions; Securities and Exchange Commission—flow of funds and national balance sheet (also assisted by the Board of Governors of the Federal Reserve System); Alfred P. Sloan Foundation — studies of productivity, employment, and price levels; U.S. Department of Commerce, Economic Development Administration — regional economic studies; U.S. Department of Health, Education, and Welfare—economics of health, and education and economic productivity; U.S. Department of Housing and Urban Development—urban economic studies; Alex C. Walker Charitable and Educational Foundation—studies of productivity, employment, and price levels.

Studies for which restricted grants provide the major portion of support usually require some additional financing from general funds. Grants for specific studies normally do not cover the full costs of initiating and developing research proposals. Many restricted grants require a sharing of project costs. And, of course, those projects approved by the Board of Directors for which specific grants are not available rely for support entirely on unrestricted income or general funds.

In October 1969, the Ford Foundation awarded the National Bureau a grant of $2,000,000 to be used for general program support over a seven-year period. During the 1969-70 fiscal year, payments on this grant provided $300,000 of the National Bureau's unrestricted income. General support grants were also received from the Richard King Mellon Foundation and the Scherman Foundation. These general fund grants provided 17 per cent of the total income for the year.

General financial support from the annual contributions and subscriptions of companies, banks, labor organizations, libraries, and individuals provided 18 per cent of total income. The interest and dividends from the investment of sustaining funds provided another 17 per cent. The remaining 4 per cent of 1969-70 income was from sales of publications and statistical materials.

Tax Status

During the past year, with the development and enactment of the Tax Reform Act of 1969, the sources of financial support for tax-exempt organizations have been of particular interest and concern. The act established new classifications for some tax-exempt organizations with different rules and requirements and with different tax results to their contributors. The manner in which the activities of organizations like the National Bureau are financed now determines whether the organization is classified as a private foundation, a private operating foundation, or an organization other than a private foundation—i.e., broadly, a public foundation.

The National Bureau's tax status was not changed by the Tax Reform Act. The National Bureau has long been recognized, by rulings of the Internal Revenue Service, as a tax-exempt organization operated exclusively for scientific and educational purposes—one of the organizations now described in section 501(c)(3) of the Internal Revenue Code, contributions to which are deductible under section 170 of the Code. The National Bureau has also received a ruling from the Internal Revenue Service that it is a publicly supported organization — or technically, "an organization referred to in section 170(b)(1)(A)(vi)." Thus, the National Bureau is an organization to which contributions were formally deductible up to 30 per cent of an individual donor's adjusted gross income and now, under the 1969 Act, are deductible up to 50 per cent of an individual donor's "contribution base."

Since the National Bureau is a publicly supported organization, it does not come within the classification of private foundations established by the 1969 Act and is not subject to the taxes and requirements imposed on private foundations. On the contrary, the National Bureau is among those organizations to which private foundations may make qualifying distributions without limitation under the act.

Douglas H. Eldridge